English in Situations

R. O'NEILL
and the Research and
Development Staff of the
Eurocentre Bournemouth

London
Oxford University Press

Oxford University Press, Ely House, London W. 1

Glasgow New York Toronto Melbourne Wellington
Cape Town Ibadan Nairobi Dar es Salaam Lusaka Addis Ababa
Delhi Bombay Calcutta Madras Karachi Lahore Dacca
Kuala Lumpur Singapore Hong Kong Tokyo

ISBN 0 19 453260 7

© *Oxford University Press 1970*

First published 1970

Fifth impression 1973

Set by H. Charlesworth & Co. Ltd.
and printed photolitho in Great Britain by
Ebenezer Baylis and Son Ltd.,
The Trinity Press, Worcester, and London

FOREWORD

Our previous four publications in the series "Teaching Languages to Adults" have been concerned mainly with teaching techniques for the language-teacher. We feel that it is also one of our tasks, however, to provide the student and teacher with actual course material. This book is designed for revision of basic patterns and structures, leading to more advanced work by a "cyclical" plan of presentation of each feature at three different levels of difficulty. It is thus particularly suitable for refresher courses or for intermediate students in general courses. A pilot-edition has already been tried out over two years under various conditions by both O.U.P. and the Eurocentres.

The book serves two primary functions. For the teacher, it should be a source of realistic situations and practice material for essentially oral presentation during the lesson. For the student it serves as a reference to and record of this oral presentation, enabling him to reconstitute the material later alone.

The way the situations are presented in class is critical to the success of this course. The basic principles of presentation are given in the introduction, but it is up to the individual teacher to exercise his own originality and talent in this vital part of his teaching. With this support, we believe the book can produce lively, realistic and successful language-learning.

Erh. J. C. Waespi
Director of the Foundation for European Language and Educational Centres

ACKNOWLEDGEMENTS

Many people helped me in writing this book. It would be impossible to mention them all, but I feel I must name the following in particular.

Roy Kingsbury and Tony Yeadon, my two colleagues in the Research and Development Department who spent many long hours suggesting material and played a considerable part in the production of this book.

Mr J. Allsop and Mr J. Andrews, the heads of the Bournemouth and London Eurocentres, who promoted the book in many ways.

Mr E Waespi, Director of the Eurocentres, who gave many facilities for the book to be tested, offered constructive criticism afterwards, and without whose support the book could not have been written.

All the many teachers in the London and Bournemouth Eurocentre who have helped with advice, criticism and enthusiasm.

Mr R. A. Close, from whose book "English as a Foreign Language" I have gained a great deal of insight into my own language, the results of which I have tried to apply here.

INTRODUCTION

TO THE TEACHER:

This book has been designed to meet the specific needs of teachers and students in refresher courses and in normal intermediate and advanced courses. It is undoubtedly most suitable for adult learners of English. The situations and vocabulary often deal with such things as work, marriage and even politics. Controversial themes are not shunned although great care has been taken not to represent any particular bias or prejudice. This is certainly not because the author and other people connected with the production of the book are without bias or prejudice. However, text-books should in no sense be propaganda. Therefore, our interests rather than our views are reflected here.

The book has been designed with four main requirements or design-criteria in mind.

      i. Easy adaptability to the teacher's needs and those of his or her class.
     ii. Clear but flexible learning-sequence.
   iii. Alternation of pace and variety of learning-activity within any one lesson.
   iv. Cyclical Progression.

Only the last perhaps needs some explanation. A fault of many structurally based courses is that they deal with a particular feature of English in one place only, and then never return to it. As the Basic Plan of the book will show, it is possible to use another approach. This approach is particularly appropriate when teaching intermediate students. There are often very basic things they have not learned to control perfectly. The teacher cannot afford to ignore what many of his students should have learned but have not. Neither can he present them to the class in the same way as he would if he were teaching complete beginners.

What is the Basic Plan of the Book?

The book deals with eleven essential concepts in English. These eleven concepts can be dealt with at three different levels of difficulty. The teacher can, at any time, go to a level of greater or lesser difficulty with a particular class.

This is made possible by the three-layer design of the book. Notice the diagram. Each layer is called a part. The three parts are labelled A, B, and C. The Units in each part run from 1 to 11.

PART A	One	Two	Three	Four	Five	Six	Seven	Eight	Nine	Ten	Eleven
PART B	One	Two	Three	Four	Five	Six	Seven	Eight	Nine	Ten	Eleven
PART C	One	Two	Three	Four	Five	Six	Seven	Eight	Nine	Ten	Eleven

The concept behind Units A One, B One and C One is the Present Simple vs. the Present Continuous. Now, there are a number of different aspects to this contrast, because each form has a number of uses. A One deals, for example, with the basic contrast of HE DOES SOMETHING EVERY DAY and HE IS DOING IT NOW. B One deals with IS/ARE DOING in the future (I'm seeing the boss tomorrow) and with the distinction between HE HAS and HE IS HAVING. C One deals with the modal SHOULD DO and SHOULD BE DOING.

It can be seen that although one is dealing throughout the three units with the same concept, the problem encountered in each is quite different. Each time, there is a different level of difficulty.

This characteristic is repeated throughout the book. A concept is treated at different levels of difficulty.

What Plan should be Adopted by the Teacher using the Book with a Class?

The teacher should work through a part, or the units in that part he or she feels the class needs. However, if the teacher finds that the material in a particular unit in the part he is working through is too easy, or too difficult, the class should be taken to the appropriate unit in the part above or below it.

What are the Criteria for Deciding whether a Unit is too Easy for a Class?

The teacher should ask these questions:

      i. Can the class manipulate the pattern at speed?
     ii. Can they use the pattern in a wide range of situations?
    iii. Can they think of situations of their own in which they naturally use the pattern?

BASIC PRINCIPLES OF PRESENTATION

1. Most of the materials, except for certain exceptions clearly identified later, should be presented orally. Only the teacher should be able to see what is in the book during the actual lesson. The class should have the book closed except during certain phases of the lesson.

2. The teacher should never feel obliged to use all the material in any unit. Certain general guide-lines for selecting the material are given later.

3. Any lesson should have changes of pace and activity in it. Suggestions as to how to use the different kinds of material in order to achieve this are also given.

4. Questions should be asked quickly and responses required at good speed. Drills should also always be done at a reasonable pace. At all times, the teacher should keep the class guessing as to who is going to have to answer next. Students should never be called upon in any fixed order. Whenever possible, indicate the student who is to respond by gesturing towards him. Do not call upon the students by name except when you have to do this in order to make them look at you.

5. As far as possible, except in the short reading- or writing-phases, maintain constant eye-contact with the whole class. Make sure you do not fix upon any particular student or students too often. It is often a good practice, for instance, to look at a student only when you are indicating he is to respond. Then, while the student is giving the response, look at the rest of the class. Look back at the student again at the end of the response to indicate whether it is correct or not.

These are the various kinds of materials you will find in any unit.

1. Problem Situations
2. Illustrative Situations
3. Progressive Substitution Drills with or without added Transformations
4. Invention Exercises
5. Practice Situations
6. Expository Material (Graphic Expositions, Grammar Notes, Special Comments)
7. Texts
8. Conversations.

The following notes explain the use and rationale of these different kinds of material, as well as the differences between them.

1. Problem Situation (usually one, sometimes two for a pattern)

Description: A short contextualised example that forces the use of the pattern under study. Questions attached. Situation always on left of page. Questions on right.

Presentation: Books shut for class. Teacher gives situation, asks questions quickly to make sure all details grasped. Later, class can read situation in class.

Rationale: Teacher may want to motivate class to look at pattern with new attention (when revising) or may want to preview nature of material. If revising, will have to convince class there is something they may think they know but still need more practice in. Problem Situation puts class in natural situation where they have to use the pattern. If they stumble, teacher says "No, that's not right. Listen to the Illustrative Situations. They will show you what pattern to use here."

Examples: See Problem Situation on page 1. Notice how questions using "What does he do?" and "What is he doing?" cannot be answered correctly if students do not realise basic difference between the two forms.

2. Illustrative Situation (between 1 and 4 per pattern)

Description: Again, contextualised examples pinpointing when to use pattern. However, the pattern itself is actually given (unlike Problem Situation). Layout the same as for Problem Situation.

Presentation: As for Problem Situation.

Rationale: Class must have chance to gain insight into when to use pattern. Situations represent typical instances. From these, they can generalise about use of pattern. Teacher may also decide to give formal rule. However, this is not enough in itself. Situations give feedback to teacher about what concept class has formed. Danger of rules alone is that they can be purely verbal and do not generate actual correct usage. Formal rules can be helpful but cannot be substituted for student's own insight.

Examples: See illustrative situations on pages 1 and 2. Notice, among other things, how some questions take the form of prompts. (Ex: Q3 for Situation (i)). Teacher can fire these at one student and make him ask other student questions. 2nd student gives answers. Student participation is increased considerably.

3. Progressive Substitution Drills

Description: A model sentence followed by a series of prompts that cause student to make sentences by changing things in original model.

Presentation: Teacher gives model and a few examples of prompts and responses. Class sees what to do from teacher's own performance. Then teacher asks class to do this, starting from model. Teacher keeps class in same rythm and page through hand-signals. The signals mark out stressed words. Class repeats in chorus. Teacher can vary this by sometimes asking only individuals to answer. Responses must be quick and teacher must not let too much time elapse between prompt and response. If drill is individual rather than chorus, teacher should again indicate who is to respond by quick gesture. Otherwise drill takes too much time, pace too slow, class forgets what to say.

Layout has model and examples of responses produced by prompts on left. On the right there are between 8 and 16 prompts.

Rationale: Drills can never, by themselves, teach a language. However, they do give necessary fluency-practice. Students often know what to say but stumble when trying to say it. Drills give practice in responding at speed, at normal pace, without having time to think about it. Thus they are a very necessary accompaniment. Also give very fast-paced phases in lesson. Teacher can break off drill at any point. Drill phase should never last more than about a minute per drill.

Examples: See drills on page 2. Notice how attention sometimes deliberately switched from main point (DO and DOES) to other things (position of object, etc.). This is done to see if class can use pattern correctly when concentrating on something else.

Notice that as book progresses, progressive drills diminish in number and are subtly changed. For instance, p. 121 introduces variations or transformations in pattern. Starts out as statement, prompt 3 changes it to question.

4. Invention Exercises

Description: Model sentence followed by a series of prompts that do not give full vocabulary for response. Prompt only suggests what sentence should be.

Lay-out as for Progressive Drills, with examples of what is to be done.

Presentation: Slower-paced. Books again closed. Teacher gives model, then fires prompts without previous signal at various members of class. More suited for individual response only.

Rationale: Gives more challenging fluency practice than does Progressive Drill. Also is first step towards student-transfer of pattern. Students have to find most of vocubulary themselves.

Examples: See invention exercise on page 12. Notice how one word generates full sentence. Variations are allowed. Teacher need not give all prompts. Some prompts more demanding than others. For instance, prompt 5 can suggest many sentences from I'M GOING TO GET UP EARLY TOMORROW to WE'RE GOING TO START THE STRIKE EARLY TOMORROW.

Invention drills become more frequent as book progresses.

5. Practice Situations

Description: Two or occasionally three very short sentences. Together they make a short situation that calls for the use of a particular pattern. Response cannot be simply mechanical.

Presentation: Books closed for class. Teacher quickly gives situation and then gestures for response. Sometimes do not ask anybody in particular to respond. Get class to volunteer response. Occasionally ask questions about situation to test comprehension. Do this unexpectedly. After presentation occasionally ask class to look at situations, and ask questions.

Rationale: Extra situations extend range of pattern. They reinforce concept of when to use it. Generate more valuable oral/aural work.

Examples: See practice situations on page 12. Notice how clues about which pattern to use are purely contextual. Purely mechanical response impossible.

6. Expository Material

Description: Brief explanation, graphic or otherwise, of grammar point.

Presentation: Simply ask class to look at exposition for reinforcement of point. Ask if there are any questions. Then go on to next thing.

Rationale: Class may need formal description of principle involved. Books offer certain typographical devices which may help teacher to get over point.

Example: Page 8, item 13. Notice symbols for Mass and Unit.

Also page 91, Item 67.

7. Texts

Description: Short passages with questions, and occasionally special exercises.

Presentation: Can be (i) purely oral, with class looking at text later, (ii) part oral and part silent reading, (iii) read throughout in chorus. Teacher can often ask class to prepare text at home and ask questions on it in class.

Rationale: Texts provide conventional contextualisation. Unlike Situations, they do not highlight specific contextual clues that call for the use of a particular pattern. However, longer length makes greater development of story-line possible. More room for information, suspense, etc.

8. Conversations

Description: Always very short conversations, with questions and occasionally special exercises.

Presentation: On tape or by teacher alone. Books can be open although we suggest that taped presentation should be done with books closed. Teacher can pause tape and shoot out questions. Also make class repeat various parts.

Rationale: The same as for Texts.

Examples: Page 172, Item 94.

COMMENTS

Although formal grammar 'rules' are usually given only in the summary at the end of the book, it has been found that with some patterns it is very helpful to include a short formal statement with the material itself. This can be read silently by the class, and then the teacher can ask a few questions to make sure the point has been made.

PRINCIPLES OF SELECTION

The nucleus of any unit consists of (i) The Illustrative Situation, (ii) The Practice Situations, (iii) at least one of the drills. Use several or all of the Illustrative Situations, depending on how much you think necessary. Then go over Practice Situations. Do one of the drills for fluency-practice. Perhaps do the drill twice; once in chorus, then individually. (Remember not to pause too long between prompts or to call upon all students by name.)

The rest of the material can be used according to discretion. If you do not use the Text in class, perhaps tell the class to read it at home and then ask questions quickly (3 or 4 minutes of lesson time) the next day.

Remember the "cyclical" progression of the book. Do not continue work with a unit if it is too easy or too difficult for your class. Rather, change to the corresponding unit in another part (A, B, C) of the course. In this lies the valuable element of flexibility in the material.

CONTENTS

CONCEPTS	UNIT	PART A
PRESENT SIMPLE vs. PRESENT CONTINUOUS	1	'They do' vs. 'They are doing.' Position of 'often' 'never' etc.
MASS AND UNIT	2	'How much' vs. 'How many' 'There is/are a lot of . . .' 'There is/are' vs. 'they are/it is.'
FUTURE AND IMPERATIVE	3	'Going to do' 'Do!' and 'Don't do!'
PAST SIMPLE, CONTINUOUS, PERFECT AND FUTURE IN THE PAST	4	'Walk/walked' etc. and 'Get/got' 'Did he . . .?' and 'He didn't' 'Was/were' and 'What . . . like?' vs. 'How . . .?' 'used to do/be/have
ADJECTIVES AND ADVERBS	5	Adjectives vs. Adverbs 'as . . . as' vs. '. . .er than' 'better' and 'worse'
PRESENT PERFECT CONTRASTED WITH OTHER TENSES	6	'did something . . . ago' 'has been/had for . . .' and 'has been doing for . . .' 'since' vs. 'for'
SPECIAL PROBLEMS OF WORD ORDER AND MODALS	7	'say'/'said' with reported speech 'tell someone something' 'could you tell me the way to . . .?'
VERB PLUS OBJECT PLUS INFINITIVE AND RELATED MODALS	8	'Would you . . .?' and 'May I . . .' 'tell someone to do . . .', and 'ask someone to do . . .' 'tell/ask/show someone how to . . .'
GERUNDS	9	hate/stop/enjoy/remember doing simple revision of 'who, 'which', and 'that' . . .
CONDITIONALS AND MODALS OF SUGGESTION ETC.	10	'Shall I . . .?' 'Shall we . . .?' 'Would you like to?' 'Would you like a . . .?' 'I'd like a', and 'I'd like to.'
PASSIVE REFLEXIVE AND RELATED CONSTRUCTIONS	11	'hurt himself' etc. (reflexives) 'wash', 'dress', 'feel.' (Non-reflexive) 'themselves/ourselves' vs. 'each other'

PART B	PART C
'is/are doing' in the future 'has/have' vs. 'is/are having'	'always does' vs. 'is always doing' 'should/can/must do' vs. 'should/can/must be doing'
'some' vs. 'any' 'very few' vs. 'very little' 'go to church/school/prison etc.' vs. 'go to THE church/school etc.'	Use and omission of definite article with concrete and abstract nouns words like 'news' etc. that never take 'a'
'I'll do it . . .' (willingness) 'I'll do it before/if/when/as soon as something happens'	'Will do until' vs. 'will have done by' 'Will do' vs. 'will be doing' 'might do' and 'might be doing' in future
'Was/were doing' vs. 'did' 'while' vs. 'during' 'during' vs. 'for'	'had done' vs. 'did' 'had no idea something was going to happen'
Position of 'very much' and 'very often' after object 'fast and hard' 'hardly/hardly (anything) at all' 'hardly ever' 'embarrassed/embarrassing'	'look/sound' etc. with adjective 'look/feel good' vs. 'look well' 'should have done' vs. 'should have been doing'
'has/have been' vs. 'was were' 'have you ever?' 'have you done that yet?' 'did it for' vs. 'has been doing it for . . .' 'It's the . . . est I've ever . . .'	'has been doing' vs. 'has done' 'had been doing' vs. 'did' 'has been' vs. 'did'
'What are you looking at?' 'What did you do that for?' 'Who/what did . . .?' 'explain something to somebody'	'supposed to do/be doing/have done' "Who knows Mary" etc. vs. "Who does Mary know?" "Isn't tall enough to dance with" etc.
'want someone to do' 'doesn't/didn't want someone to do' 'mustn't vs. 'don't/doesn't have to' 'Don't you think you should . . .?'	'make someone do' vs. 'let someone do' 'get someone to do' 'will/won't be able to do' and 'will have to do'
'stop/remember doing' 'stop remember to do' 'by/for/of doing'	Verb plus Object plus Preposition plus Gerund Patterns ('stop him from doing' etc.) 'try doing' vs. 'try to do' 'difficulty in doing' etc.
'would/wouldn't do if I were you.' 'would do if did/didn't' 'wish plus would do/were/had/did'	'It's time someone did' 'Would have done if had done.' 'wish had done.'
'has/have been done' 'have something done' 'has been done' vs. 'was done'	'Is being done' 'Might/needn't/should have been done' had (experienced) something done.'

UNIT A ONE

THEY DO vs. THEY ARE DOING
OFTEN/NEVER, etc. Questions and Negatives

1 DOES vs. IS DOING

Problem Situations

i. Mr. Collins is a businessman. He gets "The Financial Times" every day and always finds it very interesting.
At the moment, he is in his office. His copy of "The Financial Times" is in his overcoat pocket.

1. Where is Mr. Collins?
2. What does he do?
3. Does he read "The Financial Times"?
4. Is he reading it?
5. Where is his copy of "The Financial Times"?

ii. Jack Carlton is a famous football-player. At the moment he is at the dinner-table. There is a large beefsteak in front of him.

1. Who is Jack Carlton?
2. Where is he?
3. Does he play football?
4. What is he doing?

2 Illustrative Situations

i. John Dallas is a film director. At the moment he is in a plane over the Atlantic. He is on his way to Hollywood. There is a glass of champagne in his hand, a smile on his face, and a pretty girl opposite him.
Question: What DOES HE DO?
The only answer is: HE DIRECTS FILMS
            or: HE IS A FILM DIRECTOR
Question: What IS HE DOING
Answer: HE IS FLYING TO HOLLYWOOD
        HE IS DRINKING A GLASS OF CHAMPAGNE
        HE IS SMILING AT A PRETTY GIRL

Question Prompts:
1. Ask and answer these questions about John Dallas:
     (a) Who (b) Where
2. Use DOES HE DO?
3. or IS HE DOING? in these questions:
   (a) films (b) a glass of champagne
   (c) to Hollywood (d) at a pretty girl

ii. Arthur Docker is on the same plane. He is a very rich man. He drives a Rolls Royce, often eats caviar, plays roulette at Monte Carlo, hunts lions and elephants in Africa, and smokes large Havana cigars. At the moment he is having a nap.
Question: What IS HE DOING?
The only answer is: HE IS HAVING A NAP
Question: What are some of the things he DOES
Answers: HE DRIVES A ROLLS ROYCE. HE PLAYS ROULETTE. HE HUNTS LIONS AND ELEPHANTS. HE SMOKES HAVANA CIGARS.

Questions and Question Prompts:
1. Is he smoking a Havana cigar?
2. Does he smoke Havana cigars?
3. What is he doing?
4. Ask and answer questions with these words:
   (a) roulette (b) lions and elephants
   (c) a Rolls Royce (d) caviar

B

iii. Jane Martin is very athletic. She is a good skier and tennis-player and is also good at golf. She has a job as a typist and she is at work now.

SHE PLAYS GOLF AND TENNIS, SHE ALSO SKIS. SHE IS NOT DOING THESE THINGS NOW. SHE IS TYPING LETTERS.

1. Where is Jane now?
2. Does she play tennis?
3. Is she playing tennis?
4. Ask if she plays golf!
5. Ask if she is playing it!
6. Does she ski?
7. What is she doing now?

iv. It is a cold winter day. Jane is in Norway and she has her skis on.
SHE WORKS IN AN OFFICE. SHE ISN'T WORKING THERE NOW. SHE IS SKI-ING.

1. Where is Jane now?
2. Has she got her skis on?
3. Does she work in an office?
4. Ask if she is now!
5. What is she doing?

3 FLUENCY PRACTICE

Do these at speed

1. Model:
	HE READS "THE TIMES"
like =	HE LIKES "THE TIMES"
we =	WE LIKE "THE TIMES"
beefsteak =	WE LIKE BEEFSTEAK

Prompts
HE PLAYS FOOTBALL
1. golf
2. like
3. music
4. study
5. the students here
6. English
7. we
8. speak
9. the airline-hostess
10. French
11. all airline hostesses
12. understand
13. I
14. they
15. German

Examples with
He/she/it IS DOING
We/they ARE DOING
I AM DOING

2. Model:
	HE IS WORKING (he's)
I =	I AM WORKING (I'm)
listen =	I AM LISTENING
they =	THEY ARE LISTENING (they're)
we =	WE ARE LISTENING (we're)
wait =	WE ARE WAITING (we're)

Prompts
THE TRAIN IS COMING (The train's)
1. the teacher
2. leave
3. the ship
4. I
5. we
6. they
7. eat
8. he
9. she
10. work
11. wait
12. read
13. I
14. they
15. you
16. Peter

4 Practice Situations

1. Situation: I am an English teacher. I am in class now.

   Response: YOU ARE TEACHING ENGLISH (you're)

   Situation: Mrs. Martin is a music teacher. She is not in school now.

   Response: SHE TEACHES MUSIC.

Now use the correct form for these situations like this

1. Tom Cheave is a great footballer. He is on the field now, and everyone's eyes are on him.
2. Howard likes Coca-Cola. There is a glass of it in his hand now.
3. Arthur has a job in a bank from 9 to 5. It is 6 o'clock.
4. It is 9.30 and Arthur is in the bank now.
5. His overcoat is on a hook near the door. There is a copy of the Daily Express in the pocket.
6. He is on the bus now, on his way home. He is very interested in an article in the newspaper.
7. Tom and Mary like plays very much. They are at the theatre now, and the actors are on the stage.
8. Tito Golo and Carla Morass are famous opera singers. They are on the stage now in the last act of 'La Bohème'.
9. I like golf. You can see me at the golf-club every Sunday. As you can see, I am in the class-room now.
10. My bank manager thinks golf is a wonderful game, too. It is the weekend and he is on the golf-course now.
11. His wife is at home. The television is on and she is in front of it.
12. Mr. and Mrs. Johnson are at the dinner-table The steak is very good. So is the wine.
13. Mr. Johnson's son, Bert. has a fast sports-car. He is in it now, on the motorway.
14. Mr. Johnson himself has a family car. It is outside now.

Invention Exercise

2. Situation: You are talking about what you or someone else is doing.

   Prompt: I/this dictionary

   Response: I AM READING THIS DICTIONARY (I'm)
   or I AM STUDYING THIS DICTIONARY.

3. Situation: You are talking about what other people or yourself do. Perhaps you or they are doing something different at the moment.

   Prompt: Harry/a car factory

   Response: HARRY WORKS IN A CAR FACTORY (Perhaps he is watching television now.)

Prompts

1. We/roulette
2. Your son/chocolate
3. The boss/lunch
4. I/a letter to my mother
5. Frank Sinatra/a film in Rome
6. Tony Parks/television
7. Jane Martin/letters
8. Mr. and Mrs. Johnson /cognac

Prompts

1. Peter and Jane/ golf every Sunday
2. Michael/French cigarettes
3. English people/big breakfasts
4. Bert/a fast sports car
5. I/French and German
6. My parents/television every evening

5 CONVERSATION

Often/never/always

Tony and Susan are a young married couple. Tony writes advertisements for a large advertising agency and Susan teaches French. They are at home now. It is evening and they are sitting in the living-room.

Tony: You know, Susan, I think we're becoming vegetables . . . cabbages!

Susan: What a strange thing to say! What do you mean?

Tony: Well . . . just look at us! You're sitting there and I'm sitting here . . . we aren't talking . . . or reading . . . we're just staring at the wall!

Susan: Turn the television on if you're bored!

Tony: Television! That's the trouble. We never go out in the evenings. We always watch television. It's terrible.

Susan: All right. What do you want to do then?

Tony: Hmm . . . I don't know . . . the Academy cinema is showing a new Swedish film this evening.

Susan: Swedish films! Ugh! I don't like them! All that sex and religion.

Tony: How do you know? You never see them!

Susan: Oh all right! We can go to the cinema this evening if that's what you want. Where's my coat?

Tony: Oh! Just a second. It's Thursday today isn't it?

Susan: That's right. So what?

Tony: Well . . . I want to watch the boxing on television this evening. I always watch it.

Now answer these questions. Listen to the first word in the question and use it in your answer, like this

Question: **Does** Tony write advertisements?
Answer: Yes, he **does**

Question: Is he writing them now?
Answer: No, he isn't.

Closed Questions
1. Do Tony and Susan watch television?
2. Are they watching television now?
3. Does Susan teach French?
4. Is she teaching French now?
5. Is the Academy cinema showing a French film this evening?
6. Is it showing a Swedish one?
7. Does Susan like Swedish films?
8. Does Tony always watch television on Thursdays?

Open Questions
1. What do Tony and Susan do every evening?
2. What are they doing now?
3. What does Tony say about the Academy cinema?
4. What does Susan say about Swedish films?
5. What is Tony's answer?
6. What does Tony say when he remembers it is Thursday?

Reproduction

Write or talk about Tony and Susan. Use these prompt-words.
1. Tony/advertisements/advertising-agency. sitting-room now.
2. thinks he and Susan/vegetables.
3. always/television. never/out any more.
4. Susan never/the piano. He never/books.

6 Invention Drill

Notice the position of words like OFTEN/ NEVER (before verb)

Model: I OFTEN/NEVER/USUALLY/DO THAT

Prompt: champagne

Response: I OFTEN DRINK CHAMPAGNE
or: I NEVER BUY CHAMPAGNE
or: I USUALLY HAVE CHAMPAGNE

Prompts
1. French cigarettes
2. tennis in the winter
3. cream in my coffee
4. a bath in the morning
5. clothes in Bond Street
6. the cinema on Friday
7. plays on television
8. boxing matches
9. caviar sandwiches
10. tea with my dinner
11. Palmolive
12. to bed late

7 Remedial Question Practice

Notice the way we form questions in the simple form

Tony likes good films.
Does Tony like good films?

You speak English
Do you speak English?

Progressive Substitution

Model: DOES TONY LIKE BOXING?
you = DO YOU LIKE BOXING?
cigars = DO YOU LIKE CIGARS?
Bill = DOES BILL LIKE CIGARS?
smoke = DOES BILL SMOKE CIGARS?

Prompts

DOES TONY LIKE BOXING?
1. football
2. play
3. you
4. understand
5. modern music
6. French
7. speak
8. Mary
9. teach
10. like
11. big breakfasts
12. cold baths
13. take
14. you

Notice the way we form questions in the continuous form

The bus is coming
Is the bus coming?

Progressive Substitution

Model: IS THE TEACHER COMING?
you = ARE YOU COMING?
leaving = ARE YOU LEAVING?
the train = IS THE TRAIN LEAVING?

Prompts

IS THE TEACHER COMING?
1. the bus
2. they
3. studying
4. you
5. leaving
6. he
7. listening
8. you
9. the class
10. watching
11. they
12. she
13. drinking champagne
14. smoking a Gauloise
15. you
16. paying attention

UNIT A TWO

HOW MUCH vs. HOW MANY
THERE IS/ARE A LOT OF . . .
THERE IS/ARE vs. IT IS/THEY ARE

8 HOW MUCH/MANY

Problem Situation

Mr. Kipling is an American tourist from Texas. He is at London airport now. He is going through Customs and the customs officer wants to know what is in his luggage. "Oh, not very much" he says. "Just some cameras, cognac, cigars, Swiss watches, gold, things like that." The customs officer wants to know the quantity of these things.

1. Who is Mr. Kipling?
2. Where is he?
3. Ask what he is doing now!
4. What does the customs officer want to know?
5. What does Mr. Kipling say?
6. Now do this
   Imagine you are the customs officer.
   Ask questions with "How much" and "How many" with these words: cameras/cigars/gold/cognac/whisky/watches/American dollars/foreign money.

9 Illustrative Situation

i. Tony and Susan want to give a party next week. Susan wants to buy everything for it now. She and Tony are talking about it now and Susan is asking questions like:
    "HOW MUCH WINE DO WE NEED? AND HOW MANY WINE-GLASSES? HOW MUCH BEER? HOW MUCH CHEESE? HOW MANY BOTTLES OF COCA-COLA? Last of all she wants to know this: HOW MUCH MONEY CAN I SPEND?

1. What do they want to do next week?
2. What does Susan want to do now?
3. What are the questions she is asking with: wine/beer/cheese/wine-glasses/bottles of coca-cola/money.
4. Now ask more questions with words like: champagne/bottles of champagne/coffee/bottles of cream/chocolate/biscuits/sugar/paper plates/butter.

ii. Jill Burton works in a small shop. Old people often come in and say things like: "Let's see . . . what do I need today? Oh yes! Some eggs, please." Jill often has to ask them questions like: "YES, HOW MANY EGGS, PLEASE?" or "HOW MANY LOAVES OF BREAD?" or "HOW MUCH BREAD?" or "HOW MUCH CHEESE TODAY?"

1. Ask where Jill works!
2. What do the old people in the shop often say?
3. What does Jill have to ask them? (eggs/bread/cheese/loaves of bread)

10 Transformation Exercise

Situation: You are Jill Burton. You have to
ask questions like this:

Old Lady: Now, let's see. I need some butter.
You: Yes. How much, please?

1. I need some tea
2. I need some eggs
3. I need some apples
4. I need some cooking-oil
5. I need some beef-steak
6. I need some coffee
7. I need some tins of dog-food
8. I need some tins of baby-food
9. I need some tomatoes
10. I need some oranges

11 FLUENCY PRACTICE

Progressive Substitution

Model: HOW MUCH BUTTER DO WE NEED?

paper plates = HOW MANY PAPER PLATES DO WE NEED?

do you want = HOW MANY PAPER PLATES DO YOU WANT?

HOW MANY PAPER PLATES DO YOU WANT?

1. have you got?
2. money
3. sugar
4. do you take?
5. pieces of sugar
6. do you see?
7. English people
8. do you know?
9. foreign languages
10. English grammar
11. **do you teach?**
12. lessons

12 Practice Situations

Examples

These situations are more difficult Use phrases like DO YOU KNOW? etc.

A man is talking to you about the English. He is saying things like: "All English people love dogs. They all hate children. They are all stupid."
You want to know what experience he has of the English. You ask
HOW MANY ENGLISH PEOPLE DO YOU KNOW?

1. You are a doctor. A patient is telling you about his bad cough. You think he is a heavy smoker.
2. You are pouring out tea for your friend. You know she likes sweet tea, but you do not know how sweet.
3. Your friend is always telling you about what is in different American newspapers.
4. Tony is telling you he thinks he is too fat. You know he is a beer-drinker.
5. Bert Johnson is a car-salesman. He says he is a very good one.
6. An old woman is telling you she thinks all students are lazy good-for-nothings.
7. Your friend is telling you about the wonderful new job Peter has. (prompts: money/hours)
8. Your friend always looks tired. (sleep)

13 Exposition

Words like "wine, coffee, butter, money" are one type of word. They go with "How much...?"

Words like "bottles of wine, cups of coffee, pounds of butter," etc. are a different type. They go with "How many...?"

There are two symbols for the two types of word.

The first is this   ▰▰   (Mass)

Here are some examples	oil	petrol	bread	butter
	gold	tobacco	milk	sugar
	soap	wood	steel	paper

All these go with HOW MUCH

The second is this   / / / / / / /   (Units)

Here are some examples	litres of oil	loaves of bread		
	sandwiches	cigars	glasses	coins
	sweets	baths	pencils	pens
	pieces of paper			

All these go with HOW MANY

14 THERE IS A LOT OF
THERE ARE A LOT OF
THERE IS/ARE vs. IT IS/THEY ARE

Illustrative Situations

i. You are talking with Mr. Kipling.
He is telling you where all his money comes from.
"It's all from oil, my friend.
THERE'S A LOT OF OIL IN TEXAS, and THERE'S A LOT OF OIL ON MY RANCH, too."

1. Where does all Mr. Kipling's money come from?
2. Why is Texas so rich?
3. What does he say about his ranch?

ii. Now he is telling you about all his oil-wells, his Cadillacs, and the beautiful women in Texas.
"THERE ARE A LOT OF OIL-WELLS ON MY RANCH, at least 30 of them!"
"THERE ARE A LOT OF CADILLACS IN MY GARAGE, too. I have at least 5!"
"If you want to see beautiful women, come to Texas. THERE ARE A LOT OF THEM THERE!"

1. What do you know about his ranch now?
2. Do you think his garage is very full?
3. What else does he say about Texas?

15 Conversation

Peter Blake is a friend of Tony's. He is telling Tony about his new job in Texas.

Peter: Texas is a long way away, of course, but the job is really very good. There aren't many like it here in England. In fact, I don't think there are any at all.

Tony: Yes, but Texas! What is there in Texas? Nothing!

Peter: You're forgetting that there's a lot of money there, money for people like me!

Tony: There's more in life than just money.

Peter: Oh? What, for instance?

Tony: Well . . . uh . . .

Peter: Besides, what you say simply isn't true! There are a lot of things besides oil-wells and rich cowboys there.

Tony: There isn't any culture, is there?

Peter: There's a good symphony orchestra in Dallas, and there are two or three very good universities in the state.

Tony: There certainly isn't any tradition there, now, is there?

Peter: Tradition? You can keep your tradition! A job with £5,000 a year is enough for me!

Now ask and answer questions about Texas. Notice how THERE is often used in both the question and answer, like this

Prompt: A lot of money in Texas.
Question: Is there a lot of money in Texas?
Answer: Yes, there is.

1. many jobs like Peter's
2. any oil/Texas
3. rich cowboys
4. culture
5. a symphony orchestra
6. any good universities
7. tradition

Invention Exercise

Now ask some more questions about other things. Notice when IS and ARE are used.

oil-wells/England = Are there any oil-wells in England?

a canteen/the school = Is there a canteen in the school?

1. students/this room
2. oil/on the moon
3. good restaurants/this town
4. sugar/this tea
5. rooms with bath/that hotel
6. good films/in town
7. a football-match/on Friday
8. mistakes/my composition

16 THERE vs. IT/THEY

Notice the difference in these situations between THERE IS/ ARE and IT IS/ THEY ARE

THERE IS (there's) . . . vs. IT IS (It's)

Situation

You are eating in a restaurant. You see a fly in your soup. You say to the waiter:
THERE'S A FLY IN MY SOUP!
Your friend sees the fly and asks: "What's that?"
Your answer is: IT'S A FLY.

1. What do you say to the waiter when you see the fly?
2. What do you say when your friend asks what it is?

THERE ARE . . . IN/ON etc., vs. THEY ARE (They're)

Situation

You and a friend are walking through a park in winter. You see two robins (a bird with a red breast) in a tree. You tell your friend:
THERE ARE TWO ROBINS IN THAT TREE.
There is also a foreign student with you. He does not know the English word for the two birds. His question is: "What kind of birds are those?" Your answer is: THEY'RE ROBINS.

1. What do you tell your friend when you see the two robins?
2. What is the foreign student's question?
3. What is your answer?

17

Now use THERE or THEY/IT for these situations

Situation: You see two black cats in the garden. You say: THERE ARE TWO BLACK CATS THERE.

Situation: Someone asks you what kind of animals they are. THEY'RE CATS.

Practice Situations

1. You are robbing a bank late at night. You suddenly see a policeman at the window.
2. Your friend (who is rather stupid) sees the policeman too and asks: "What's (or "Who's") that?"
3. You are talking to a friend when you see an ink-spot on his shirt.
4. He does not know what kind of spot it is, so you tell him.
5. The customs officer notices two parcels in your luggage. The parcels contain books. He asks: "What are these?"

6. You and a friend have a room in a student's hostel. A minute ago, you saw two letters in your friend's post-box. You tell your friend:
7. The letters are birthday-cards. You ask what they are, and the answer is:
8. Tony is coming home late at night with his wife. They are still outside. Suddenly he sees a light in their bedroom.
9. Tony is sure it is a burglar. What does he tell the police on the telephone? (There is a public telephone on the corner.)
10. His wife sees a car she thinks is a police-car. He knows the car is only a taxi.

UNIT A THREE

is/are/am GOING TO DO
DO! DON'T DO! (Imperative Forms)

18 Problem Situation

Before it rains, the clouds in the sky usually get darker and darker. Peter and Jane are walking through the park now. Peter notices that the clouds are getting darker. What does he say to Jane?

1. What usually happens before it rains?
2. What does Peter notice?
3. Is it raining?

19 Illustrative Situations

Now study i Bill always gets up at 7. It is almost 7 now. Bill
these situations   is still in bed, his eyes are open and he is not asleep now. HE IS (he's) GOING TO GET UP IN A FEW MINUTES.

1. When does Bill always get up?
2. Is it 7 now?
3. Where is Bill?
4. Is he asleep?
5. What is going to happen in a few minutes?

ii Mary is tired after a hard day's work. She wants to have a hot bath. She is in a bathroom now. She is standing by the bath, and the hot water is running into it.
SHE IS (she's) GOING TO GET INTO THE BATH IN A MINUTE.

1. What does Mary want to do?
2. Is she having a bath now?
3. Where is she standing?
4. What is she going to do?
5. When?

iii The Boeing 707 is on the runway. All the passengers are inside now, the door is closed and the engines are roaring.
IT IS (it's) GOING TO TAKE OFF.

1. Is the plane in the air?
2. Where are the passengers?
3. Tell me about the door?
4. And the engines?
5. What can you say about the plane?

20 FLUENCY PRACTICE

Practise these at speed

Progressive Substitution

Model: THE PLANE IS GOING TO TAKE OFF

land = THE PLANE IS GOING TO LAND

We = WE ARE GOING TO LAND

Prompts

THE PLANE (The plane's) IS GOING TO TAKE OFF

1. land
2. it
3. we
4. leave
5. the train
6. stop in a minute
7. I
8. eat at 12
9. watch television this evening
10. she
11. have a test tomorrow
12. we

Invention Exercise

the plane = THE PLANE IS GOING TO LAND SOON

or IT IS GOING TO TAKE OFF AT 6.30 etc.

lunch = WE ARE GOING TO HAVE LUNCH IN A MINUTE.

or I'M GOING TO EAT LUNCH IN TOWN TODAY

Prompts

1. a new car
2. a bath
3. a test
4. Peter and Jill/a baby
5. early tomorrow
6. the new Continental restaurant
7. lamb again for dinner
8. my hands

21

Now use GOING TO for these

Situation: Paul is standing by the bath. The hot water is still running into it but it is almost full.

Response: HE IS GOING TO HAVE A BATH.

or HE IS GOING TO TURN OFF THE WATER.

or HE IS GOING TO GET INTO THE BATH.

Practice Situations

1. Peter is sitting in the train. He is taking a newspaper out of his briefcase.
2. The zebra is dead, and the tiger is standing over it.
3. It is November and all the leaves on the trees are brown.
4. The telephone in the sitting-room is ringing. Mary is coming down the stairs.
5. Shabinski, the great pianist, is walking onto the concert-platform. The audience is waiting.
6. The train is still standing at the platform, but all the passengers are inside now and the guard is waving a green flag.
7. Tony has 5,000 Spanish pesetas. He is in an English bank now.
8. The customs officer does not believe you when you tell him there are only books in your luggage.
9. Tony is alone this evening. He likes boxing-matches and there is one on television at 8. It is 7.30 now.
10. Charles is a bank robber. He has a revolver in his pocket and he is going into a bank.

22 CONVERSATION

GOING TO DO revised. DO/DON'T DO!
(imperative forms) introduced.

Mr. and Mrs. Bashford, a very snobbish couple, are sitting on a train. The train is waiting at the station.

Mr. B: Look at the time! When is this train going to leave? It's already five minutes late.

Mrs. B: Now, don't get impatient, darling. Are you sure?

Mr. B: Of course I'm sure. This is the 4.05 to London and it is now 4.10 . . . no . . . 4.11.

Mrs. B: Well don't get angry with me, darling. Look at that guard on the platform. Tell him.

Mr. B: A very good idea! (opening window and shouting) Guard! Guard! Come over here, please.

Guard: Yes, sir. What can I do for you?

Mr. B: Why are we waiting here?

Guard: Why are we waiting here?

Mr. B: Don't just repeat my question! Answer it.

Guard: (slowly, deliberately) Now keep calm sir. Don't shout! It's not that I don't want to answer your question. It's only that I don't really understand it. It's a very strange question.

Mr. B: A strange question! What do you mean? Look at the time! When is this train going to leave?

Guard: At 4.25, sir.

Mr. B: At 4.25! Now see here! I'm a very important man and I have some very important friends. One of them is the head of this railway and I'm going to tell him about this!

Guard: I don't care who you are, sir, or what you're going to do. This train is going to leave at 4.25. It always does.

Mr. B: What? Are you telling me that the 4.05 always leaves 20 minutes late?

Guard: 4.05? I see. You want to go to London, don't you, sir?

Mr. B: Don't ask stupid questions. Of course I do! Why do you think I'm on this train?

Guard: Well, sir. This isn't the 4.05 to London. It's the 4.25 to Bristol. The 4.05 always leaves from platform 3. This is platform 5. You're on the wrong train, sir.

1. Where are Mr. and Mrs. Bashford?
2. What is Mr. Bashford's first question about the train ("leave")
3. What does Mrs. Bashford say when he gets impatient?
4. What does the guard say when Mr. Bashford gets angry?
5. What exactly does Mr. Bashford say when the guard repeats his question?
6. What does the guard say when Mr. Bashford says he is a very important person and that he is going to tell the head of the railway about all this?
7. Mr. Bashford thinks the guard's last question ("You want to go to London, don't you, sir?") is stupid. What does he say?
8. Why is the guard's last question not a stupid one?

Reproduction

Do not look at the text. Can you remember parts of the conversation? Use these words as help.

Mr. B: (to Mrs. B) time! When/train/leave?
Mrs. B: impatient. guard over there.
Mr. B: (to guard) over here! Why/waiting?
Guard: Why/waiting?
Mr. B: repeat! Answer!
Guard: understand. strange.
Mr. B: Strange? What/mean? the time! When / leave?
Guard: 4.25.
Mr. B: important man. friends. one/head. tell him about this.
Guard: care who/or what. This train/4.25. always.
Mr. B: telling me/4.05/always 20 minutes late?
Guard: London, sir?
Mr. B: stupid questions! Of course. Why/on this train?
Guard: 4.25 to Bristol.

23 DO! DON'T DO! (Imperative Forms)

Make sentences like COME HERE! etc.

Invention Drill

time = LOOK AT THE TIME!
window = OPEN THE WINDOW!

1. this milk
2. your homework
3. this newspaper
4. my question
5. the door
6. the light
7. your hands
8. the car in front

Invention Drill

Now make sentences like DON'T SHOUT!

the door = DON'T CLOSE THE DOOR!
out in the rain = DON'T GO OUT IN THE RAIN!

1. foolish questions!
2. nervous!
3. to bed so late!
4. such terrible stories!
5. so many television programmes!
6. so many sweets!
7. that terrible restaurant!
8. that stupid man!

Now make sentences like COME HERE! or DON'T SHOUT! for these situations

1. There is a television programme you want to watch. Your friend is sitting near the television set. The set is not on.
2. You are a teacher. You are showing a student his homework. It is full of mistakes.
3. Your friend is shouting at you.
4. You are sitting in a doctor's waiting-room with your friend. He is getting impatient.
5. You have a secretary. You want to dictate a letter. She is in the other room.
6. You are washing the floor. It is still wet. Your friend wants to come into the room.
7. You are getting petrol for your car at a petrol station. Your friend is going to light a cigarette.

UNIT A FOUR

WALK/WALKED and GET/GOT (reg. and irreg. past)
DID HE . . . ? HE DIDN'T . . . (Question and Negative)
WAS/WERE and WHAT . . . LIKE? vs. HOW . . . ?
USED TO DO/BE/HAVE

24 Problem Situations

i. Richard West works in an office 5 days a week.
    He usually gets up at 7.30, has a shower and
    then has breakfast. He starts work at 9, lunch
    at 1, and then goes home at 5.30. In the even-
    ing he usually reads or watches television.

    1. Where does Richard work?
    2. When does he usually get up?
    3. What does he do after he gets up and before
       he goes to work?
    4. Tell me about his work-day!
    5. What does he do in the evening?
    6. Now do this

    Yesterday (Monday) was a typical day for
    Richard. Tell me what he did. Use these prompts:
    (i) up/7.30. (ii) a shower and then breakfast.
    (iii) work/9 (iv) lunch at 1 (v) home at 5.30
    (vi) in the evening/a book and television.

ii. Richard wants a change. He often says "Every
    day I do exactly the same thing! Yesterday I
    GOT UP at 7.30, HAD a shower and then HAD
    breakfast. I STARTED work at 9 and ATE
    lunch at 1. Then I WENT home at 5.30. In the
    evening I READ a book and then WATCHED
    television.

    1. When did he get up?
    2. Did he have a shower and have breakfast
       before he went to work?
    3. When did he start work?
    4. When did he eat lunch?
    5. When did he go home?
    6. Did he only read last night?
    7. Now do this

    Use these prompts (given orally by teacher,
    books closed) to ask the same questions
    yourself.
    (i) up at 7.30? (ii) a shower? (iii) breakfast?
    (iv) work at 9? (v) lunch at 1? (vi) home/5.30?
    (vii) a book? (viii) television?

25 Work/Worked (regular forms)

Illustrative Situations

Richard worked until 5.30 yesterday and then travelled home on the bus. His wife cooked a steak for dinner. She also prepared a nice salad. After dinner she washed the dishes and Richard listened to the radio for a bit. Then they both watched a television programme.

1. What did Richard do until 5.30 yesterday?
2. What did he do then? (on the bus)
3. What were the two things his wife did for dinner? (a steak/a salad)
4. Then she did one thing and he another. What? (the radio/the dishes)
5. What did they both do then?

26 Get/Got (irregular forms)

Jane Martin usually gets up early but she got up very late yesterday. She usually has a small breakfast but she had a very big one yesterday. She usually puts on a simple dark dress and goes to work, but yesterday she put on a very unusual white dress and then went to church. She usually says 'Hello' to Peter in the office. Yesterday she said 'I love you'. They usually eat lunch in the canteen. Yesterday they ate in a very expensive restaurant. Peter and Jane usually go home in different directions. They went home in the same direction yesterday. They also usually sleep in different beds, but yesterday they slept in the same bed. Peter and Jane Martin got married yesterday.

1. Jane usually gets up early; what about yesterday?
2. She usually has a small breakfast; what about yesterday?
3. She usually puts on a simple dark dress; what did she do yesterday?
4. Did she go to the office yesterday?
5. Did she say only 'Hello' to Peter?
6. Did they eat in the canteen?
7. They usually go home in different directions; tell me about yesterday!
8. Did they sleep in different beds yesterday?
9. What happened yesterday?

27 FLUENCY PRACTICE

He Watched/Did he Watch?

Transformation Exercises

i. A: I watched television on Monday.
   B: OH, DID YOU WATCH IT ON TUESDAY
   TOO?

1. I worked very late on Monday.
2. I walked home on Monday.
3. I washed the dishes on Monday.
4. I learned a lot on Monday.

5. I listened to the news on Monday.
6. I played football on Monday.
7. I prepared the meal on Monday.
8. I answered all the questions on Monday.

He Got/Did He Get?

ii. A: I got to work late yesterday.
    B: DID YOU GET TO WORK LATE THIS
    MORNING, TOO?

1. I got up late yesterday.
2. I had a steak for breakfast yesterday.
3. I came to work at 10 yesterday.
4. I saw Jane on the bus yesterday.

5. I ate a sandwich in the morning-break yesterday.
6. I took a taxi to work yesterday.
7. I slept late yesterday.
8. I went to church before work yesterday.

28 Didn't do

Invention Exercise

Notice that DIDN'T DO (negative form) is formed in the same way as questions are.

the bus this morning = I DIDN'T CATCH
THE BUS THIS
MORNING.

1. a big breakfast
2. a television
3. any work
4. the radio
5. to work late

6. a cold bath
7. the newspaper
8. the dishes
9. to church
10. all the questions

Transformation Exercise

Make questions with WHY DIDN'T . . . ? with these new verbs.

A: Jane usually writes a lot of letters in the
   morning. She wrote a lot yesterday.
B: WHY DIDN'T SHE WRITE A LOT
   TODAY?

1. Peter usually catches the 8.30 bus. He caught it yesterday.
2. We usually see Jane on the bus. We saw her yesterday.
3. The boss usually reads all his letters in the morning. He read them yesterday morning.
4. The bell usually rings at 10. It rang at 10 yesterday.

5. The milkman usually brings the milk early. He brought it early yesterday.
6. The cat usually drinks a lot of milk. It drank a lot yesterday.
7. Jane usually does a lot of work in the morning. She did a lot yesterday.
8. Peter usually reads the paper in the morning. He read it yesterday.

C

29 CONVERSATION

Was/Were. More Examples of DIDN'T DO

Mr. Collins was in Zurich this morning. It is now twelve o'clock noon and he is at London airport now. He's going through Customs.

Customs Officer: Have you anything to declare, sir?
Mr. Collins: Anything to declare? No! Uh . . . nothing!
Customs Officer: I see, sir. Please open your suitcase.
Mr. Collins: But . . . I didn't buy anything at all in Zurich.
Customs Officer: Uh huh Hmm. What's this under this sweater here?
Mr. Collins: What?
Customs Officer: Three bottles of brandy!
Mr. Collins: But . . . but that's impossible. They weren't there when I packed the bag this morning! I'm sure I didn't put them there!
Customs Officer: And a box of cigars.
Mr. Collins: That wasn't there, either! Really! I didn't buy any cigars at all!
Customs Officer: And what's this. An electric clock.
Mr. Collins: Impossible. There wasn't a clock in my case this morning.
Customs Officer: And I suppose this perfume wasn't there, either?
Mr. Collins: No, it wasn't! Really. I didn't get any perfume for my wife.
Customs Officer: Well, sir, when you smuggle things you lose them. And you pay a fine, as well.
Mr. Collins: A fine? How much?
Customs Officer: I don't know, sir. But when they take the money away from you you can forget you ever had it. Just tell yourself it wasn't in your wallet this morning.

Listen to these model questions and answers

Question: *Did* Mr. Collins open his case?
Answer: Yes, he *did.*

Notice the first word in the question is used in the answer

Question: *Was* there a sweater in it?
Answer: Yes, there *was.*

Now use these prompts to ask and answer questions yourself, like this

Prompt: Mr. Collins/Zurich this morning?
Question: *Was* Mr. Collins in Zurich this morning?
Answer: Yes, he was.

1. any bottles of brandy/his case
2. cigars
3. perfume
4. a clock
5. Mr. Collins/nervous
6. a fine/smuggle things

30 FLUENCY PRACTICE

Do these at speed **WAS/WERE**

Progressive Substitution

Model: THE PROGRAMME WAS AWFUL LAST NIGHT.

the meal = THE MEAL WAS AWFUL LAST NIGHT.

THE PROGRAMME WAS AWFUL LAST NIGHT
1. the spaghetti
2. yesterday
3. the weather
4. terrible
5. all right
6. Bill
7. in a bad mood
8. the children
9. the teacher
10. late
11. we
12. I
13. you
14. full of energy
15. very funny
16. the film

Progressive Substitution

Do these questions at speed, too. Model: WAS THE FILM GOOD LAST NIGHT?

WAS THE FILM GOOD LAST NIGHT?
1. interesting
2. the programme
3. very long
4. yesterday
5. the lessons
6. hard
7. the dictation
8. the test
9. the tests

31 WHAT . . . LIKE?

Illustrative Situation

Peter North is a journalist. He was in Mexico City last week but he is in London now. He is talking to a friend. His friend wants to know about the city, the weather, the food, etc. These are the questions he asks.
WHAT WAS MEXICO CITY LIKE?
WHAT WAS THE WEATHER LIKE?
WHAT WERE THE PEOPLE LIKE?
WHAT WAS THE FOOD LIKE?

1. Ask questions with
   (a) where/last week? (b) now? (c) who/ talking to?
2. What does his friend want to know?
3. Ask the same questions he asked with
   (a) the weather (b) the food (c) the people (d) the city
4. Suppose Peter's friend wants to know about other things. What are his questions with
   (a) the girls (b) the hotel (c) the beer (d) the political situation

32 Practice Situations

Think of questions for situations; like this Your friend went to the theatre last night.
You ask: WHAT WAS THE PLAY LIKE?

1. July can be a very fine month in Ireland. Sometimes, however, there is a lot of rain. Your friend was in Ireland last July.
2. You want to know about Dublin. Was it beautiful, ugly, or what?
3. You also want to hear about the traffic. Was it heavy, better than in England, light, etc.?

4. Some people say the Irish are very friendly. Others say the opposite. You want to know your friend's impression.
5. You want to know about the hotel he was at. Was it good, bad, comfortable, etc.?
6. Some people say prices in Ireland are higher than in England, others say they are much lower. What did he think?

33 HOW WAS . . . ?

Illustrative Situation

Notice what we say when we want to know about someone's health. Peter is still in the pub in Fleet Street. Now he and his friend are talking about a Mexican journalist they both know. His name is Ricardo and Peter's friend wants to know if Ricardo was in good health, happy or unhappy, etc.
His question is: HOW WAS RICARDO?

Ricardo has 10 children. Peter's friend wants to know about them, too.
HOW WERE ALL HIS CHILDREN?

1. Who are Peter and his friend talking about?
2. Ask questions with: (a) name (b) how many children
3. What is the exact question Peter's friend asks about Ricardo?
4. What does he say when he wants to know about Ricardo's wife? What is his question?

34 Invention Exercise

Now invent questions with WHAT? . . . LIKE? or HOW? like this. the weather = WHAT WAS THE WEATHER LIKE?

Ricardo =   HOW WAS RICARDO?

1. the beer in Mexico
2. your hotel
3. Ricardo's mother
4. His baby daughter
5. your hotel room
6. the girls
7. the food
8. all our other friends
9. the architecture
10. the new sports-stadium
11. the Olympic games
12. Juan (another friend)
13. Pedro and Maria
14. the bull-fights

35 Used to Do/Be

Illustrative Situations

i. Charles Gripp was a bank robber once. The police caught him in 1968 and he is in prison now. Before 1968 Charles drove a large car, robbed banks, had a lot of money and had arguments with his wife all the time. He did a lot of things then but he does not do any of those things now and he never sees his wife. HE USED TO BE A BANK ROBBER. HE USED TO ROB BANKS, DRIVE A BIG CAR, AND HAVE ARGUMENTS WITH HIS WIFE ALL THE TIME, BUT HE DOESN'T DO ANY OF THOSE THINGS NOW.

1. Is Charles still a bank robber?
2. Where is he now?
3. Has he still got a lot of money?
4. What are some of the other things he does not do now?
5. Now make three or four sentences with "used to".

ii. *Notice how the verb between HE and ANY MORE changes here.* Sam Smith was a very funny comedian once. People used to laugh at his jokes. He made a lot of money and had a good life. All this is over now. HE USED TO BE VERY FUNNY BUT HE ISN'T ANY MORE. HE USED TO MAKE A LOT OF MONEY BUT HE DOESN'T ANY MORE. HE USED TO HAVE A LOT OF FRIENDS BUT HE HASN'T ANY MORE.

1. Is Sam still a funny comedian?
2. Ask more questions with "still" with these words: at his jokes/a lot of money/
3. Now make at least four sentences with "used to" about Sam.

36 Invention Exercise

Make your own sentences. Pay attention to the problem of "but it DOESN'T/ISN'T/HASN'T anymore".

London/terrible fog = LONDON USED TO GET TERRIBLE FOG BUT IT DOESN'T ANY MORE.

1. the English/the radio a lot
2. This pop-group/popular
3. children/in factories
4. Charles/at night
5. Britain/an empire
6. Charles/good clothes
7. Sam's jokes/funny
8. Sam/a Rolls Royce

UNIT A FIVE

GOOD/BAD QUICK/SLOW CAREFUL/CARELESS (adjectives)
vs. WELL/BADLY QUICKLY/SLOWLY CAREFULLY/
CARELESSLY (adverbs)
As . . . . . . As vs. . . er Than (comparatives)
BETTER and WORSE (irregular comparatives)

37 GOOD/BAD vs. WELL/BADLY

Problem Situation

Mr. and Mrs. Butler both have cars. Mr. Butler has an accident almost every other month. Mrs. Butler never has accidents.

1. How often does Mr. Butler have accidents?
2. Ask the same question about Mrs. Butler.
3. What sort of driver is Mr. Butler?
4. How does he drive?
5. Ask the two last questions about Mrs. Butler.

38 Illustrative Situations

i. Carla Morass, the famous opera singer, sang at the opera house last night. The audience liked her very much. They clapped and clapped at the end.
SHE IS A GOOD SINGER. SHE SANG WELL LAST NIGHT.

1. Ask what Carla did last night! (and answer!)
2. Ask where!
3. What did the audience do?
4. What sort of singer is she?
5. How did she sing?

ii. When Tony dances, it is always bad. He steps all over Susan's feet. Susan is very different. She never makes a mistake when she dances.
TONY IS A BAD DANCER. HE DANCES BADLY.
SUSAN IS A GOOD DANCER. SHE DANCES WELL.

1. What does Tony do when he dances?
2. Does Susan ever do things like this?
3. What sort of dancer is Tony and how does he dance?
4. Ask those two questions about Susan!

iii. Bobby Greston, the great footballer, had a very bad game yesterday. He made a lot of mistakes.
HE IS A GOOD FOOTBALLER. HE USUALLY PLAYS WELL. HE PLAYED BADLY YESTERDAY.

1. What sort of game did Bobby have yesterday?
2. Did he make many mistakes?
3. How does he usually play?
4. Ask if he did yesterday!

39 Progressive Substitution

Do these at speed.

Model:

	HE PLAYED VERY WELL LAST WEEK	
you =	YOU PLAYED VERY WELL LAST WEEK	
spoke =	YOU SPOKE VERY WELL LAST WEEK	
yesterday =	YOU SPOKE VERY WELL YESTERDAY	

HE PLAYED VERY WELL LAST WEEK

1. last night	7. very badly
2. she	8. I
3. danced	9. drove
4. then	10. acted
5. sang	11. they
6. you	12. spoke

40 Practice Situations

Say how the people in these situations usually do things and how they did them yesterday.

When Carla Morass sings, people usually like her and clap afterwards. This did not happen when she sang yesterday.
SHE USUALLY SINGS WELL. SHE SANG BADLY YESTERDAY.

1. Shabinsky, the great pianist, played yesterday. He is always good and was yesterday too.
2. Mr. Smith taught us yesterday. His lessons are usually very good but the lesson yesterday wasn't.
3. Mr. Butler drove into town yesterday. He usually makes a lot of stupid mistakes when he drives but he didn't yesterday.
4. Tony spoke at a businessmen's lunch yesterday. He is usually not very good when he speaks, but he was yesterday.
5. Mr. Green taught us yesterday, too. His lessons are always bad. We all fell asleep yesterday.
6. Jane went ski-ing yesterday. She is usually very good when she skis, but she made a lot of mistakes yesterday.

41 Do something Well/Badly (Adverb after Object)

Illustrative Situation

Notice the position of WELL and BADLY here.

Peter and Jane both play tennis, but Peter is not very good at it. Jane, however, is a very good player. In fact, when they played yesterday, Jane beat Peter.
JANE PLAYS TENNIS WELL but PETER PLAYS TENNIS BADLY.

1. Is Peter good at tennis?
2. Ask if Jane is!
3. What happened yesterday?
4. How does Peter play tennis?
5. Ask if Jane plays it badly! (and answer)

Invention Exercise

Use WELL or BADLY in sentences of your own with these words.

My friend/English = MY FRIEND SPEAKS ENGLISH WELL

1. My mother/all my food
2. Carla/that last song
3. You/that last exercise
4. Shabinsky/Mozart
5. The teacher/grammar
6. The comedian/that joke

42 Do it QUICKLY/SLOWLY
CAREFULLY/CARELESSLY

Illustrative Situation

Tom and Anthony are both customs officers at London airport. When Tom looks at a suitcase, it takes him only a few seconds to see what is inside it. It takes Anthony much longer to do this. It often takes him 10 minutes.
TOM WORKS QUICKLY. ANTHONY WORKS SLOWLY.

1. Where do Tom and Anthony both work?
2. How long does it take Tom to see what is inside a suitcase?
3. Ask how long it takes Anthony to do this!
4. How does Tom work?
5. How does Anthony work?

When Mrs. Butler drives, she is usually very careful. She never goes too fast, stops at all the red lights, and pays attention to the traffic. Yesterday she had an argument with her husband and could not concentrate afterwards. She did several foolish things and almost had an accident.
SHE USUALLY DRIVES CAREFULLY but SHE DROVE CARELESSLY YESTERDAY.

1. What are some of the careful things Mrs. Butler usually does when she drives?
2. What happened yesterday?
3. How does she usually drive?
4. Ask if she did yesterday! (and answer)

43
Use QUICKLY/ SLOWLY/ CAREFULLY or CARE- LESSLY in these situations, like this

Robert did a test yesterday. He thought about each answer a long time. HE DID THE TEST VERY CAREFULLY.

1. Bert Johnson drove in heavy traffic yesterday. He did not pay attention to the other cars.
2. I read a 200 page book yesterday. I read it in about an hour.
3. Burt Johnson read a short article in the paper. It took him an hour.
4. Bobby Greston ate a steak in 2 minutes yesterday.
5. Mr. Collins spoke to his wife on the phone from Zurich yesterday. He had a lot to say and he said it in a very short time.
6. Lord Kane, the diplomat, got a very important letter yesterday. He studied every word and sentence in it.

7. When Jane types, there are never any mistakes in the letter.
8. Tony held a very expensive vase in his hands. He did not want to drop it.
9. Robert and Eric both had a test yesterday. It took Robert one hour to finish it. (It was very long) It took Eric three hours.
10. Tony spoke to a foreign customer on the phone yesterday. The customer's English was very poor but he understood Tony. Why do you think he understood him?

Dark/Darker than . . . etc. vs. As Dark as

Mrs. Bashford is in a department store. She is looking for a sweater for her husband. The salesman is showing her some.

Mrs. Bashford: I always choose my husband's clothes very carefully. He dresses very well!

Salesman: (politely) Yes, madam. I'm sure. Now, you said a size 38, didn't you? Something like this perhaps? It's a very good sweater!

Mrs. Bashford: Perhaps, but I don't really think it's good enough for my husband! Haven't you anything better?

Salesman: Better than this, madam? (laughing nervously a bit) Well . . . uh . . . there's this grey sweater.

Mrs. Bashford: I don't think I like that shade of grey. It's not dark enough.

Salesman: I see. You want something darker than this . . . like this, perhaps?

Mrs. Bashford: (thinking) Hmm . . . you know, I don't really think I like grey at all. It's too . . . dull.

Salesman: I see. Now this green sweater is brighter than the grey one.

Mrs. Bashford: No. I don't like green, either.

Salesman: Well . . . let me see . . . there's this red sweater.

Mrs. Bashford: Good heavens, no! My husband never wears red! It's too bright.

Salesman: (confused) So you want something darker than the light grey, brighter than the dark grey but not as bright as the green or the red sweater?

Mrs. Bashford: Exactly! And please hurry up. I really haven't much time.

Salesman: Something like this blue sweater?

Mrs. Bashford: Blue . . . hmm . . . yes, I think I like that. How much does it cost?

Salesman: £8

Mrs. Bashford: £8! Good heavens! Haven't you anything . . . anything . . . uh . . .

Salesman: Cheaper than this, madam? Only this other blue sweater. It costs £4.

Mrs. Bashford: Now that's exactly what I'm looking for. That's much nicer than all the others. Why didn't you show it to me before?

Salesman: (angrily) But I did, madam! It was the first one you saw!

1. What does Mrs. Bashford always do when she buys her husband's clothes?
2. Why doesn't she like the first sweater?
3. What are the two things wrong with the grey sweater?
4. Ask and answer why Mr. Bashford never wears red!
5. Ask and answer why Mrs. Bashford tells the salesman to hurry up!
6. What does she want when she hears the price of the blue sweater?
7. Why does the salesman get angry?

45 Reproduction

Retell part of the conversation without looking at the text!

Prompts

Mrs. B:	I always/my husband's clothes. dresses.
Salesman:	Something like . . . ? very good.
Mrs. B:	Perhaps but/enough. better?
Salesman:	grey.
Mrs. B:	not dark . . .
Salesman:	I see. darker/this. like this . . . ?
Mrs. B:	don't really think/at all. dull.
Salesman:	This green/much brighter/grey.
Mrs. B:	No/either.
Salesman:	let me . . . this red.
Mrs. B:	My husband never . . . It's . . .
Salesman:	So/want something darker/light grey/brighter/dark grey but . . .
Mrs. B:	Exactly! hurry up. much time.
Salesman:	this blue?
Mrs. B:	like that. cost?
Salesman:	£8
Mrs. B:	anything . . . uh . . . ?
Salesman:	cheaper/this? Only/blue. £4
Mrs. B:	exactly what . . . much nicer/the others. Why . . . ?
Salesman:	But . . . the first one . . .

46 Darker than

Transformation Exercise

Make sentences like the one the salesman makes here

Mrs. Bashford: That sweater is not dark enough.
Salesman: I see. YOU WANT SOMETHING DARKER THAN THAT.

1. That sweater is not bright enough.
2. It isn't cheap enough.
3. That car is not big enough.
4. That test is not hard enough.
5. That curry is not hot enough.
6. That coat is not warm enough.

47 as — as

Now make sentences like the one Mrs. Bashford makes here.

Salesman: I see. You want something cheaper. Now this sweater costs only £1.
Mrs. Bashford: OH, NO! NOT AS CHEAP AS THAT!

1. Something darker, madam? Perhaps this black sweater?
2. Something brighter, madam? Perhaps this red sweater?
3. Something bigger, madam? This sweater is made for very fat men.
4. Something smaller, madam? Perhaps this boy's sweater?
5. Something warmer, madam? Like this sweater? We call it Siberia.
6. Something dearer, madam? This costs £100.

Notice when
"as . . . as" is
used and when
"than" is used.

Model: IS THIS CHEAPER THAN THAT?
cheap = IS THIS AS CHEAP AS THAT?
bigger = IS THIS BIGGER THAN THAT?

IS THIS CHEAPER THAN THAT?

1. good	7. brighter
2. warm	8. hard
3. warmer	9. harder
4. nice	10. dark
5. bright	11. nicer
6. new	12. darker

49 BETTER/WORSE THAN

Illustrative Situation

Notice the two
irregular forms,
BETTER and
WORSE.

i. Two students are talking about the weather in England. One of them is saying that the weather is not just bad, but terrible. The other does not agree.
"IT'S NOT AS BAD AS YOU SAY IT IS" he says. "IT'S BETTER THAN THAT!"

1. What are the students talking about?
2. What is one of them saying?
3. Does the other agree?
4. What does he say?

ii. Two students are talking about a professor's lecture. One of them is saying it was very bad. "Bad?" the other says. "IT WAS WORSE THAN THAT! IT WAS TERRIBLE!"

1. What are they talking about?
2. What does the first student say?
3. What does the second student say?

50 FLUENCY PRACTICE

Use ISN'T/ARE AS GOOD/BAD AS . . .
    IS/ARE BETTER/WORSE THAN . . .

Progressive Substitution

Model: THE WEATHER ISN'T AS BAD AS THAT.
better = THE WEATHER IS BETTER THAN THAT.
The food = THE FOOD IS BETTER THAN THAT.
good = THE FOOD ISN'T AS GOOD AS THAT.

THE WEATHER ISN'T AS BAD AS THAT.

1. The food	7. The lectures
2. The students	8. worse
3. better	9. This sweater
4. worse	10. My room
5. good	11. bad
6. The film	12. My English

UNIT A SIX

DID SOMETHING . . . AGO and more Reg. and
Irreg. Pasts
HAS/HAVE BEEN/HAD FOR . . . and HAS/HAVE
BEEN DOING SINCE vs. FOR

51 Did something . . . ago

Problem Situation

Study the situation. See if you can ask and answer the right questions. It is 10 o'clock in the morning. Richard West is at work. He got up at 6 this morning. He had breakfast at 7, and came to work at 8.

1. What time is it in the situation?
2. Richard came to work at 8. Can you ask and answer a question about this with HOW LONG AGO?
3. It is 10 now and he got up at 6; again ask and answer a question with HOW LONG AGO?
4. He came to work at 8; ask and answer HOW LONG AGO?

52 Illustrative Situations

Harry Evans is a young factory-worker. Every evening at 5 o'clock exactly the same thing happens. A bell rings at 5. The men stop work, turn off their machines, run out, put their overcoats on, and hurry home. It is now 7 o'clock, and the factory is empty. TWO HOURS AGO a bell RANG. The men STOPPED work, TURNED OFF their machines, RAN out, PUT their overcoats ON and HURRIED home.

1. What always happens at 5 o'clock in the factory?
   (bell. work. machines. out. overcoats. home.)
2. What happened at 5 o'clock this evening?
3. It is now 7. Ask questions with "How long ago did . . . ?

At 5 o'clock, Harry always buys an evening paper when he leaves the factory and then goes home on his motorbike. He gets home at 5.30 and always washes his hands and face, takes off his work-clothes and puts on a good shirt. He eats quickly. He leaves home at 6.30 and meets his friends in town. It is 7 now. TWO HOURS AGO Harry BOUGHT a paper when he LEFT the factory and WENT HOME on his motor-bike. AN HOUR AND A HALF AGO he GOT home, WASHED, TOOK OFF his work-clothes and PUT ON a sports-shirt. He ATE quickly. HALF AN HOUR AGO he LEFT home and MET his friends in town.

1. Ask if Harry always does these things at 5: (a paper. the factory. on his motorbike.)
2. What happens at 5.30? (home. hands and face. work-clothes. shirt)
3. What does he always do at 6.30? (home. friends)
4. What did Harry do at 5 this evening?
5. What did he do at 6.30?
6. Now ask some questions with "How long ago . . . ?"

53 FLUENCY PRACTICE

Progressive Substitution

Notice the question-form Do these at speed.

Model = HOW LONG AGO DID THE BOSS LEAVE?

get here = HOW LONG AGO DID THE BOSS GET HERE?

you = HOW LONG AGO DID YOU GET HERE?

HOW LONG AGO DID THE BOSS LEAVE?

1. the train	9. they
2. the plane	10. we
3. take off	11. learn this
4. land	12. he
5. she	13. get up
6. you	14. go to work
7. eat	15. have lunch
8. come here	16. you and she

54 Invention Exercise

Now say things you did. Use AGO with the prompt.

up = I GOT UP 6 HOURS AGO

1. a letter from my mother	5. breakfast
2. a letter to my mother	6. my old friend Max
3. to England	7. something to eat
4. my first English lesson	8. these shoes

Practice Situations

Study the situations. Make sentences with ONLY . . . AGO for them.

Situation: The lesson started at 9 and it is now 9.01. "You're late again" the teacher says. What does the student answer?

Answer: BUT THE LESSON STARTED ONLY A MINUTE AGO!

1. Tony's shoes are worn out. He bought them in January and it is only February now. Why is he angry?
2. Peter wants to leave the cinema. He and Jane came at 7, and it is 7.30 now. What does she say?
3. A friend invites you to lunch. You had lunch at 12 and it is 1 now. What do you say?
4. Mary's little boy is hungry again. He had a sandwich at 5. It is 5.15 now. What does she say?
5. The plane for Zurich left at 1, and it is 1.05 now. Can you still catch it? Why not?
6. A customer telephoned the manager at 12. He was not there. At 12.35 he came back. What did his secretary say?
7. Jill met a soldier at a dance on Friday. Now it is Sunday, only 2 days later and she wants to marry him. What does her mother say?
8. Your friend went out at 2. At 2.05 you got to his hotel. What does the hotel clerk say when you ask for him (your friend)?

"HAS/HAVE BEEN/HAD FOR . . ."
and "HAS BEEN DOING FOR . . ."

55 Problem Situation

There is an old man who works in the same office as Jane does. He started there when he was 20 and he is 60 now. He has exactly the same job as when he started. He is a clerk.

1. How old is the old man now?
2. How old was he when he started?
3. Has he still got the same job?
4. What sort of job is it?
5. Ask and answer two questions about him. (Use **how long**)   (a) a clerk (b) the same job.

56 Illustrative Situations

i. The old man, Mr. Jenkins, is in the boss's office now. The last time he got a rise was two years ago. He wants another one. The boss is asking questions like this:
"HOW LONG HAVE YOU BEEN WITH US NOW?" "HOW LONG HAVE YOU HAD THE SAME JOB?" "HOW LONG HAVE YOU BEEN EARNING THE SAME MONEY?"

1. Where is Mr. Jenkins now?
2. Ask why (and answer).
3. Ask the same questions the boss is asking. Use these words: with us/job/the same money.

ii. Sam Smith, the comedian, is 60, too. He became a comedian when he was 20. When he first became a comedian, he bought a book of jokes and funny stories. He still has that book and he still tells the same jokes and funny stories. Other comedians often say "Poor old Sam" "HE HAS (He's) BEEN A COMEDIAN FOR 40 YEARS NOW AND HE HAS (He's) HAD THAT BOOK FOR JUST AS LONG. HE HAS BEEN TELLING THE SAME JOKES FOR 40 YEARS! (That's why nobody laughs at them any more).

1. How old is Sam and when did he become a comedian?
2. When did he buy his book of jokes and funny stories?
3. Ask questions with "still" with these words: that book/jokes/people laugh
4. Now ask (and answer) questions with "How long . . . ?" a comedian/that book/same jokes and stories.

iii. One of Tony's friends, Paul, used to be a teacher. He did not earn a very good salary then. Three years ago he got another job in industry and immediately got a very good salary. He has a very good job now.
HE HAS BEEN IN INDUSTRY FOR THREE YEARS NOW. HE HAS HAD A GOOD JOB FOR THREE YEARS AND HAS BEEN EARNING A GOOD SALARY ALL THAT TIME.

1. Ask questions about Paul with these words: a teacher/a poor salary
2. Ask what he did three years ago! (and answer)
3. Ask about his job now.
4. Ask questions with "How long" with these words: in industry/a good job/a good salary.

57 FLUENCY PRACTICE

Progressive Substitution

Do these at speed. Notice also the change in HAS or HAVE.

Model: I HAVE (I've) HAD THIS JOB FOR 3 YEARS

been here =   I HAVE (I've) BEEN HERE FOR 3 YEARS

he =   HE HAS (he's) BEEN HERE FOR 3 YEARS

an hour =   HE HAS BEEN HERE FOR AN HOUR

I HAVE HAD THIS JOB FOR 3 YEARS

1. this coat	9. she
2. been here	10. had that car
3. two weeks	11. you
4. had this cold	12. we
5. two months	13. ten years
6. been in this town	14. this house
7. he	15. they
8. four years	

Progressive Substitution

Do at speed! Ask questions with HOW LONG?

Model: HOW LONG HAVE YOU BEEN HERE?

had that cold = HOW LONG HAVE YOU HAD THAT COLD?

he =   HOW LONG HAS HE HAD THAT COLD?

been away =   HOW LONG HAS HE BEEN AWAY?

HOW LONG HAVE YOU BEEN HERE?

1. those students	7. he
2. those books	8. we
3. she	9. they
4. had that job	10. been married
5. you	11. had that house
6. been in this class	12. been away

Invention Exercise

Use these words to make questions with "HOW LONG HAVE/HAS... BEEN DOING?

Sam/those terrible jokes = HOW LONG HAS SAM BEEN TELLING THOSE TERRIBLE JOKES.

1. the children/that stupid game
2. Carla/Italian opera
3. you/English
4. the teacher/English
5. you/in this town
6. Mr. Jenkins/that old jacket
7. he/£15 a week
8. Jane/in that office

58 **Practice Situations**

Bill Parks is in his lorry. He got into it at 9 and it's 12 now.
HE HAS (He's) BEEN IN HIS LORRY FOR 3 HOURS. HE HAS BEEN DRIVING FOR 3 HOURS.

1. Jane came into the office at 9. It is 11 now. She is working.
2. Sam went into the library 2 hours ago and got a book called "Great Jokes". He is still there.
3. Tony caught a bad cold 2 days ago. He immediately went to bed. He is still there. He coughs a lot.
4. Peter and Mary walked onto the station platform half an hour ago. They are waiting for a train.

5. The famous heart surgeon went into the operating theatre 8 hours ago. He is still there.
6. Eric arrived in England 3 months ago. He is studying English.
7. Eric and all the other students are in the lecture hall. They are doing a test. It started 4 hours ago.
8. Peter and Mary are married now. When they got married 2 months ago, they bought a house and are living there now.

59 **"Since" vs. "For"**

Illustrative Situation

Dr. Cantor is a heart surgeon. He is operating now. He began at 8 this morning and it is now 4 o'clock.
HE HAS BEEN OPERATING FOR 8 HOURS. HE HAS BEEN OPERATING SINCE 8 O'CLOCK.

1. What is Dr. Cantor doing now?
2. Ask when he began!
3. What time is it now?
4. Make two sentences, one with "since" and one with "for"

60 **Simple Discrimination**

Notice that we use FOR with LENGTHS of TIME and SINCE with POINTS in TIME.

Prompt: Monday
Response: SINCE
Prompt: 2 Days
Response: FOR

1. 1968
2. 3 years
3. the end of the war
4. the beginning of the lesson
5. 30 minutes
6. 20 years
7. a long time
8. 1620
9. hundreds of years
10. the death of my mother
11. the year I bought this house
12. the last few months

Progressive Substitution

Model: I'VE BEEN WAITING A LONG
           TIME
9 o'clock = I'VE BEEN WAITING SINCE 9
           O'CLOCK.
she =   SHE'S BEEN WAITING SINCE
           9 O'CLOCK.
Have you = HAVE YOU BEEN WAITING
           SINCE 9 O'CLOCK?

I'VE BEEN WAITING A LONG TIME

1. living here
2. She
3. working here
4. 1969
5. doing that
6. 10 o'clock
7. the last two hours
8. saying that
9. years and years
10. reading that paper
11. many years
12. Have you
13. teaching here
14. the school began
15. he

61 TEXT

This is a letter from a girl to her best friend.
The girl is on her honeymoon. She and her
husband are aboard a banana-boat sailing to
Jamaica.)

Dear Daphne,
What a terrible idea it was to take this cruise.
Never make the same mistake yourself. Take
your honeymoon on dry land! When we left
England, the weather was very nice. It was
warm and sunny. As soon as we sailed out of
Southampton harbour, black clouds covered
the sun and it became cold. That was 9 days ago,
and the weather is still miserable.
Roger became very sea-sick a few hours after we
got on the ship. He immediately went to bed
and he is still there. The ship's doctor says it is
the worst case of sea-sickness in his experience.
I am not very well either. I caught a cold 5 days
ago and I still have it. I am afraid I became very
depressed when I got on this boat, too. I am
depressed now. Oh, how I hate boats and the
sea! The only good thing about this cruise is
the ship's doctor. He is a very nice young man
with a beard. He loves the sea! He became a
ship's doctor when he left medical school 5
years ago and he says he does not want to do
anything else. I cannot understand it.
I hope Roger gets better. He is really terribly
sick. Oh, well, I am glad I bought all those
detective novels in Southampton 9 days ago!

          Love,
          Phyllis

1. How long ago did the weather become miserable?
2. What happened to Roger as soon as they got on the ship?
3. Where is Roger now?
4. When did Phyllis first become miserable?
5. When did she catch that cold?
6. When did the ship's doctor leave medical school?
7. What does Phyllis do to kill the time?
8. Now ask and answer questions about Roger, Phyllis, and the ship's doctor. Use "How long . . . ?" with these words:
(a) the weather/miserable (b) Roger/sea-sick
(c) Roger/bed (d) Phyllis/depressed (e) Phyllis that cold (f) the doctor/a ship's doctor
(g) Phyllis/detective novels.

D

33

UNIT A SEVEN

**SAY and REPORTED SPEECH (Present into Past Transformation)
TELL SOMEONE SOMETHING
CAN YOU TELL ME THE WAY TO . . . ?**

62 "SAY . . ."

Problem Situation

Mrs. Bashford met an old friend yesterday. "How's your husband" was the old friend's first question. Mrs. Bashford smiled. Her exact answer was:
"Oh, he's very well. He's a very important man, now. He has a very important job and does very important work." Her friend was very impressed.

1. Who did Mrs. Bashford meet yesterday?
2. What is her friend's first question?
3. What was Mrs. Bashford's exact answer? (well. important man. job. work)
4. Now begin your answer to the last question with "Mrs. Bashford said . . ."

63 Illustrative Situations

i.   Bert Johnson met a girl at a dance last week. He danced with her and said things like: "I'm a racing-driver. I earn a lot of money. I have a Rolls Royce. I live a dangerous life." A few days later the girl found out none of these things was true. In fact, Bert is a car salesman, he does not earn very much money, he has a very old sports car, and he lives a rather boring life. When the girl saw Bert again, she said this.
"You're a liar. YOU SAID YOU WERE A RACING-DRIVER, THAT YOU HAD A ROLLS ROYCE, THAT YOU EARNED A LOT OF MONEY AND THAT YOU LIVED A DANGEROUS LIFE. Those were all lies!"

1. Bert met a girl; ask where and when!
2. What were some of the exact things he said? (racing-driver. money. Rolls Royce. dangerous)
3. Ask and answer questions about Bert beginning with "Is" or "Does he really . . . ?"
4. What did the girl say when she met him again? (liar. racing-driver. Rolls. money. life)

ii. A factory needs workers. Yesterday Bill read their advertisement in the paper. It said these things:
"We are a very large firm, pay very high wages, and have a good pension-scheme."
Bill is at the factory today. He now knows that all those things are not true. At this moment he is saying these things to the manager:
"YOU SAID YOU WERE A VERY LARGE FIRM. but you are really a small one!
YOU SAID YOU PAID HIGH WAGES but they are really very low.
YOU SAID YOU HAD A GOOD PENSION SCHEME. You really haven't one at all."

1. Did the advertisement say the firm was large or small?
2. What are the exact words?
3. What did the advertisement say about the wages?
4. What are the exact words?
5. What did the advertisement say about the pension-scheme?
6. What are the exact words?
7. What exactly is Bill saying at the moment about:
(a) large firm (b) high wages (c) good pension-scheme?

64 Test Situation

Albert Oppenstein is one of the world's greatest mathematicians. However, when he was young, he was not a good student. These are the exact words one teacher used about him.
"The boy is stupid! He never does his homework. He never listens to me! He never answers my questions and he always comes to school late. The boy has no future."

1. Who is Albert Oppenstein?
2. Tell me what a teacher said about him. Use HE SAID + :
(a) stupid (b) homework (c) listen (d) his questions (e) to school late (f) no future

65 FLUENCY PRACTICE

Invention Exercise

Say things with IS/HAS/DO, etc. with these words.

Then say what you said!

The weather = "THE WEATHER IS TERRIBLE"
I SAID THE WEATHER WAS TERRIBLE.

1. the station/near the school
2. Rockefeller/a lot of money
3. a cup of tea every morning
4. a lot of homework every evening
5. French and Spanish
6. television every evening
7. "The Times" in the morning
8. about 10 cigarettes a day

66

Make sentences with SAID for these situations

Situation: "I know 10 languages" Ted said, and the export company gave him the job. Why?

BECAUSE HE SAID HE KNEW 10 LANGUAGES

Practice Situations

1. The words of the advertisement were "Our prices are very low". In fact they are really very high. Why did you go to the shop?
2. "The car has a very good engine," were the salesman's words; but later you found the opposite. Why did you buy it?
3. "I have a big house in California" the soldier said, and she married him. It was really very small. "Liar," she said, later. Why?
4. "The food is very good in that restaurant" were your friend's exact words, so you went there. Why?
5. "I know the way" Robert said. They both got lost. Why did Robert's friend go with him?
6. "Do you take shorthand?" was the question. "Yes, I do", was the answer. Why did he give her the job?
7. "Do you love me?" was the question, and "Yes, very much" was the answer. Why did she marry the man?
8. "Diamonds are my favourite toys" the blonde said, and so the old millionaire bought her some. Why?

67 TELL SOMEONE SOMETHING

Problem Situation

When Charles Grigg (the bankrobber now in prison) first met his wife, he said a number of things, like:
"I love you" "You are the only girl for me" and "I don't want anyone else but you".

1. When did Charles say this?
2. What exactly did he say?
   (love. only girl. anyone else.)
3. Now make sentences showing not only what he said but who he said it to.

68 Illustrative Situations

i. Robert, a language student, had a test yesterday. In the middle of it, his head began to ache. He got up and went over to the teacher. "I have a terrible headache" he said. The teacher's answer was: "All right. You can go out."
ROBERT TOLD THE TEACHER HE HAD A HEADACHE AND THE TEACHER TOLD HIM HE COULD GO OUT.

1. What happened in the middle of the test?
2. Ask (and answer) what Robert did!
3. What were his exact words and the teacher's exact answer.
4. What did Robert tell the teacher and what did the teacher tell him?

ii. Mr. Kipling (the tourist from Texas) went up to a policeman. "I want to see the Queen!" he said. The policeman nodded and was very polite. Well, sir" he said "She lives in Buckingham Palace but you can't see her today, I'm afraid. She's in Scotland".
MR. KIPLING TOLD THE POLICEMAN HE WANTED TO SEE THE QUEEN AND THE POLICEMAN TOLD HIM SHE LIVED IN BUCKINGHAM PALACE BUT THAT HE COULD NOT SEE HER TODAY BECAUSE SHE WAS IN SCOTLAND.

1. Ask (and answer) what Mr. Kipling told the policeman!
2. What did the policeman tell Mr. Kipling? (Buckingham Palace. today. Scotland.)

iii. Mr. Collins met an old friend for lunch yesterday. They talked a lot about old times. Suddenly Mr. Collins remembered he had an important business appointment. His own watch was broken so he asked his friend the time. "3.30" was the answer. "I'm awfully sorry but I have to go now. I have an appointment" Mr. Collins said.
WHEN HIS FRIEND TOLD HIM THE TIME MR. COLLINS TOLD HIM HE WAS SORRY BUT HE HAD TO GO BECAUSE HE HAD AN IMPORTANT APPOINTMENT.

1. Ask these questions
   (a) When/an old friend (b) What/suddenly remember (c) Why/his friend/the time.
2. Now make sentences with "told" (the time. sorry. go. appointment.)

69 FLUENCY PRACTICE

Progressive Substitution

Model: HE TOLD HER THE PRICE
the time = HE TOLD HER THE TIME
I =   I TOLD HER THE TIME

HE TOLD HER THE PRICE
1. them	7. the name of the film
2. I	8. her
3. her	9. it was good
4. the way to the school	10. me
5. he	11. you were here
6. us	12. us

Invention Exercise

Now make a sentence with TOLD or SAID If you hear a word like HIM, use TOLD. Use SAY if you do not hear a word like HIM.

him/tourist = I TOLD HIM I WAS A TOURIST.
a tourist =   I SAID I WAS A TOURIST.

1. them	7. him/nervous
2. a teacher	8. hello
3. her/very rich	9. Good-bye
4. a foreigner	10. them/angry
5. hungry	11. you/here
6. nervous	12. her/ill

70

Now make sentences with TOLD for these situations

Situation: The girl asked Tom about the film. "Wonderful" he said.
Response: HE TOLD HER IT WAS WONDERFUL.

Practice Situations

1. Robert asked his teacher about his mark in the test. "Very bad" was the answer.
2. "You are a very good student" the teacher said. Robert was pleased.
3. The doctor looked at Jane and said: "You have a very bad cold!"
4. The doctor looked at Tony and said "You're too fat!"
5. Mrs. Butler put another cigarette in her mouth. It was her 30th that day. "You smoke too much" her husband said.
6. The mechanic looked at Bert's car and said "The engine is worn out!"
7. Jane was already in the pool. "The water's very warm" she shouted, so Tony jumped in.
8. The salesman wanted £500 for the car. "The price is too high" Sam said, and walked out of the shop.
9. The film-actor looked at the film-actress and said: "You have beautiful eyes!"
10. The teenager wanted a drink but the barman looked at him and said: "You're too young!"
11. Jane asked the time. "It's five o'clock" was Mary's answer.
12. "Do this homework!" the teacher said. The student said "It's too difficult."

71 CONVERSATION

Mr. Kipling, the tourist from Texas, is in London. He is walking along a busy street. He wants to go to Oxford Street but he does not know the way.

Mr. Kipling: Excuse me. Could you tell me the way to Oxford Street?

Stranger: Certainly. I'm going that way myself. Come with me.

Mr. Kipling: That's very kind of you. Are you a real Londoner?

Stranger: Well . . . I suppose you could say that. I was born here.

Mr. Kipling: Well, I think it's a very nice little town.

Stranger: Little? You mean . . . small! London?

Mr. Kipling: Now don't misunderstand me. I said it was a nice small town. That's what I like about it. Everything's so small. I went to see Buckingham Palace yesterday. One of my friends in Texas was here last year and he told me it was small but I didn't know it was that small! I mean . . . my ranch-house back in Texas is bigger than that.

Stranger: (sarcastically but politely) Of course, you realise that our buildings are . . . small . . . only because we build them so quickly.

Mr. Kipling: Quickly? But I read a book about England last week and it said this was the country of tradition and slow change where everything happened slowly.

Stranger: Oh, no! The exact opposite. We do things much faster here than you do in Texas!

Mr. Kipling: (getting a bit aggressive) What? You're telling me that you do things here faster than we do in Texas?

Stranger: Oh yes. I mean. Everybody says so, don't they? (suddenly) Hmm! That's strange.

Mr. Kipling: What's strange?

Stranger: That tall building over there. That skyscraper.

Mr. Kipling: Say! Now that is a tall building. At least 30 storeys. Of course it isn't as tall as the buildings in Dallas . . . or New York. But . . . what's strange about it?

Stranger: Well . . . I came this way only yesterday and it wasn't here!

72 Special Exercise

Use the model COULD YOU TELL ME THE WAY TO . . . ? In sentences of your own. Suppose you want to go to:
  i Victoria Station
 ii the Post Office
iii the bus station
 iv at least 3 other places you know of

1. Where did Mr. Kipling want to go?
2. Why did he have to ask someone?
3. What were his exact words when he asked?
4. What was the first thing he said about London?
5. What did his friend from Texas tell him about Buckingham Palace?
6. What did the book Mr. Kipling read last week say about England?
7. What did the Englishman say when Mr. Kipling said all the buildings were small in England?
8. What were the exact words the Englishman used after Mr. Kipling asked him what was strange about the skyscraper?

UNIT A EIGHT

WOULD YOU/MAY I? (and phrasal verbs like "Turn ON/OFF etc."
TOLD and ASKED SOMEONE TO DO
TELL/SHOW/ASK etc. SOMEONE HOW TO DO

73 WOULD YOU?...MAY I?
(and phrasal verbs like Turn on/off/up/down)

i. Illustrative Situations

Susan is washing the dishes in the kitchen. She has only a few more to do. She wants to watch television in a minute. Tony is in the sitting-room but the television is not on.
"WOULD YOU TURN THE TELEVISION ON?" she shouts.

1. What is Susan doing?
2. How many more has she to do?
3. What does she want to do in a minute?
4. What does she shout to Tony?

ii.
Tony was at Peter's house yesterday. Susan was not with him and he wanted to phone her.
"MAY I USE YOUR PHONE?" he asked Peter. The radio was on in another room and it was so loud Tony could not hear Susan very well on the phone. "WOULD YOU TURN THE RADIO DOWN A BIT?" he asked Peter.

1. Where was Tony yesterday?
2. What did he want to do?
3. What exactly did he say when he asked?
4. Why couldn't he hear Susan very well on the phone?
5. What did he say to Peter?

74 FLUENCY PRACTICE

Progressive Substitution

Model:	WOULD YOU TURN THE RADIO ON?	
off =	WOULD YOU TURN THE RADIO OFF?	
May I =	MAY I TURN THE RADIO OFF?	

WOULD YOU TURN THE RADIO ON?

1. the lights	9. the heating
2. off	10. on
3. the machines	11. the lamp
4. the television	12. Would you
5. down	13. off
6. the music	14. May I
7. May I	15. the record-player
8. up	

75 TOLD/ASKED him etc. TO DO

i. Illustrative Situations

Richard usually drives to work along Bristol Road. Yesterday, however, there was a bad accident there and the road was blocked. A policeman stopped his car and said. "I'm sorry sir, you'll have to go the other way. Turn right, then left."
THE POLICEMAN TOLD HIM TO GO THE OTHER WAY (there was no alternative; we cannot say ASKED)
HE TOLD HIM TO TURN RIGHT AND THEN LEFT (instructions).

1. Why couldn't Richard use Bristol Road yesterday?
2. What exactly did the policeman say?
3. What do you think Richard said when he told a friend about this later?

ii. An extremely important customer rang up the director of Europa Export yesterday. The director was not there. His secretary said this: "I'm awfully sorry; the director isn't here. Do you think you could phone later?"
SHE ASKED HIM TO PHONE LATER.

1. What kind of customer was the man?
2. What exactly did the secretary say?
3. What do you think she said when the director came in later?

76 Practice Situations

Study the situations; use ASKED or TOLD

Situation: The policeman looked at the gangster and shouted: 'Put your hands up!'
HE TOLD HIM TO PUT HIS HANDS UP.

Situation: When the policeman saw the lord he said: "Wait just a moment, please"
HE ASKED HIM TO WAIT.

1. The window was open. The teacher said something very politely to the student next to it.
2. When the teacher saw a student reading a newspaper in the middle of the lesson, he got angry and shouted, "Put it away!"
3. When the plane landed the stewardess said "Would all passengers please leave by the front door?"
4. Just before the plane landed she said "Would all passengers please put out their cigarettes?"
5. The secretary was on the phone when I went into the office. She looked up and said, "Would you wait just a minute, please?"
6. Mary's son did not want to put his toys away. She got very angry.
7. The head waiter noticed that one of the waiters had a dirty shirt on. "Change it at once," he shouted.
8. The head waiter saw Lord F come in. He turned to one of the waiters and said, "Give him good service."
9. The film star was very particular about her hair. "Do it very carefully," she said. The hairdresser nodded.
10. There was something wrong with the racing car. "Look at the engine" the driver said to the mechanic angrily.

77 FLUENCY PRACTICE

Progressive Substitution

Model:	SHE ASKED HIM TO PHONE LATER.	SHE ASKED HIM TO PHONE LATER

come =	SHE ASKED HIM TO COME LATER.
I =	I ASKED HIM TO COME LATER.
next week =	I ASKED HIM TO COME NEXT WEEK.
told =	I TOLD HIM TO COME NEXT WEEK.

1. tomorrow   7. write
2. after dinner   8. him
3. told   9. do it
4. I   10. immediately
5. them   11. leave
6. next week   12. soon

78 SHOW/TELL/ASK him/her/etc. HOW TO DO

Problem Situation

Larry is a young engineer in India. At the moment he is showing an Indian a new machine and is telling him about it.
"Now, to use the machine, do this . . . "he is saying.

1. What does Larry do?
2. What is he doing?
3. What exactly is he saying?
4. Answer this
   Before the Indian can use the machine, Larry must show him something and tell him something; what?

79 Illustrative Situations

i. Peter is giving a party this evening. His friend does not know how to get to Peter's house, so Peter is telling him now.
"Turn left when you come to Churchill Avenue, then turn right when you come to Park Road. Then . . ."
HE IS TELLING HIM HOW TO GET THERE.

1. Why is Peter telling his friend all this?
2. What is Peter telling him?
3. Suppose you have the same problem as Peter's friend; ask Peter to do the same.

ii. Peter's friend does not really understand. Peter has a map on the table now and he is showing him.
HE IS SHOWING HIM HOW TO GET THERE.

1. What has Peter on the table now?
2. Ask what he is doing with it! (and answer)
3. How exactly do you think his friend asked him to do this?

iii. I had a flat tyre yesterday. I tried to change it myself but I couldn't because I did not really know how. I finally rang up my friend Tony. Tony knows a lot about such things.
I ASKED HIM HOW TO DO IT AND HE TOLD ME HOW TO DO IT.

1. What exactly was my problem?
2. Why couldn't I change it?
3. Why did I ring up Tony?
4. What did he do?
5. Did I ask him to change the tyre himself?
6. What did I do, then?

80 FLUENCY PRACTICE

Progressive Substitution

Do these at speed. Notice all the variations.

Model:	DID YOU SHOW HIM HOW TO DO IT?
why don't you =	WHY DON'T YOU SHOW HIM HOW TO DO IT?
can you =	CAN YOU SHOW HIM HOW TO DO IT?
tell =	CAN YOU TELL HIM HOW TO DO IT?
get there =	CAN YOU TELL HIM HOW TO GET THERE?

DID YOU SHOW HIM HOW TO DO IT?

1. would you		9.	learn more English
2. me		10.	he told
3. use this thing		11.	showed
4. get there		12.	to do it
5. could		13.	her
6. to the station		14.	him
7. tell		15.	them
8. us		16.	me

81

Make a sentence with SHOW or TELL or ASK for these situations, like this.

Situation: A secretary does not know how to use a new machine. The representative of the firm that makes them is demonstrating it.

Response: HE IS SHOWING HER HOW TO USE IT

1. A man asked me where the bus station was. I said: "Go down the road, then turn right."
2. Larry is training 2 Indian machinists. He is operating a machine and they are watching.
3. A sergeant has two soldiers in front of him. He is taking a rifle to pieces, bit by bit.
4. Bert is trying to fix his brakes. He has a problem so he is going to phone a friend who knows a lot about such things.

5. Maria is an Italian au-pair girl. She is making spaghetti and the woman she works for is watching carefully.
6. The man who installed my new T.V. set pointed out all the controls and demonstrated them.
7. A week ago I had no idea how to do the new dance. Then Jane demonstrated it for me.

Two old men are sitting on a bus. They are talking.

First Old Man:	Did you see that schoolgirl who got off then?
Second Old Man:	What about her?
First Old Man:	She looked more like a boy than a girl!
Second:	I think it's the other way around. All the boys look more like girls these days. It's all that long hair!
First:	The trouble is these days they don't teach the girls how to cook or how to take care of children or even how to keep house!
Second:	My granddaughter's going to university. She's learning how to build bridges and things like that! Fancy that! A girl learning how to be an engineer!
First:	Things aren't what they used to be, are they?
Second:	No, they aren't. Everything's upside down these days. People haven't even got good manners any more. Look at the way children act.
First:	That's right! Why don't they teach the girls to behave like ladies and the boys to behave like gentlemen!
Second:	Exactly!
Bus Conductor:	Excuse me. Would one of you give a passenger your seat. She's a mother with a baby and you're nearest the door. It'll only be for a few minutes!
First:	What? Give up my seat? Me!
Second:	Tell her to stand! I'm not giving up my seat to anyone!

1. What are some of the things one of the men thinks girls should learn? (cook/children/house)
2. What does the other man say about his granddaughter?
3. What is the first old man's question beginning with "Why don't they . . . ?" (girls/like ladies etc.)
4. Now mention some of the things you learned how to do in school.
5. What are some of the things you think schools should teach girls how to do?
6. What are some of the things you think everyone who gets a "modern" education should learn how to do?

UNIT A NINE

hate
stop
enjoy   **DOING**
remember

**Simple revision of WHO/WHICH/THAT
(contact clauses)**

83 Problem Situations

i. Richard went to a film yesterday. It was very
funny and he laughed a lot. In one scene a man
threw a pie in a woman's face. Richard laughed
and laughed and laughed, he could not stop.

1. Ask what kind of film Richard went to.
2. What happened in one scene?
3. Ask what Richard did?
4. Could he stop?
5. Now answer this
   Richard laughed and laughed and couldn't
   stop; he couldn't stop what?

ii. Paul White teaches small boys. He hates it. He
has, however, one great compensation, and that
is his garden. When he comes home from school,
tired and very often angry as well, he puts on
old clothes and works in the garden. He really
enjoys this and he always feels better afterwards.

1. What does Paul do?
2. Does he like it?
3. What does he do when he comes home from
   school?
4. How does he feel afterwards?
5. Now answer these
   (a) There is one thing that Paul does that he
       hates; what is it?
   (b) There is something else he does that he
       enjoys; what is it?

STOP DOING

Illustrative Situations

i. Tony was a heavy smoker 5 years ago. Then
cigarettes went up in price and the doctor told
him it was bad for his health so he stopped. He
does not smoke any more now.
HE STOPPED SMOKING 5 YEARS AGO

1. Is Tony a heavy smoker?
2. Why did he stop?
3. What exactly did he stop doing?
4. Ask when!

ii. The teacher is giving a lecture, but 2 students in
the back of the room are talking. He says this to
them:
PLEASE STOP TALKING

1. Is everyone in the room paying attention to
   the lecture?
2. What are 2 students doing?
3. What does the teacher say?

Variations

1. Peter and Jane played tennis yesterday but
it started raining in the middle of their match.
What did they do?
2. Mary's little son has a toy drum which he
beats all the time. What does she say when the
phone rings?

3. Robert is studying at the moment but it is
almost dinner-time. What is he going to do in a
few minutes?
4. Robert often misses his bus in the morning.
He always runs out of the house. What does he
do when he sees he is too late?

84   When we give advice to other people, we often
say YOU OUGHT TO or WHY DON'T YOU:
suppose your friend smokes a lot, coughs a lot
and never has any money. Give him advice.

Progressive Substitution

*Now make
sentences
starting from
the model.
Notice the
variations.*

Model: YOU OUGHT TO STOP
SMOKING
drinking = YOU OUGHT TO STOP
DRINKING
shouting = YOU OUGHT TO STOP
SHOUTING
Please =   PLEASE STOP SHOUTING
We ought = WE OUGHT TO STOP
SHOUTING

YOU OUGHT TO STOP SMOKING
1. going there   7. laughing
2. Please   8. saying that
3. shouting   9. doing that
4. they ought to   10. you ought to
5. talking   11. eating so much
6. Please   bread
                       12. working so hard

85 HATE DOING

Illustrative Situation

Jill wants to earn some money so she works in a
factory. She does not like it at all because it is
old and dirty and the work is boring. The only
thing that keeps her there is the money.
SHE HATES WORKING THERE

1. Ask why she works in the factory (and
   answer).
2. Ask why she hates it.
3. What exactly does she hate?

Variations

1. Harry operates a machine and does exactly
the same thing all day. Ask if he hates it.
2. When Arthur was a young boy the worst
thing in his life was that he had to go to school.
Ask a question with HATE about him.

3. Jill hasn't got a car. She takes the bus and
often has to wait for it. She hates this. Ask and
answer a question with WHAT.
4. Give at least 3 examples of things you hated
doing when you were younger.

86 ENJOY DOING

Illustrative Situations

i. Jane is a very athletic kind of girl. She is a very
good swimmer. She swims a lot every week-end
and always enjoys it.
SHE ENJOYS SWIMMING

1. What kind of girl is Jane?
2. Ask what kind of swimmer she is.
3. What does she do every week-end?
4. Why?

ii. She also enjoys football very much. She does
not actually play herself, but every Saturday
she watches a match somewhere.
SHE ENJOYS WATCHING FOOTBALL

1. What other sport does she enjoy?
2. Do you mean she actually plays football
herself?
3. What is it, then, that she enjoys?

iii. She got a small but very fast sports-car from her father last year. (He's very rich.) She drives it a lot. She loves fast cars.

1. What did she get last year?
2. Ask who from!
3. What is it that she enjoys?

Variations

1. Eric is a student of architecture. He was in Florence last year. He walked through the streets and looked at the buildings.
What did he enjoy doing?
Now ask someone else if they enjoy things like this.
2. Tony walks a lot. He enjoys it but his wife doesn't. Why doesn't she want to go with him now? (He is getting ready to walk through the woods.)

3. When a person is going to do something that we think he will enjoy, we say:
"I think you'll enjoy . . ."
Your friend is going to listen to a good record of yours; what do you say just before you play it?
4. Most women cook. Some enjoy it and others do not. Think of a typical question one women could ask another woman!

87 Invention Exercise

Make sentences of your own with these words

football = I ENJOY WATCHING FOOT-BALL
or I DON'T ENJOY PLAYING FOOTBALL

1. television
2. in the garden
3. detective novels
4. classical music
5. languages
6. homework
7. in the school canteen
8. exercises in the language-lab.
9. my car at night
10. in the park
11. English beer
12. by ship

88 REMEMBER DOING

Illustrative Situation

In the story on the next page you will also find an example of REMEMBER DOING. Study the situation in which we use it.

Mr. Butler put an important letter on his desk at home yesterday, and now it is not there. His wife wants to know if he is sure he put it there. His answer is:
"Oh, yes, I definitely REMEMBER PUTTING it there."

1. What does his wife want to know?
2. Is Mr. Butler sure he put it there?
3. What does he say to show he is sure?

89 REMEMBER DOING

Invention Exercise

Make sentences of your own with REMEMBER DOING

that book a long time ago =
I REMEMBER READING THAT BOOK A
LONG TIME AGO

1. that film last year
2. this word in the last lesson
3. all my money in my coat pocket
4. a toy horse for Christmas when I was 5
5. in that park last summer
6. in that hotel 4 summers ago
7. a steak in that restaurant
8. very late one night

90 TEXT

L. K. Fontana is a Cambridge Don. He is also a famous writer. 30 years ago he wrote a strange fantasy called "King of the Circles." It was about strange people called "Bobbins" who live in holes in the ground. The book is very popular now, especially in America. In a recent interview on television, Mr. Fontana said this about himself.

"I know some people think I'm some kind of philosopher. Actually, I'm a very ordinary kind of person and I enjoy very ordinary things. For instance, the first thing I say after getting up in the morning is always: 'Ah, good! I'm still alive. Now I can enjoy smoking for another 24 hours.' I probably enjoy smoking too much. My doctor once told me I ought to stop. 'What?' I said, 'Stop smoking? Why don't you ask me to stop living, too?'
Good simple food is another great pleasure. I really enjoy seeing, smelling, touching, and then, finally, eating a good pork pie . . . or good mashed potatoes . . . or simple English cheese, not too new. I also enjoy drinking good English beer.
There are things I hate, too. For instance, I hate getting up early in winter. I also hate eating watery vegetables. Nasty overcooked things! Most of all, however, I hate marking test papers. All poor professors have to do it in the summer. That's how 'King of the Circles' started, you know: I had to stay up late marking one night, and then, around 3 in the morning, I just could not go on. Suddenly I saw a blank piece of paper and I can remember writing the first sentence of the book on it. 'Once upon a time, there was a deep hole and a Bobbin lived in it.' "

1. What is the first thing he says after getting up in the morning?
2. What did his doctor tell him to do?
3. What was his answer?
4. Is eating food the only thing he enjoys about it?
5. What does he say about beer?
6. Ask if he enjoys getting up early in the morning (and answer).
7. Now ask (and answer) the same question about watery vegetables.
8. What about test-papers?
9. What did he have to do one night?
10. What can he remember doing when he saw that blank piece of paper?

91 **This is a simple revision of WHO/WHICH and THAT**

Examples:

That's the man WHO loves Jane.
That's the bus WHICH goes to the town-centre.

Books sometimes tell us to use WHO for people and WHICH for things in sentences like these
WHICH, however, often sounds unnatural
You can usually use THAT for both people and things. Study this

92 **Transformation Exercise**

Situation: You are pointing to a person or a thing. You are telling your friend something about that person or thing.
Prompt: That's the doctor. He gave me the tablets.
Response: THAT'S THE DOCTOR THAT (th't) GAVE ME THE TABLETS.
Prompt: That's the car. It won the race.
Response: THAT'S THE CAR THAT (th't) WON THE RACE.

1. That's the man. He stole my car.
2. That's the football club. It won every game last year.
3. That's the school. It has the best reputation.
4. That's the man. He's going to end the war.
5. That's the factory. It makes good cameras.
6. That's the shop. It sells foreign books.
7. That's the girl. She told me about you.
8. That's the teacher. He is going to give the lesson.
9. That's the word..It sounds unnatural.

93 **Progressive Substitution**

Notice how WHO and THAT are both used for people; WHO, however, is never used for things

Model: THAT'S THE MAN THAT MAKES CHOCOLATE.
who =   THAT'S THE MAN WHO MAKES CHOCOLATE.

THAT'S THE MAN THAT MAKES CHOCOLATE
1. sells chocolate
2. the shop that
3. buys old books
4. the student that
5. who
6. the teacher who
7. has a good reput-ation
8. the firm that
9. repairs radios
10. the shop that
11. the man that
12. who
13. gives money away
14. the organisation that
15. helps old people

94 omission of WHO or THAT

That's the man. I saw him.
THAT'S THE MAN I SAW

That's the bed. Napoleon slept IN it.
THAT'S THE BED NAPOLEON SLEPT IN.

Notice that in a certain type of sentence, we often leave out words like THAT/WHO, etc. and especially
In the second part of our sentences without WHO or THAT there is already another word like HE or SHE or WE ("I" in the first sentence and "NAPOLEON" in the second). In such cases it is not necessary to use THAT or WHO. The best way to understand this is to do some examples yourself

95 Transformation Exercise (all without THAT or WHO)

Notice also where words like IN go

Prompt: That's the dress. I want to buy it.
Response: THAT'S THE DRESS I WANT TO BUY.
Prompt: That's the house. Peter lives in it.
Response: THAT'S THE HOUSE PETER LIVES IN

1. That's the book. I want to read it.
2. That's the man. I want to see him.
3. That's the girl. I want to marry her.
4. That's the man. I love him.
5. That's the Rolls Royce. I want to have it.
6. That's the word. I don't know it.
7. That's the thing. I can't understand it.
8. That's the girl. I saw her.
9. That's the bed. I slept in it.
10. That's the house. I live in it.
11. That's the school. I study at it.
12. That's the girl. I danced with her.
13. That's the idiot. I talked to him.
14. That's the picture. You're looking at it.
15. That's the chair. You're sitting in it.
16. That's the bomb. You're sitting on it.

96

We must use THAT or WHO in these sentences. In the others it is not necessary.

Now last of all compare the sentence with WHO (or THAT) and the sentence without WHO (or THAT)

That's the man. He teaches.
THAT'S THE MAN WHO TEACHES
That's the man. I teach him.
THAT'S THE MAN I TEACH
That's the cheese. It smells.
THAT'S THE CHEESE THAT SMELLS
That's the cheese. You smell it.
THAT'S THE CHEESE YOU SMELL

Now you do it.

97 Transformation Exercise (mixed)

That's the man. I love him =
THAT'S THE MAN I LOVE
That's the man. He loves me =
THAT'S THE MAN THAT LOVES ME!

1. That's the woman. I hate her.
2. That's the woman. She hates me.
3. That's the teacher. I like him.
4. That's the teacher. He likes us.
5. That's the bomb. It killed a million people.
6. That's the man. He had an accident.
7. That's the film. I saw it.
8. That's the steak. I want it.
9. That's the music. I love it.
10. That's the music. It's popular.
11. That's the money. I lost it.
12. That's the man. Mary loves him.
13. That's the man. He loves Mary.
14. That's the hotel. I live in it.
15. That's the city. I was born in it.
16. That's the city. It was famous before the war.

E

UNIT A TEN

SHALL I?
SHALL WE?
WOULD YOU LIKE TO?
WOULD YOU LIKE A...?

Conversation
I'D LIKE TO DO
I'D LIKE A...

98 Illustrative Situations

i. You see an old lady at the railway station. She is carrying a heavy suitcase but you can see it is much too heavy for her. You say to her:
SHALL I CARRY THAT BAG FOR YOU?

1. Ask what the old lady is doing (and answer).
2. Is it a light suitcase?
3. What do you say to her?

ii. You and your friend are on the motorway. He is driving. He is very tired because he has been driving a long time. You say:
SHALL I DRIVE?

1. Who is driving the car?
2. Why is he tired?
3. What do you say?

iii. You are staying at your friend's house. You are both tired and are going up to your bedrooms. There is still a light on in the sitting-room and no-one is there. You say:
SHALL I TURN THE LIGHT OFF?

1. Where are both of you going?
2. Are all the lights off?
3. Who's in the sitting-room?
4. What do you say?

99 Progressive Substitution

Do these at speed!

Situation: You want to help a person in some way. You ask if that person wants your help.

Model: SHALL I CARRY THAT BAG?

SHALL I CARRY THAT BAG?
1. that box
2. open
3. the door
4. close
5. the window
6. your suitcase
7. take
8. the gramophone
9. turn on
10. the radio
11. the light
12. turn off
13. the engine
14. look at
15. the tyres
16. put some air into

100 Practice Situations

Make sentences with 'SHALL I?'

1. You are going to classroom T and so is a teacher, but she has a lot of books in her hands. What do you say?
2. You and your friend are going out of the house. The radio in your friend's room is still on. He is outside; you're not.
3. The teacher is trying to talk but a lot of noise is coming from the street and the window is open. You are next to it.

4. Your friend cannot do a problem. You already know the answer.
5. The train is going to leave in a few minutes. Robert is going to get himself a magazine. He sees his girl friend has nothing to read. What does he say?
6. Two men are trying to push a car. They are finding it very difficult. What do you say?

101 SHALL WE ......?

Illustrative Situations

Now study the meaning of SHALL WE?

It is lunch time and 2 students want to eat somewhere in town. One of them has an idea. He wants to know if the other student thinks it is a good one. He says:
SHALL WE HAVE A SANDWICH AND SOME BEER IN A PUB?

1. How many students are there?
2. What do they both want to do?
3. Where does one of them want to eat?
4. How does he find out if the other student thinks this is a good idea?

It is Saturday evening and Tony and Susan want to go out somewhere. Neither of them knows where, but then Tony has an idea. He says:
I KNOW! SHALL WE GO TO A CONCERT?

1. What do both Tony and Susan want to do?
2. Do we know yet if Susan wants to go to a concert?
3. Ask if Tony wants to!
4. What does he say?
5. When he says this, is he also asking if Susan wants to do this?

It is late at night at 10 Downing Street. The Cabinet is there. 3 or 4 of them are arguing about one particular point and now the Prime Minister wants to go to bed. He says:
"Well, Gentlemen. SHALL WE END OUR DISCUSSION NOW and talk about this again tomorrow?"

1. Ask how late it is! (and answer).
2. What is happening?
3. What does the Prime Minister want to do?
4. What does he say?

102 Practice Situations

Make sentences with SHALL WE ....? for these situations.

1. You and some other people are sitting inside on a rainy day. You are all bored. Suddenly you see a pack of cards.
2. You and your friend are hungry. There is a Greek restaurant nearby. You think it is a good restaurant.

3. You and your friend have to get somewhere in London. You know it is quickest by Underground.
4. Robert and his girl-friend want to go out. He knows there is a good film at the cinema. What does he say?

103 Invention Exercise

Situation: You have an idea about what you and another person (or people) can do together.
Model: SHALL WE ....?
this point tomorrow = SHALL WE DISCUSS THIS POINT TOMORROW?

1. the cinema this evening?
2. a drink somewhere?
3. another television programme? (this one is terrible).
4. in the new French restaurant?
5. a game of tennis?
6. at the table over there?
7. the bus to school?
8. a taxi?
9. this question some other time?
10. a walk in the park?
11. lunch now?
12. the dance on Friday?

WOULD YOU LIKE A . . .?
WOULD YOU LIKE TO DO?

104 **Illustrative Situations**

i. Robert is speaking to a girl called Claudia. He wants to take her out this evening. She does not know this yet. His question is:
WOULD YOU LIKE TO GO OUT THIS EVENING?

1. Who is Robert speaking to?
2. What does he want to do?
3. What is his exact question?
4. Suppose he wants to go for a walk with her; what does he say?

ii. Tony is going to give a party next Friday. He wants to ask his friend to it. His exact words are:
WOULD YOU LIKE TO COME TO MY PARTY next Friday?

1. Ask when Tony is going to give his party.
2. Who does he want to ask to it?
3. What are his exact words?

iii. A number of students are having a drink in a country pub. One student notices that one of the girls is not drinking anything. He wants to get her something, so he asks:
WOULD YOU LIKE A DRINK?
Her answer is: "Yes, please."
His next question is:
WHAT WOULD YOU LIKE?

1. What are the students doing?
2. Ask where!
3. What does one student notice?
4. Ask what he wants to do!
5. What is his exact question?
6. What is her answer?
7. What does he say then?
8. Suppose he is going to light a cigarette when he notices she is not smoking; what does he say?

105 **Progressive Substitution**

WOULD YOU LIKE A CIGARETTE?

Notice when we say TO DO and when we do not.

Notice also that TO is pronounced T' (weak)

Model: WOULD YOU LIKE A CIGARETTE?
a cup of coffee = WOULD YOU LIKE A CUP OF COFFEE?
see my pictures = WOULD YOU LIKE TO SEE MY PICTURES?

1. a cigar
2. another
3. use my telephone
4. go to his wedding
5. eat in a Wimpy bar
6. some more sugar
7. some salt on your chips
8. see the language-lab.
9. some garlic on your steak
10. another glass of Beaujolais
11. look at my wine-cellar
12. take a later train

Think of sentences with WOULD YOU for these situations

1. You are giving a party. A guest isn't eating anything and you have a tray of sandwiches.
2. You often give people lifts. You are driving along a lonely country road when you see an old woman walking along it in the rain.
3. Robert has 2 tickets for the concert but nobody to go with. Then he sees Claudia. What does he say?
4. Peter's boss has come to dinner. Peter notices that his wine-glass is empty. What does he say to his boss?
5. Peter knows his boss has heard a lot about his house but has never seen all of it. What does Peter say after dinner?

6. Robert wants to take his girl-friend to a Spanish restaurant. What does he say to her.
7. Bert's new sports car is outside the pub. He sees a friend in the pub who is interested in sports cars. What does Bert say?
8. Jane is walking through the park with her grandfather. He seems to be getting tired. What does she say when she sees a bench?
9. Your friend is leaving your house. It is raining and he has no umbrella. You have an extra one. What do you say?
10. Mrs. Butler loves children. She is walking home with a bag of sweets in her hand when she sees the neighbour's little boy. She asks . . .

106 CONVERSATION

Listen to the conversation. (or read it)

Robert is talking to a girl called Claudia. He likes her very much. He wants to take her out this evening.

Robert: Would you like to go out somewhere this evening?
Claudia: Somewhere? Where?
Robert: Well . . . . I don't know exactly. Shall we see a film perhaps?
Claudia: A film? Which one?
Robert: Well . . . . There's a new Swedish film at the Continental.
Claudia: No. Bert told me it wasn't very good.
Robert: Bert? Who's Bert?
Claudia: He's that car salesman I told you about.
Robert: Oh . . . that one.
Claudia: Yes. He has a new sports car.
Robert: Now, let's see . . . .
Claudia: You really must meet him, you know!
Robert: Would you like to eat in that new Indian restaurant?
Claudia: No. Bert and I were there last week. I didn't think much of it.
Robert: Well, shall we have a Chinese meal somewhere?
Claudia: No. I'm going to have a Chinese meal tomorrow.
Robert: Oh?
Claudia: Yes, with Bert. I always go out with Bert on Saturday night.
Robert: But that's tonight! It's Saturday today!
Claudia: What? Oh dear. I'm so sorry.
Robert: You mean . . . .
Claudia: I'm afraid I thought it was Friday. Isn't that funny?
Robert: Yes, very. Very amusing.

1. Does Robert know exactly where he wants to go when he first asks Claudia?
2. What does he say to her?
3. How does he suggest seeing a film?
4. Why doesn't she want to see it?
5. How does he ask her to eat in the new Indian restaurant?
6. When was she there?
7. Ask what she thought of it!
8. What exactly does he say when he mentions the Chinese restaurant?
9. Why doesn't she want to eat there?
10. What does she always do on Saturday night?
11. What day is it in the situation?
12. Ask what day she thought it was!

107 I'D LIKE A . . .
      I'D LIKE TO . . .

Illustrative Situations

i.   Tony is in a restaurant. He is ordering now. He says:
    I'D LIKE A STEAK, PLEASE.

1. Where is Tony?
2. What is he doing?
3. What exactly does he say?

ii. Mrs. Mavis is very poor. She lives in a small house with a very old and tiny kitchen. She enjoys going into the large department stores and looking at all the large, modern model kitchens there. She often says:
    I'D LIKE A KITCHEN LIKE THAT, SOME DAY

1. Tell me about Mrs. Mavis's house and kitchen!
2. What does she enjoy doing?
3. What else does she enjoy doing?
4. What does she often say?

iii. An American diplomat made a long distance telephone call to the President of the United States yesterday. He had some important information for him. However, the President did not answer himself. One of his assistants did. The diplomat's information was for the President only, so he said:
    HELLO? I'D LIKE TO SPEAK TO THE PRESIDENT, PLEASE.

1. What did the diplomat do yesterday?
2. Ask why! (and answer).
3. Who answered his call?
4. Why didn't he give his information to him?
5. What did the diplomat say?

108 Invention Exercise

Notice again when we say TO DO and when it is not necessary. Pronounce TO as T' (weak)

another cup of tea = I'D LIKE ANOTHER CUP OF TEA PLEASE.

the news on = I'D LIKE TO LISTEN
the radio   TO THE NEWS ON THE RADIO

1. the director of the school
2. a bigger room (this one is too small)
3. spring in Paris
4. a long-distance call to Moscow
5. a tie to go with this pullover
6. the new film at the Continental
7. television this evening
8. a long, hot bath

109 Situation: You are at Mrs. Bashford's tea-party. You notice that your cup is not really clean. One of Mrs. Bashford's maids is there. I'D LIKE A CLEAN CUP, PLEASE.

Now make sentences with I'D LIKE A . . . or I'D LIKE TO . . . for these situations

1. You are not satisfied with your room in the hotel because it is too small. You are talking to the manager.
2. You are Mrs. Bashford's cocktail party but have nothing to drink. The waiter is going by with a tray of champagne cocktails.
3. The salesman says he cannot give you your money back for the thing you bought. You know that the manager can.
4. You want some salt for your steak and the waiter is just going by.
5. You must telephone someone right away, and the only telephone in the school is in the office. You are there now.
6. You and another friend are going past a cinema on your way to work. You notice that there is a very good film on.
7. You are having a drink in a pub. You notice that your glass is cracked.
8. Only the director of the firm can answer your question. His secretary answers the telephone.

UNIT A ELEVEN

Reflexives HURT HIMSELF, etc.
(story) non-reflexives like WAS/DRESS/FEEL, etc.
THEMSELVES/OURSELVES vs. EACH OTHER

110 **Problem Situation**

Tony and his wife went on a tour of a television studio last week. In one room there was a camera at one end and a television set at the other. Tony looked at the set and saw a very familiar face. It was his own face!

1. Ask where Tony and his wife went last week.
2. What was there in one room?
3. What did Tony see when he looked at the set?
4. Now do this
   The face Tony saw was his own; who did he see? All the people in the room had exactly the same experience; who did they see?

Study and repeat these words with the teacher several times!

MYSELF HERSELF HIMSELF YOURSELF OURSELVES THEMSELVES

Also notice when SELF becomes SELVES

Examples (repeat aloud)
I CUT MYSELF YESTERDAY. SHE HURT HERSELF. YOU'RE GOING TO BURN YOURSELF! THE BABY BURNED ITSELF. BILL CAN LOOK AFTER HIMSELF. CAN THEY LOOK AFTER THEMSELVES? WE AMUSED OURSELVES.

111 **CUT MYSELF**

Illustrative Situation

My bread-knife is not very sharp. I always have to use a lot of energy to slice a loaf. Yesterday I suddenly felt a pain in my finger. When I looked at it I saw blood.
I CUT MYSELF YESTERDAY

1. Suppose you are the person in this situation; where did you feel the pain?
2. What did you see when you looked at your finger?
3. What happened yesterday?

Variations

1. You see a child playing with a knife and you think you know what is going to happen. What exactly do you say to the child?
2. Ask the person next to you if he or she ever did this as a child (and answer).

3. There is blood on your friend's chin. Ask him a question with HOW.
4. Why are knives dangerous in the hands of children?
5. Margret is slicing some bread but she is thinking about something else. What do you think is going to happen?

112 HURT HERSELF

Illustrative Situation

Mrs. Mavis went to the shops yesterday. The
pacement was very icy and she slipped. The fall
was very painful. She can still feel it.
SHE HURT HERSELF

1. Ask where she went!
2. Tell me about the pavement!
3. Was the fall painful?
4. What did she do to herself?

Variations

1. Mrs. Mavis told you she slipped and fell
yesterday. What did you ask her?
2. You slipped and fell yesterday, but it was
not painful. Later your friend asked you if you
were all right. What did you say?

3. You see a child playing with a dangerous toy.
You think you know what is going to happen.
What do you say about the child?
4. And what do you say when you speak direct-
ly to the child?

113 CONTROLLED HIMSELF

Illustrative Situation

Richard was late for work last week, and his
boss was very sarcastic. Richard became very
angry. He wanted to say something very sarcastic, too, but he didn't.
HE CONTROLLED HIMSELF

1. Why did Richard get angry?
2. What did Richard want to say?
3. Ask if he did!
4. What did he do?

Variations

1. When a person does one thing and you think
another thing is better, you often say YOU
OUGHT TO . . .
What do you say to a friend who often gets
very angry?
2. When you give orders in English, you use the
form DO THIS or COME HERE or SIT DOWN.
What did the General say to the Captain yesterday when the Captain got angry?

3. Jane's boss is also very sarcastic. Yesterday it
was too much, and she said what she felt. What
couldn't she do?
4. Mr. Butler has a huge appetite. When he sees
food, he goes wild and eats and eats. What can't
he do?
5. He goes to a psychiatrist every Friday now.
What is the psychiatrist teaching him to do?

114 Going to BURN YOURSELF

Illustrative Situation

A small child is playing near a gas-fire. (Many
English homes have them in the sitting room.)
It is interested in the fire and wants to touch it.
Its mother sees this and says:
'No! Don't touch it! YOU'RE GOING TO
BURN YOURSELF'.

1. Where is the child playing?
2. What does it want to do?
3. What does its mother say?

Variations

1. The child actually touched the fire yesterday. It cried with pain. What did it do yesterday?
2. What can children do to themselves if there is an open fire in the room?
3. I picked up a lighted cigarette by the wrong end yesterday. What happened?

4. You see a small boy playing with a cigarette lighter. What do you say about the child?
5. What do you say to the boy?
6. Three or four children are playing with matches. Why is this dangerous?

115 LOOK AFTER THEMSELVES

Illustrative Situations

Human babies are helpless for a long time. Young animals can do everything for themselves when they are a year old. However, a one-year-old baby cannot wash itself, dress itself, or, sometimes, even feed itself.
BABIES CANNOT LOOK AFTER THEMSELVES

1. Can most babies feed themselves?
2. Ask about young tigers.
3. Can a child wash itself?
4. Ask about young cats.
5. Can a child dress itself?
6. Ask about a man with boxing-gloves on.

Variations

1. What happens sometimes to very old people?
2. Ask the person next to you if he or she could do that when he was 5.

3. What do mothers teach their children to do?
4. Ask (and answer) when a cat learns to do this.

116 Progressive Substitution

Do these at speed!

Model: SHE KILLED HERSELF

SHE KILLED HERSELF

1. cut	9. controlled
2. you	10. I
3. I	11. hurt
4. looked at	12. she
5. she	13. the baby boy
6. we	14. washed
7. amused	15. fed
8. he	

Progressive Substitution

Now do this at speed.

Model: HE BURNED HIMSELF

HE BURNED HIMSELF

1. she	9. the boy can't
2. hurt	10. look after
3. going to	11. the old man
4. you	12. a lot of old people
5. did you	13. I can
6. control	14. can you
7. you ought to	15. we can
8. wash	16. amuse

Special Note:

Words like MYSELF/YOURSELF/HERSELF, etc. (reflexive pronouns) are used much less in English than reflexive pronouns (sich/si/se) are used in other languages. This is probably because they are longer in English than in most other languages.

In the text you will find a number of words that are not reflexive in English but are in most European languages.

Some words like WASH/DRESS/SHAVE are used with HIMSELF, etc., only with children or in situations where, for some reason, it is difficult to do these things.

117 TEXT

Robert felt bad this morning. He got up, washed and shaved and dressed very slowly and then got himself some breakfast. He usually has a large breakfast but this morning he did not feel hungry at all, so he had only a piece of toast and a cup of coffee.

Robert has an important examination in a few weeks and he wanted to prepare for it. He sat down after breakfast and looked at his books, but he could not concentrate. After a while he looked at himself in the mirror. What he saw was not very nice. His eyes were red and he was also very pale. Just then his sister knocked on the door.

'What you need is fresh air," she said. "You study too much."

They went for a walk in the park and sat in the warm spring sun for a while. Afterwards Robert felt much better and found he could concentrate on his books.

Use WASH/CONCENTRATE/IS PREPARING/ FEEL/etc. for these situations;

1. How did Robert feel this morning?
2. What did he do immediately after he got up?
3. Ask if he did these things quickly! (and answer)
4. Ask (and answer) why he did not have a large breakfast today!
5. Robert has an examination soon; what did he want to do after breakfast?
6. Ask (and answer) if he did this!
7. Why not? What couldn't he do?
8. Ask if he could after his walk in the park!
9. How did he feel afterwards?

Use WASH/CONCENTRATE/IS PREPAR-ING/FEEL/etc. for these situations

118 Practice Situations

1. Robert is trying to read the book in front of him but his brain is very tired.
2. Jane is in the bathroom with soap and a sponge in her hand.
3. She does this every morning at 7.
4. Peter has a headache and a pain in his stomach.

5. Three students are in the library now with their books. Their exam is next week.
6. What is it that good students do and bad students often do not?
7. Suppose you are a teacher; tell a bad student what it is important to do.
8. Ask the person next to you if he or she did this for the last exam!

119 THEMSELVES/OURSELVES vs. EACH OTHER

Illustrative Situations

i. Tony and his wife were both at the television studio. They both were in the room with a camera at one end and the television set at the other. Tony saw his own face and his wife saw her face.
THEY SAW THEMSELVES

1. Who did Tony see?
2. Who did his wife see?
3. So, who did they see?

ii. After, this, Tony saw his wife on the screen (the part of the set where the picture is) and Tony's wife saw him.
THEY SAW EACH OTHER

1. Who did Tony see then?
2. Who did his wife see?
3. So, who did they see?

iii. Philip went to the Art Gallery in Liverpool yesterday (there is a very good one there). He saw his old friend Sandra there. She saw him, too. When he saw her, he waved to her. She waved back.
THEY SAW EACH OTHER AND THEY WAVED TO EACH OTHER.

1. Who did Philip see at the Art Gallery?
2. Ask if she saw him!
3. What did he do when he saw her?
4. Ask if she did, too?
5. He saw her and she saw him; what is the shorter way of saying this?
6. Who did they wave to.

Variations

1. If Peter knows Barbara, and Barbara knows Peter, who do they know? Ask a question about the 2 of them with LIKE.
2. What do we say about 2 people if one hates the other and vice versa? Ask (and answer) if Romeo and Juliet did.

3. If I help you and you help me, who do we both help? Do you think people ought to do this? Ask if they always do.
4. Philip is going to see Sandra tomorrow at 8. Who are they both going to see at 8? What exactly does Philip ask if he wants to know where and when (use SHALL here).

120 Transformation Exercise

Think about the difference! She saw him and he saw her = THEY SAW EACH OTHER
Use EACH OTHER or THEMSELVES /OURSELVES. He saw himself; she saw herself = THEY SAW THEMSELVES

1. She knew him and he knew her.
2. She liked him and he liked her.
3. He amused himself and she amused herself.
4. I am watching you and you are watching me.
5. You can look after yourself and I can look after myself.

6. I'm going to see Mary and she is going to see me in London.
7. You talked to me about it and I talked to you.
8. She can help me and I can help her.

UNIT B ONE

IS/ARE DOING in the future
HAS/HAVE vs. IS/ARE HAVING
Introduction of Irregular Past Participles (in conversation)

1 IS/ARE DOING in the future

Problem Situation

Robert was on his way home yesterday when he saw a large poster in front of the concert hall. It said: 'Concert by great international pianist LEO SHAMINSKI Thursday next!' Robert knows his girl-friend thinks Shaminski is marvellous, so naturally he told her the news.

1. When is Shaminski's concert?
2. What does Robert's girl-friend think of Shaminski?
3. What did Robert do after he saw the poster?
4. Now do this
   What exactly do you think Robert said when he told her about Shaminski next Thursday?

2 Illustrative Situations

i. The term at the Language Institute is almost over. Paula is a student there. Her bags are packed and she has a ticket for tomorrow's plane. She is speaking to one of her teachers: I want to say goodbye. I'M LEAVING TOMORROW.

1. Is the term over?
2. Ask if Paula's bags are packed!
3. Has she a ticket for a plane?
4. Ask when that ticket is for!
5. What exactly does she say to her teacher?

ii. Two Generals have a problem and the only person who can really deal with it is the President. As it happens, one of the Generals has an appointment with him for next week. He says: I'M SEEING THE PRESIDENT NEXT WEEK.

1. Who is the only person who can deal with the problem?
2. Is one of the Generals going to make an appointment?
3. Why not?
4. What exactly does he say to the other General?

iii. Richard and his wife often give parties. Everything is ready for their party on Saturday. They made most of the arrangements some time ago. However, there are 2 or 3 people Richard forgot to invite, so he is phoning them now. His words are always the same:
"Hello. WE'RE GIVING A PARTY ON SATURDAY! Can you come?"
Sometimes his first question is:
"ARE YOU DOING ANYTHING ON SATURDAY?" (he wants to find out if they have any other plans.)

1. What are Richard and his wife doing on Saturday?
2. Ask if they often do!
3. When did they make most of the arrangements?
4. Why is Richard phoning now?
5. What exactly does he say first?
6. How does he find out if the people have other plans?

3 Special Comment
We use IS/ARE DOING like this when we are sure about the thing because arrangements for it are already made.

Invention Exercise

Now make sentences of your own with I'M . . . ING TOMORROW, etc.

dinner out this evening = **I'M HAVING DINNER OUT THIS EVENING.**

(Situation) = I phoned my friend this morning and asked her out. She said it was all right. We are meeting after work.

1. the cinema this evening
2. to Istanbul next Monday
3. a test next week
4. a driving lesson at 5
5. a new car tomorrow
6. the boss on Tuesday
7. the night express to Paris
8. dinner at Chez Marcel

4 Practice Situations

Now make sentences for these situations

Situation: Peter went to Victoria Station this morning and reserved a berth on the night boat to Calais.
Response: **HE IS CATCHING THE NIGHT BOAT TO CALAIS.**
or: **HE IS TAKING THE NIGHT BOAT TO CALAIS.**

1. Paula went to the BEA ticket office this morning and bought a ticket to next Friday's plane to Prague.
2. Max phoned the President about a problem. The President was very interested and invited Max to dinner this evening.
3. Terry sees his mother every Sunday. It is Sunday tomorrow.
4. Margaret has a new job. Her first day in it will be next Monday.
5. Jill and Bert have a date this evening. Trafalgar Square is their meeting place.
6. You received an invitation to your best friend's wedding a month ago. You accepted. The wedding is tomorrow.
7. You rang up your friend and arranged to see a film this evening after work.
8. Tony and his wife eat out every Friday. It is Friday tomorrow.
9. The Prime Minister has a ticket in his pocket for this evening's plane to Moscow.
10. Mrs. Mavis has an appointment with the doctor tomorrow.

5 HAS/HAVE vs. IS/ARE HAVING

Problem Situation

Bert often has the same nightmare. In it, a huge cat, 3 or 4 times larger than he is, chases him down a street and catches him. He always wakes up just before the cat puts him into its mouth.
It is the middle of the night now and Bert is asleep, but in his mind that cat is chasing him. In a second he is going to start screaming.

1. Is a cat really chasing Bert?
2. What do you call a dream like this?
3. Ask if he often has such dreams!
4. Is Bert awake now?
5. What is he going to start doing in a second?
6. Now do this
   Bert often has nightmares; what can you say about him at this moment? (In this situation)?

6 Illustrative Situations

i. **In front of Bert's house, there is a sports car. It belongs to Bert.**
   HE HAS A SPORTS CAR

1. Ask who that car belongs to!
2. So, what can you say about Bert?

ii. **It is 7 a.m. now and Bert is in the bathtub. The water is warm, and Bert is singing.**
   HE IS HAVING A BATH. HE HAS ONE EVERY MORNING.

1. Where is Bert now?
2. He is doing two things; what are they?
3. How often does he have a bath?

Mona Fire, the film-star, wants to become a better actress. A drama teacher comes to her house every morning.
SHE HAS A DRAMA TEACHER.

1. Who is Mona Fire?
2. Is she satisfied with herself?
3. What else can you say about her?

Mona is with her drama teacher now. She is acting a scene from 'Hamlet'. Her teacher is going to criticise her in a second.
SHE IS HAVING A DRAMA LESSON. SHE HAS ONE EVERY MORNING.

1. Ask who Mona is with now!
2. What is her teacher going to do in a second?
3. What are the two things Mona is doing?
4. How often does she have a drama lesson?

7 Special Comment

One of these two different uses of HAVE means to do something. The other does not mean to do something. When HAVE means to do something, it has a continuous tense. Do not accept the explanation some books give about the other HAVE. Some books say the other HAVE means POSSESS. Situation iii shows this explanation is misleading. (Page 65)

Concentrate only on the examples in which HAVE means to do something. In those examples, remember that there is a continuous form that must be used and is used very frequently when the situation demands it.

Study the examples. Identify those in which HAVE means to do something.

(a) I have a cold bath every morning.
(b) We have a very nice house.
(c) He has a bad cold.
(d) I have an egg for breakfast every morning.
(e) She has very nice eyes.
(f) He has a music lesson every Monday.

8 Invention Exercise

With some words we can think both of what a person has and what he or she IS DOING

Make examples with IS . . . ING when you hear such a word.

If a word suggests only HAS make such an example.

steak = HE HAS STEAK TWICE A WEEK.

blonde hair = HE HAS BLONDE HAIR.

1. a cold bath
2. a solid gold bath-tub
3. a ride on his horse
4. a horse
5. a poodle and a cat
6. a lamb chop for dinner
7. a cup of tea
8. a Ming porcelain tea-cup
9. a music lesson
10. a music teacher
11. a good character
12. a conversation with the Pope
13. a pleasant dream
14. an antique bed

9 Situation: There is a green sports car in front of Mary's house. It belongs to her. SHE HAS A SPORTS CAR.

Make sentences with HAS/ HAVE or IS/ ARE HAVING for these situations

Situation: There is a cup of coffee in front of her now on the breakfast table. SHE IS (she's) HAVING A CUP OF COFFEE.

1. There is a car in front of Mrs. Collins' house. Her husband gave it to her for Christmas.
2. She can't drive it yet. That's why she's in a car now with a driving-teacher.
3. Mr. Collins is at work. He is in the conference room with several other men.
4. It is lunch time now and Mr. Collins is in a restaurant with some customers.
5. It is 8 o'clock in a Peking language institute. Three students are in a classroom with an English teacher.
6. There is an Irish passport somewhere with that teacher's name on it.

7. Whenever President MacGull goes abroad, a doctor goes with him. He is President MacGull's private doctor.
8. President MacGull is on the operating-table now. There are 10 doctors around him.
9. Burt is under the shower. The water is very hot.
10. Tony and Susan do not often have argument but they are both very angry now and are saying nasty things to each other.
11. They often go to a house in the country at week-ends. It belongs to them.

10 CONVERSATION

Tony and Susan have gone to a very expensive restaurant. They are looking at the menu now.

Susan: I hope we haven't made a mistake in coming here. I mean, we could have gone to a cheaper restaurant and had something like fish and chips.

Tony: Fish and chips? I hate fish and chips! We eat fish and chips when we can't afford anything else. In fact, we've come here because they haven't even got fish and chips on the menu!

Susan: Look. The waiter's coming. You order first, Tony.

Waiter: Good evening. Would you like to order now?

Tony: Yes. I think I'll have the steak cooked in red wine and . . .

Waiter: I'm terribly sorry, sir. We've run out of steak. It's coming in tomorrow.

Tony: Oh! Well, I'll order something else, then. Have you made up your mind, yet, Susan?

Susan: Yes. I'd like the "scampi provencale".

Waiter: Scampi, madam. I really am most awfully sorry, but we've run out of scampi, too. They're coming with the steak, tomorrow.

Susan: Oh, dear! What a pity. I haven't eaten scampi for a long time. Have you found something else, Tony?

Tony: Yes. I'll have the "veal, Spanish style".

Waiter: Oh? (laughing nervously) Now, that is a pity, sir.

Tony: What: You mean you've run out of veal, too?

Waiter: I'm afraid so, sir. It's coming tomorrow, too.

Tony: Well, what about the "chef's special chicken casserole", then. I suppose you've run out of chicken, too!

Waiter: Oh, no, sir. We haven't run out of chicken but . . .

Tony: Well, that's one good thing at least!

Waiter: Uh . . . I'm afraid, sir, that the only person who can cook the chicken casserole is the chef, sir.

Tony: Yes? Well?

Waiter: And . . . uh . . . he's gone into hospital sir. He's having an operation tomorrow. He's coming back to work next month.

Tony: (very angry now) Good Lord! No steak, no scampi, no veal, not even a chef! What can we eat, then?

Waiter: Well, sir, it's not on the menu but I can recommend it. It's very good, sir, and I know because I'm doing the cooking myself.

Tony: What's that?

Waiter: The fish and chips, sir. Try the fish and chips. I'm afraid they're the only thing we have, sir.

1. What does Susan say at the beginning? (mistake in coming here, etc.)
2. Why haven't they gone to a cheaper place and had fish and chips?
3. What does the waiter say when Tony orders steak?
4. What else do Tony and Susan order and what does the waiter say each time?
5. Why is Susan so disappointed when she hears she can't have scampi?
6. Why can't they have the chef's special chicken casserole?
7. What does the waiter finally recommend?

F

11 Special Exercises

Use these prompts to make a conversation. Then use the conversation as a model for more conversations with the extra prompts given below.

Tony: think/like/steak in red wine.
Waiter: terribly sorry. afraid/out of steak. tomorrow.

Extra prompts (for Tony's part)
  i. Old English roast beef
 ii. Roast pork
iii. beef casserole
 iv. scampi American style

Study these irregular past participles. (Regular ones are no problem because they are formed exactly as is the past form of a regular verb; an "ed" is added to the base) Compare them with the past forms.

  i. I've (have) *made* a terrible mistake. I *made* it a moment ago.
 ii. Tony and Susan've just *come* in. They *came* in a second ago.
iii. We've *run* out of steak. We *ran* out of it this afternoon.
 iv. I've often *eaten* scampi. I *ate* some only yesterday.
  v. The cook's (has) *gone* into hospital. He *went* in yesterday.
 vi. I've *found* a good restaurant. I *found* it last week.

Now cover the examples and see if you can remember them with the help only of these prompts.
  i. a terrible mistake. a moment ago.
 ii. Tony and Susan/in. a second ago.
iii. steak. this afternoon.
 iv. often/scampi. only yesterday.
  v. The cook/into hospital. yesterday.
 vi. a good restaurant. last week.

Note: More irregular participles will be introduced systematically in the next five units.

UNIT B TWO

SOME vs. ANY
VERY FEW vs. VERY LITTLE
"Go to THE CHURCH" vs. "Go to CHURCH" etc.
More Irregular Past Participles (in Text)

12 SOME vs. ANY

i. **Problem Situation**

Mr. Burton has a new house and he wants a lawn in front of it. He knows you cannot make a lawn without grass-seed. He has no idea how much he needs. He is in a garden-shop now.

1. Is there a lawn in front of Mr. Burton's new house?
2. Does he know how much grass-seed he needs?
3. Where is he now?
4. Now do this
   What is he going to say about what he needs before he tells the man how big his lawn is?

ii. The man in the shop usually has a lot of grass-seed in his shop. He usually keeps it in a large bag, but somebody bought it all yesterday and that bag is empty.

1. Where does the man keep all his grass-seed?
2. Is that bag full or empty?
3. Why?
4. Now do this.
   What exactly does he say to John?

13 Illustrative Situations

i. Flight BC 245 to New York is only half-way there, but the stewardess is already having trouble with a group of men. They are drunk. They are talking loudly and telling silly jokes. The stewardess is talking to the pilot now.
WE HAVE SOME VERY DIFFICULT PASSENGERS BACK THERE!

1. Who is the stewardess talking to?
2. Why?
3. What is wrong with the men?
4. Does the stewardess say how many there are?
5. What exactly does she say?

ii. One of the passengers wants some French cigarettes. This particular airline never carries them. The stewardess can only say this:
"I'm sorry, WE HAVEN'T ANY FRENCH CIGARETTES."

1. What does one of the passengers want?
2. Does the airline ever carry them?
3. What does the stewardess say?

iii. Tony always gives his wife roses on her birth-
      day. It is her birthday today and Tony is in a
      flower-shop. Before he buys the roses he wants
      to look at them carefully. He does not even
      know exactly how many he is going to buy yet.
      The first thing he says is:
      "I'D LIKE SOME RED ROSES, PLEASE."

1. Why has Tony come into the shop?
2. What does he want to do before he buys the
   roses?
3. Ask if he knows how many he wants yet!
   (and answer)
4. What exactly does he say first?

iv.   Tony looked at the roses carefully and a minute
      ago he told the girl to wrap a dozen of them. He
      wants to pay for them now, but for some
      reason his wallet is empty. He is very embarrassed
      and has to say this:
      "I HAVEN'T ANY MONEY! It must be in my
      other wallet."

1. Does Tony know how many he wants?
2. What did he do only a minute ago?
3. What does he want to do now?
4. Why can't he?

14 Practice Situations

*Make your own
sentences with
HASN'T ANY
and NEEDS
SOME for these
situations.*

Situation: Tony wants to write a letter but the
            box where he keeps his writing
            paper is empty.
            HE HASN'T ANY PAPER.
            HE NEEDS SOME PAPER.

*Notice that
SOME is
pronounced
S'M.*

1. Mary wants to make a cup of tea but the
packet is empty.
2. She wants to make an omelette. She broke
the last egg this afternoon.
3. Peter wants to buy a new car. His bank
account is down to nothing.
4. Bert wants to drive into the country but
his petrol tank is empty.
5. He would really like a cigarette, but he gave
his last one to a friend.
6. The French Foreign Legionnaire is thirsty
and alone in the desert. There is a hole in his
water-bottle.

7. The guerilla soldiers have to walk through the
jungle without shoes.
8. They have to fight Government troops with
their bare hands.
9. Mr. Collins often says he cannot live without
his pipe, but his tobacco-pouch is empty now.
10. Mary wants to take a bath but her young
son threw the soap away a minute ago.
11. Mary wants to make a cake but she used all
the sugar this morning.
12. The General wants to attack. All his men
are dead.

15 VERY FEW vs. VERY LITTLE

Illustrative Situation

Alfred White (an old man who lives next door to Tony and Susan) used to smoke ten cigars a day and drink a lot of whisky. Then he had a heart-attack and his doctor told him to smoke and drink less. Now he smokes about three cigars a week and has a small glass of whisky once a week, on Sunday.
HE SMOKES VERY FEW CIGARS AND DRINKS VERY LITTLE WHISKY NOW.

16 Practice Situations

Notice that one type of word takes HOW MUCH and also VERY LITTLE

Situation: Alfred smoked only 3 cigars last week.
Question: HOW MANY CIGARS did he smoke?
Answer: VERY FEW.

the other type takes HOW MANY and also VERY FEW.

Situation: Alice does not like bread. She never eats more than half a slice of it.
Question: HOW MUCH BREAD does she eat?
Answer: VERY LITTLE.

Now both ask and answer questions for these situations

1. Mrs. P. drinks alcohol only at Christmas and then never more than a glass of sherry.
2. Tim smokes about 2 cigarettes a day.
3. Hugo knows some English people, but only about 2 or 3.
4. The only exercise Mr. A. gets is when he works in the garden on Sundays.
5. Sam knows some Italian, but only things like "spaghetti", "Arrivederci", "Grazie".
6. The German words he knows are "Ach", "Mein Gott", "Bier", "Fraulein" and "Geld".
7. Edna isn't actually a vegetarian but eats meat only once or twice a year.
8. Joe spends some time at home but never more than one evening a week.
9. Stanley gets about 4 hours sleep a day.

10. Betty and Sandra never do more than a page of homework in the evening.
11. In the whole of last term Roger did exactly 2 pages of homework.
12. Old Professor Moore sees perhaps 2 or 3 students in a whole term.
13. He gave only 2 or 3 interesting lectures last year.
14. Stuart saw only 3 or 4 films last year.
15. Some teachers earn no more than bus-drivers do.
16. In the year Terry spent in Paris he learned exactly 3 French words.
17. Old Mrs. Samuels never gets more than 2 letters a month.
18. Mrs. Collins got only 3 Christmas cards last year.

17 CHURCH, etc., versus THE CHURCH, etc.

i. Problem Situations

Study the Problem Situations with the teacher. Notice when we say THE and when we do not

Mrs. Mavis is a very religious woman. It is Sunday morning and she is just leaving home. She has a Bible in her hand.

1. What kind of woman is Mrs. Mavis?
2. What is she doing now?
3. Ask (and answer) if she has anything in her hand!
4. Now do this
   Where do you think she is going?

ii. Mrs. Mavis is at church now. However, only a few seconds ago, someone shouted "Fire!" The place really is on fire, but the priest is telling everyone to be calm. It is not a bad fire, and everyone is leaving in an orderly manner. Nobody is hysterical.

1. Where is Mrs. Mavis now?
2. What happened only a few seconds ago?
3. What is the priest doing?
4. What is everyone doing?
5. Now do this
   Only a mile away, the fire-engine is already on the road; where are they going?

18 Hospital

Illustrative Situations

i. Jane became very ill at the office yesterday. The manager could see it was something very serious, so he immediately phoned for an ambulance. It came within minutes.
IT TOOK HER TO HOSPITAL.
SHE'S IN HOSPITAL NOW.

1. What happened to Jane at the office yesterday?
2. What did the manager do?
3. What happened then?
4. Where is she now?

ii. Richard is a good friend of Jane's. He is very worried about her. He is going to see her this evening.
HE'S GOING TO THE HOSPITAL THIS EVENING.

1. What is Richard going to do this evening?
2. Where exactly is he going?
3. Now do the variations.

Variations

1. Bert had a bad accident a few days ago. He lost a lot of blood. Where is he now. What did the ambulance do? His girl-friend comes to see him every day; where does she come?
2. Nora Hanley is in an ambulance now. (She's going to have a baby.) Where is she going? Her husband is going to see her there. Where is he going?
3. Peter's wife is ill and he is visiting her now. Where is he? Where is she?
4. Jane had a serious operation but she is much better now and is leaving today. What is she leaving?
5. Doctor Kidd is going home now. What is he leaving?
6. There is something wrong with a machine in the operating-theatre and the manufacturer is sending an electrician. Where are they sending him? What does the electrician say to his wife?

19 School

Tim is a school-boy. He goes there every morning. The milkman goes there, too. He delivers milk.
TIM GOES TO SCHOOL EVERY MORNING. THE MILKMAN GOES TO THE SCHOOL EVERY MORNING.

1. What does Tim do every morning?
2. Ask (and answer) if the milkman does.
3. What does the milkman do every morning?

Variations

1. It is almost 9 a.m. and Tim is leaving home; ask and answer a question with WHERE.
2. The milkman has 100 bottles of milk for the pupils there and he is going in the same direction; ask a question with WHERE.
3. One day last year there was a fire there. What did the fire-engine do?

4. Tim came home with a very bad report yesterday, and his mother wants to see the headmaster about it; ask a question about her with WHERE.
5. You and your friend both study at a language school; ask your friend when he or she is going tomorrow!

20 Prison

Ted is a thief. The police caught him again a few days ago. This morning in court the judge said "5 years!" Ted is in a black van now. A policeman is sitting beside him.
HE'S GOING TO PRISON.

1. What does Ted do for a living?
2. What happened a few days ago?
3. What happened this morning?
4. Where is Ted now?
5. Ask (and answer) a question about Ted now!

Variations

1. The judge sent him there for 3 years; ask (and answer) WHERE!
2. Ted is there now; where?
3. His wife is visiting him today: where is she?
4. What happens in your country if a man is a thief and the police catch him?

5. All Ted's friends are there; ask and answer WHERE!
6. Every visiting day a lot of women come; where are their husbands?
7. Jeff is also a thief but his prison term is over today and he is coming out. What is he coming out of?
8. Ask if it is easy to escape from such a place!

21 (Invention) Special note

These words are often used without THE. Make examples of your own with them.

(a) With TO and AT
university/Medical School/Primary School/College/church/school/work

(b) With TO and IN
bed/class/school/church/prison/hospital/court

These words are always used with THE after "TO", "AT" and "IN". Again, make your own examples!

(c) With TO, AT and IN
the bank/the station/the post office
the concert/the theatre/the cinema/the airport
the office/the garage/the shops/the hairdresser's/the chemist's/the greengrocer's

22 TEXT

"A Remarkable Old Man"

Mr. Gregory Gale is one of the few people in England who are 100 years old, but this is not the only thing that makes him remarkable. On the day of his birthday, he played a game of tennis and went for a long walk. A few days later a radio reporter came to his house and asked him if he had any "secrets of long life". This is what Mr. Gale said.

"No, I don't know any "secrets" like that, but there are a few simple rules of good life. I've always kept them all my life. The first is this: 'Don't listen to those fools who tell you you have to give up all the pleasures of life!' That's absolute nonsense!

The second is to enjoy all the pleasures of life in moderation. For instance, I've always smoked a few good cigars every day. Not many, mind you! Only two or three! I've also always drunk a little good wine with my meals, perhaps two or three glasses.

The third rule is to take a little exercise every day. I've always taken a little every day and on Saturdays I've always played a little tennis or golf.

There's really only one thing in which I haven't been very moderate. I've had twenty children, but I've also had four different wives, all at different times, of course.

1. How old is Mr. Gale and what did he do on the day of his birthday?
2. What did a radio reporter ask him and when?
3. Ask questions about Mr. Gale (and answer the Use these words as question prompts.
   (a) secrets of long life (b) simple rules of good life (c) the first rule (d) the second rule
   (e) the third rule (f) one thing/hasn't been moderate.
4. Ask questions with either "very much" or "very many". Then answer with either "very little" or "very few"
   Example wine = A: Does he drink very much wine?
                 B: No, very little.
   (a) glasses of wine (b) exercise (c) tennis
   (d) cigars.

23 Special Exercise

Study these irregular and regular participles. They were all used in the text. Compare the past forms.

  i. I've always *kept* these rules. I *kept* them even when I was very young.

  ii. I've always *drunk* a little good wine with my meals. I *drank* some yesterday.

  iii. I've always *taken* a little exercise. I *took* some this morning.

  iv. I've *had* twenty children. I *had* my first when I was seventeen.

Now cover the examples and see if you can remember them from these prompts.

  i. rules

  ii. good wine

  iii. exercise

  iv. twenty children

UNIT B THREE

I'LL DO IT (willingness and promises)
I'LL DO it BEFORE/IF/WHEN AS SOON AS something HAPPENS
(simple tense after IF/WHEN etc.)
More irregular Past Participles (In Conversation)

24 I'LL DO (willingness)

Problem Situations

Susan is at a friend's house. The telephone is
ringing and Susan's friend cannot answer it because she is busy with a baby upstairs. Susan
is going to answer it herself.

1. Where is Susan?
2. Ask a question about the telephone! (and answer)
3. Ask if Susan's friend can answer it herself!
4. What is Susan going to do?
5. Now do this:
   What do you think Susan is going to shout up to her friend just before she answers it?

25 Illustrative Situations

i. P. C. Foyle (a policeman) was in the town-centre
half an hour ago when a man suddenly ran out
of the bank. Someone else shouted "Stop him!"
and Foyle ran after him. The man had a
revolver. He turned round and shot Foyle
in the heart.
Everyone at the police station is shocked. "His
wife doesn't know yet", someone says. The
inspector is there.
I'LL TELL HER, he says.

1. Where was P.C. Foyle half an hour ago?
2. What did the man run out of?
3. Ask (and answer) what Foyle did!
4. What happened then?
5. Ask if his wife knows!
6. What does the inspector say when he hears this?

ii. Peter's wife has a terrible headache. She hasn't
any aspirin. Peter says:
I'LL GO OUT AND GET YOU SOME.

1. Ask what's wrong with Peter's wife! (and answer)
2. Why doesn't she take an aspirin?
3. What does Peter say?

iii. Paula (the language student) has a sports car. It
has a flat tyre. The car is in front of school, now,
and her friend, David, is looking at it.
I'LL CHANGE IT FOR YOU he says.

1. Ask what's wrong with Paula's sports car!
2. Where is the car?
3. What is David doing?
4. What does he say?

26 I'LL do it BEFORE/WHEN/IF/AS SOON AS
(it DOES
(you DO, etc.

Problem Situation

A man's car needs a small repair. He is at the garage with the car now. He is going to come back for it later. The mechanic must repair it before that.

1. What does the man's car need?
2. Where is he now?
3. What is the man going to do?
4. What must the mechanic do?
5. Now do this
   The mechanic promises to do this: what exactly does he say?

27 BEFORE it DOES

Illustrative Situation

Notice the form of the verb (DO/BE, etc.) after BEFORE

It is a cold, foggy winter day. The weather report says the fog is going to get worse. Mrs. Collins is phoning Mr. Collins. He is at work. She is worried about him because bad accidents often happen on the roads, especially after it gets dark. "Don't worry" he says. "I'LL GET HOME BEFORE IT GETS DARK".

1. Ask about the weather!
2. What does the weather report say?
3. What is Mrs. Collins doing and why is she worried?
4. What does Mr. Collins say?

28 Practice Situations

Make sentences with the pattern for these situations

Situation: The party is going to begin at 8.
You'll come earlier.
I'LL COME BEFORE THE PARTY BEGINS.

1. The film is going to begin at 8. You'll get to the cinema earlier.
2. The train is going to leave at 8. You'll be at the station before then.
3. Your boss is going home at 6. You'll finish all the letters earlier.
4. It's going to get dark soon. You'll leave the beach before then.
5. You are going to leave England. You'll buy some books first.
6. The lesson is going to end soon. You'll finish the dictation before that.
7. Your sister is going to New York next week. You'll give her your guide book before then.
8. The petrol tank is almost empty. You'll stop at a petrol station.
9. You think your car is going to break down. You'll sell it before then.
10. You are going to Mexico. You'll learn Spanish first.

29 Invention Exercise

Now make sentences of your own with these words

Swedish/to Sweden = I'LL LEARN SWEDISH BEFORE I GO TO SWEDEN.

1. the airport/the plane
2. to school/the first lesson
3. some English clothes England
4. my old car/a new one
5. this dirty room/the guests
6. this letter/the teacher
7. all these letters/lunch
8. a lot of English/ home

30 WHEN it DOES

Illustrative Situation

Tom is making a long-distance call to his girl friend. His girl friend is going to come to London tomorrow. Her train will get into Euston Station at 10. She does not know London at all. Tom tells her this:
"Don't worry. I'LL BE THERE WHEN THE TRAIN GETS IN!"

1. Where is Tom?
2. What is he doing?
3. When will his girl friend's train get in?
4. Will Tom be there?
5. When?
6. What exactly does he say?

31 Practice Situations

Suppose you are in these situations. Make sentences for them.

Situation: Your friend is going to arrive at Waterloo Station. You'll be there.
I'LL BE AT THE STATION WHEN YOU ARRIVE.

1. You're going to get some money from home. You'll pay your friend back then.
2. You are sure you are going to get rich. You'll buy your mother a car then.
3. You have to go to the post office. You'll buy some stamps then.
4. You are going to be in Prague. You'll send your friend a postcard.

5. You are going to see the boss. You'll discuss your friend's problem.
6. You are going to see the manager. You'll complain about the food.
7. The rain is going to stop. You'll go out then.
8. You are going to buy a new car. You'll sell your friend your old one.

32 Invention Exercise

Now make sentences with I'LL ... Use these words.

see you/back from my holiday = I'LL SEE YOU WHEN I COME BACK FROM MY HOLIDAY.

1. phone you/in London next week.
2. another loaf of bread/to the shop
3. lunch at the Hilton/ money from home
4. English papers every day/back to Spain
5. my mother a letter/a bit of free time.
6. some more stamps/to the post office
7. to the Folies/in Paris again
8. your concert/in London next year

33 IF it DOES

Illustrative Situation

An American marine in Asia has a prisoner. The prisoner is a guerrilla soldier and the marine thinks he is going to run away, or at least try to. The marine says this:
I'LL SHOOT YOU IF YOU RUN!
I'LL SHOOT YOU IF YOU EVEN MOVE!

1. What does the marine think the prisoner is going to do?
2. What does he say to him?

34 Practice Situations

Make sentences with the pattern for the situations. Situation: Perhaps it is going to rain. You'll cancel the picnic then.
I'LL CANCEL THE PICNIC IF IT RAINS.

1. Perhaps the sun is going to shine. You'll sit in the garden then.
2. It is possible that you are going to get a rise. You'll buy a car then.
3. There is a chance you'll go to Boston. You'll visit your uncle there then.
4. Some people say cigarettes are going to get dearer. You'll smoke fewer.

5. Perhaps the boss will give you a rise. You'll stay then.
6. Some people say taxes are going to go up. You'll emigrate to Canada.
7. There is a chance you'll fail the exam. You'll take it again.
8. Perhaps you are going to miss the bus. You'll take a taxi then.

35 AS SOON AS it DOES

Illustrative Situation

The director of a firm is waiting for an important customer. The customer is going to arrive any minute, and the director does not want to keep him waiting. His secretary knows this. She is speaking to the director now.
"Don't worry! I'LL TELL YOU AS SOON AS HE COMES, SIR."

1. Who is the director waiting for?
2. What doesn't he want to do?
3. What are his secretary's exact words?

36 Practice Situations

Make sentences with the pattern for the situations. 1. What do you think the director's exact words were when he told his secretary what to do?
2. In fact, when the customer came, she did not do this; ask and answer what she did not do!
3. The first thing N. did after his plane landed was to phone his wife; what did he do and when?
4. The President of the United States is waiting for some very important information. What must the telegraph operator at the White House do?

5. The Prime Minister of Dragola is on the phone to London. He is very ill and an ambulance is waiting at the airport; what is going to happen?
6. All the students are very hungry and the canteen is next door. The bell is going to ring; what is going to happen?
7. Ask and answer if this always happens!
8. Ask about yesterday!
9. The film is going to end in a minute; your last bus is going to leave soon, too. What are you going to do?

37 CONVERSATION

"One Last Chance"

The manager of a small and not very successful furniture factory is talking to an important customer.

Customer: All right. I'll give you one last chance. That's this order. No more mistakes like last time! The furniture you sent wasn't even what I ordered.

Manager: Now, don't worry. That won't happen again.

Customer: I hope not! Remember! This order is very important and I must have it next week.

Manager: Certainly. We'll send it immediately. We've always sent you your orders on time before, haven't we?

Customer: No! You haven't! You once sent me one six months late! Another thing. This order must arrive in perfect condition. Pack everything in good, strong packing cases.

Manager: Of course we will! I'm sure you'll agree that's one thing we've always done in the past.

Customer: Oh no, you haven't Just remember you won't get any more orders from me if you don't this time. One last thing. Write my name clearly on the address labels.

Manager: You mean . . . we haven't always written it clearly before?

Customer: No. That's about the only good thing you have done before, I suppose. Just do it again, that's all.

Manager: Certainly. I'll do that myself.

Customer: The goods must come to the right address, to me personally and not to someone else, do you understand?

Manager: Of course. I'll see to that myself. The goods will be there at the time you want them, at the place you want them, and in the condition you want them. We won't make any mistakes.

Customer: Good. That's all.

Manager: Thank you, Mr. Harden, and good bye, Mr. Harden.

Customer: What did you say?

Manager: I said thank you and . . .

Customer: No, Not that! The name.

Manager: Mr. Harden.

Customer: Harden? My name isn't Harden. It's Marden. "M" as in "man", not "H" as in "ham"!

Manager: (trying to laugh it off) Of course. Mr. Marden. How silly of me. Just a slip of the tongue, that's all.

Customer: Don't worry about it.

Manager: That's very kind of you, Mr. Marden.

Customer: I didn't mean that. I meant it won't be necessary for you to worry about my name any more. I'll get the goods from soemwhere else. The order's cancelled. Good bye!

1. Give some of the reasons the customer is not satisfied with the furniture factory.
2. What are some of the things he says the manager must do?
3. What are some of the things the manager says when he hears what the customer wants?
4. Try to remember the manager's responses to these sentences
   i. The furniture you sent last time wasn't even what I ordered.
   ii. Pack everything in good, strong packing cases.
   iii. You've always written my name clearly before; just do it again!
   iv. The goods must come to me personally and not to someone else!
5. What explanation does the manager give when he gets the customer's name wrong?
6. Why won't it be necessary for the manager of the factory to worry about the customer's name any more?

Participles

Study these participles and compare them with
their past forms.
  i. We've always *sent* your orders on time. We
     sent the last one on time.
 ii. That's one thing we've always *done* before.
     We *did* it last time.
iii. We've always *written* your name clearly
     before. We *wrote* it clearly last time.

Now cover the examples and reproduce from
these prompts.
  i. orders. ii. thing iii. your name.

Guided Paired Conversation

Imagine conversations between two people,
perhaps a customer and the manager, or a
teacher and a student, or a doctor and a patient,
etc. One person begins using "must" or
"mustn't" with the prompt words. The second
person answers using "will" or "won't"
Example: this test = A: YOU MUST PASS THIS
                        TEST!
                     B: DON'T WORRY. I'LL
                        PASS IT.

Prompts

  i. all the homework
 ii. the next train
iii. here at 8 tomorrow
     morning
 iv. any mistakes
  v. these goods
 vi. a good mark in your
     next test
vii. this medicine four
     times a day
viii. these secrets to
     anybody

UNIT B FOUR

WAS/WERE DOING vs. DID
WHILE vs. DURING
WHILE vs. FOR
More Irregular Participles (in Text)

39 WAS/WERE DOING vs. DID

Problem Situation

I watched television yesterday evening. One of
the programmes was very interesting but the
phone rang in the middle of it. It was my friend.

1. What did I do yesterday evening?
2. What happened in the middle of one
   programme?
3. Who was it?
4. Now do this
   What do you think I was doing when the
   phone rang?
   What do you think I did?

40 Illustrative Situations

i. Mr. Collins got to the airport early. He sat in
the lounge for a while. Then they called out his
flight and he went to his plane.
HE WAS SITTING IN THE LOUNGE WHEN
THEY CALLED OUT HIS FLIGHT.
HE WENT TO HIS PLANE WHEN THEY
CALLED OUT HIS FLIGHT.

1. What did he do when he got to the airport?
2. What was he doing when they called out his
   flight?
3. What did he do when they called out his
   flight?

ii. I gave an English lesson this morning. In the
middle of it a bird flew in through the window.
Naturally I stopped the lesson.
I WAS GIVING AN ENGLISH LESSON
WHEN THE BIRD FLEW IN.
I STOPPED THE LESSON WHEN IT FLEW
IN.

1. What happened in the middle of the lesson?
2. What was I doing?
3. What did I do?
4. What do you think the students did?
5. What do you think they were doing?

iii. Nimbo is a circus clown. His tricks are rather
silly and not very original but a lot of people
always laugh at them. Last night, for instance,
Nimbo suddenly began to dance with a monkey.
Then he stepped on a banana skin, slipped
and fell down.
HE WAS DANCING WHEN HE STEPPED
ON THE BANANA SKIN.
HE SLIPPED AND FELL DOWN WHEN
HE STEPPED ON IT.

1. Was this a very original trick?
2. What was he doing when he stepped on the
   banana skin?
3. Ask and answer a question with "WHO . . .
   WITH?"
4. Ask and answer what he did when he stepped
   on it!

41 Invention Exercise

The clown/tricks/down = THE CLOWN WAS
DOING SOME TRICKS
WHEN HE FELL
DOWN.

1. home/my old friend
2. a bath/the phone
3. dinner/a telegram
4. in the garden/a
   plane
5. at the bus stop/rain
6. home on my bike/
   an accident
7. a book/a strange
   insect
8. television/a thief
   through the back
   door

42 Practice Situations

Listen to or study the situations. Ask and answer only WHAT WAS.. ..DOING? questions for all of them.

Situation: William opened the text book and
began to study but then the bulb
in his reading lamp went and he had
to get another one.

Question: WHAT WAS HE DOING WHEN
THE BULB WENT?

Answer: HE WAS STUDYING.

1. Mary had a bath last night. In the middle of it the phone rang. She went downstairs and answered it.
2. Robert went to the bus stop and waited. Then his friend came by in a car and he got in.
3. Carla Morass sang well last night, but in the middle of the aria someone threw an egg. She got very angry.
4. Peter walked up and down on the platform. Then the train came and he got in.
5. Robert began to eat the apple. Then he saw the worm. He threw the apple away.
6. Tony worked in the garden for several hours but then it began to rain. He went inside.
7. The demonstrators shouted slogans for hours. Then the police told them to move. They all sat down.
8. Robert fell asleep in the middle of the lecture. His friend shook him and he woke up.

43 Now go over these situations again. This time ask
"WHAT DID (he/she/they) DO?" questions and
answer them.

44 WHILE vs. DURING

Examples

Notice the type of word after WHILE and the type of word after DURING in the examples

A bird flew in DURING THE LESSON
This happened WHILE I WAS TEACHING
He went out DURING THE FILM
He came in WHILE WE WERE WATCHING
the film.

Simple Discrimination

The concert =   DURING THE CONCERT
I was listening = WHILE I WAS LISTENING

1. the play
2. I was looking at it
3. the game
4. I was playing
5. the festival
6. the lecture
7. we were writing
8. the dictation

9. our honeymoon
10. they were away
11. the demonstration
12. they were standing there
13. they were shouting
14. the march
15. the last war
16. I was in the Army

Practice Situations

Make sentences
with both
WHILE and
DURING for
these situations
Notice the form
(tense) that
we use with
WHILE.

Situation: We had a picnic yesterday. It began to rain in the middle of it.
IT BEGAN TO RAIN DURING THE PICNIC.
IT BEGAN TO RAIN WHILE WE WERE HAVING A PICNIC.

1. Mary had a dancing lesson yesterday. She fell down in the middle of it.
2. Shabinski the pianist gave a concert last night. A few minutes after he began a woman fainted.
3. We all had a party last night. The police came in the middle of it.
4. There was a good film on television last night but I watched only part of it because the set broke down.
5. The rector of the university gave a speech yesterday. The students booed several times.

6. The demonstrators marched down the road. Somebody threw a stone at one point.
7. The diplomat's dinner began at 7 and ended at 10. A lot of people in the streets outside died of hunger in that time.
8. The doctor turned the radio on and listened to the first part of the concert. Then the phone rang.
9. We were at a dance last night. In the middle of it someone shouted "Fire!"
10. Greston played very well in most of the football match, but he hurt his leg at one point.

45 DURING vs. FOR

Examples

Notice the type
of word we use
after DURING
and the type of
word we use
after FOR

I was in the Army DURING THE WAR
I was in the Army FOR FIVE YEARS
She was in hospital DURING HER ILLNESS
She was in hospital FOR SEVERAL WEEKS

G

Use DURING
or FOR for
these words **Simple Discrimination**

the voyage = DURING THE VOYAGE

six months = FOR SIX MONTHS

1. three years
2. the summer
3. the last century
4. the last lesson
5. fifty minutes
6. fifty years

7. the last act
8. the war in Algeria
9. six years
10. the battle
11. the air raid
12. the last thirty years

Invention Exercise

Now make
sentences of
your own with
these words. America/four weeks = I WAS IN AMERICA
FOR FOUR WEEKS.

America/the last riots= I WAS IN AMERICA
DURING THE LAST
RIOTS.

1. in Japan/the Korean war
2. Tokyo/several months
3. only water/the meal
4. in hospital/a month
5. my last job/three years
6. Paris/the last crisis

7. in the other room/your talk
8. out the window/the lesson
9. a sherry/the flight
10. the plane/12 hours
11. another class/the first few days
12. my friend/the test

46 TEXT

"The Ghost of Glenn Avenue"

This is part of a radio-programme called "Radio Investigator", a programme that investigates strange things.

Narrator: Glenn Avenue is a street in the town of Waring, Essex. A number of people who live in Glenn Avenue say they have seen and heard and even felt a ghost. Mr. Friend, who lives at number 8, begins the story.

Mr. Friend: Last Monday evening I was watching television around ten o'clock when I heard a knock at the door. I got up and opened it but there wasn't anybody there.

Narrator: But that isn't strange, is it? Children have often knocked on my door or rung my doorbell and then have run away.

Mr. Friend: Just a second! I haven't told you everything yet! Around eleven I was getting into bed when I heard the window open behind me. Before I could turn around, someone turned the light off. I was trying to find the switch when I suddenly felt a hand. It wasn't a human hand! I can tell you that! I shouted and found the switch again, but when I turned the light on, the room was empty. Nobody could have come in and gone out of the window so fast!

Narrator:	Mrs. Betty Smiles lives at number 28. This is her story.
Mrs. Smiles:	I was lying in bed around 10.30 Monday evening. My husband was doing some work downstairs. Suddenly I heard a noise at the window. I always sleep with it open. Then I saw two eyes in the darkness. I heard a strange laugh! I screamed, My husband ran into the room but the thing was gone by then. I've never heard or seen anything like it before! (Becoming hysterical) It wasn't human, I tell you!
Narrator:	I've spoken to a number of people on Glenn Avenue with similar stories. I am sure they are not lying. I could not understand it. Then, a few hours ago, I got a phone-call from Waring Town Zoo. I went and spoke to one of the officials, Mr. Harry Ford.
Mr. Ford:	Eustace is one of our cleverest chimpanzees. They're very intelligent animals, you know. Eustace here can open windows from the outside and turn lights on and off and do all sorts of things. He's very fast, too.
Narrator:	Has Eustace ever escaped, Mr. Ford?
Mr. Ford:	Yes. That's why we asked you to come here. He escaped on Monday evening. The next morning two little boys were playing when they saw him in a tree. They climbed the tree and caught him. We'd like to thank the boys publically, on this programme. Their names are Freddy Jones and Marcus Miller. They both live on Glenn Avenue.

1. What was Mr. Friend doing when he heard a knock and what did he do?
2. Ask the same two questions about him when he heard the window open.
3. What was he doing when he felt a hand?
4. What did he do?
5. What was Mrs. Smiles doing and what did she do shen she heard a noise?
6. Ask the same two questions about her husband when she screamed.
7. Ask the same two questions about the two little boys when they saw the chimpanzee.
8. What do you think is the explanation for "The Ghost of Glenn Avenue"?

Reproduce the story without looking at the text.
Use only these prompt words.
  i. Mr. Friend/television/knock on the door. up/
     open/nobody.
 ii. Later that evening/into bed/the window.
     Before/round/the light off.
iii. trying/switch/a hand. a human hand. shout/
     light on again/empty.
 iv. Nobody/in and out so fast.
  v. Mrs. Betty Smiles/in bed/noise at the window.
     two eyes. strange laugh. scream. husband/
     some work downstairs. upstairs. thing gone.

Irregular Past Participles

Study these participles. Compare them with the
past forms.
  i. He says he has (he's) *seen, heard,* and even
     felt a ghost.
     He says he *saw* and *heard* one last night. He
     felt it, too!
 ii. I've *told* you this story before. I *told* you it
     yesterday.
iii. Children have often *rung* my doorbell and
     then have *run* away. One *rang* it and *ran*
     away only yesterday.
 iv. Someone has just *come* in. He *came* in a
     second ago.
  v. I've *spoken* to everybody in Glenn Avenue.
     I *spoke* to them yesterday.

Now cover the examples and reproduce them
from these prompts.
  i. He/a ghost. last night.
 ii. this story before. yesterday.
iii. Children/often/my doorbell. only yesterday.
iv. Some/just/in. a second ago.
  v. Everybody in Glenn Avenue. yesterday.

UNIT B FIVE

POSITION of VERY OFTEN/VERY MUCH as adverbs
FAST/HARD as adjectives and adverbs
HARDLY as adverb of degree
Adjectives with -ING and -ED endings
(Embarrased/Embarrassing, etc.)

48 does something VERY OFTEN/VERY MUCH
(position after object)

Illustrative Situation

Bernard Ruston is a philosopher. His 3 great
loves in life are mathematics, argument and
wine. He never drinks more than a glass or two
at once, but he likes it very much, particularly
red wine.
HE NEVER DRINKS VERY MUCH WINE
BUT HE LIKES WINE VERY MUCH.

1. How much wine does he drink?
2. How much does he like wine?
3. Ask and answer questions with:
   DO YOU LIKE . . . VERY MUCH?
   with (a) tea (b) caviar (c) expensive soap

49
Notice the position of VERY MUCH and also VERY OFTEN in these examples.

| He likes | good food | very much |
| He watches | television | very often |

50 Invention Exercise

Now make sentences of your own with VERY MUCH or VERY OFTEN Use these words

steak =
or =

I LIKE STEAK VERY MUCH
I DON'T EAT STEAK VERY
OFTEN

1. cowboy films
2. English chocolate
3. Bach and Mozart
4. pop music
5. letters from home

6. ice in Vermouth
7. the cinema
8. the film last night
9. spaghetti
10. arguments with my parents
11. foreign restaurants

51 FAST/HARD as adjectives and as adverbs

Illustrative Situations

i. Nurse Connor works in a hospital. She has to lift people into bed, run about a lot, and do all sorts of things.
THE WORK IS HARD. SHE WORKS VERY HARD.

1. What are some of the things she has to do?
2. What can you say about the work?
3. What can you say about the way she works?

ii. **Bert** Johnson drives a sports car. He often does over 100 miles an hour in it. The police can never catch him.
THE CAR IS VERY FAST. HE DRIVES VERY FAST.

1. What type of car does he drive?
2. How fast does he go sometimes?
3. Why don't the police stop him?
4. What is the car like?
5. How does he drive it?

Variations

1. Tony worked in the garden yesterday. He moved almost a ton of earth. What was the work like? Tell me how he worked yesterday!
2. Ask and answer questions about (a) most doctors, (b) a doctor's work, (c) all students, (d) this exercise.
3. What do some people often say when they compare English workers with Continental or American ones.
4. Ask the person next to you if he or she did yesterday.

5. Some planes now fly at Mach 2 (twice the speed of sound). What kind of planes are they? Tell me about the way they fly!
6. Ask and answer questions about (a) the buses here, (b) French trains, (c) French taxi-drivers.
7. Ask the person next to you if he or she thinks it is dangerous to do so.
8. Tell me if you enjoy it! Ask someone else!

52 HARDLY

Illustrative Situations

i. Tony and Susan had an argument last week. She lost her temper and shouted at him but he kept calm. He said only a few words. HE HARDLY SPOKE.

1. What happened last week?
2. What happened when Susan lost her temper?
3. What did Tony do?
4. Did he speak a lot?

ii. Mrs. Collins is often alone in their big house in the country because he is often away on business. She was alone last night and during the night she often thought she heard noises. She is very tired this morning.
SHE HARDLY SLEPT LAST NIGHT.

1. Why is Mrs. Collins so often alone?
2. Ask if she was last night!
3. What happened during the night?
4. Why is she so tired today?

53 HARDLY does ANYTHING AT ALL
HARDLY does ANY . . . AT ALL
HARDLY EVER DOES

Illustrative Situation

Notice the kind of words we often use with HARDLY

Arthur Docker had a terrible hangover this morning. His butler brought him his usual heavy breakfast in bed. He looked at it, took a few bites, and then groaned.
He HARDLY ate ANY breakfast AT ALL.
He HARDLY ate ANYTHING AT ALL.
This is unusual because he HARDLY EVER loses his appetite.

1. What was wrong with Arthur this morning?
2. What kind of breakfast did his butler bring him?
3. Ask and answer how much of it he ate!
4. Say the same thing with ANYTHING.
5. Why is this unusual?

54 Invention Exercise

Make sentences of your own with HARDLY . . . ANY . . . AT ALL

breakfast yesterday = HE HARDLY ATE ANY BREAKFAST AT ALL YESTERDAY

1. homework last night
2. tea this morning
3. free time last week
4. films last year
5. new clothes last Spring
6. football matches last season
7. champagne last night
8. presents last Christmas

55 HARDLY EVER

Illustrative Situation

Before Tony got married he used to play football every Saturday. Now he does the shopping on Saturday and plays football perhaps once or twice a year.
HE HARDLY EVER PLAYS FOOTBALL NOW.

1. Ask these questions
(a) Tony/still football every Saturday? (b) What /Saturday now? (c) How often/football/now?

56 Invention Exercise

Make sentences of your own with HARDLY EVER.

the cinema = I HARDLY EVER GO TO THE CINEMA

1. the beach in winter
2. that old coat
3. taxis
4. bed after midnight
5. programmes like that
6. that paper
7. my old friends
8. table tennis

Now make at least four more sentences. Make real examples of things you hardly ever do.

Depress-
Interest-   ING vs. ED
Bor-

57 Depress-/ING vs. . . . ED

Problem Situation

Lucy Boggs lives in a slum in Liverpool. She
wants to get out of it. Everything about the
slum depresses her. She hopes to marry someone with money.

1. Where does she live?
2. What does she want to do?
3. Ask and answer if the slum depresses her!
4. Now do this
   If a book or a film or anything depresses you
   what kind of thing is it?
   How does Lucy feel when she looks at the
   slum?

58 Bor
Interest   /ING vs. . . . ED

Illustrative Situation

Sam is the only person who thinks his jokes are
funny. When he tells them, people smile politely
at first but they then yawn and try to change
the subject. He never notices.
PEOPLE ARE BORED BY HIS JOKES.
HIS JOKES ARE VERY BORING.
SAM IS A VERY BORING PERSON.

1. What do people do at first when Sam tells
   his jokes?
2. What happens then?
3. Ask if he ever notices!
4. What do people think of his jokes?
5. How do they feel?
6. What do they think of Sam?

59
*Now practice
using them
with these
words*

1. football
2. jazz (some/all)
3. discussion about
   politics
4. mathematics
5. books about
   travel
7. foreign languages
8. gangster films
9. cowboy films
10. Bach
11. Marxism
12. the financial page of
    the Times

(+ your own examples)

60 amus/ING vs. ED

Susan saw a film yesterday. In it, a fat man with
a huge red nose slipped on a banana skin. When
he got up, someone threw a pie in his face.
Everybody in the cinema laughed, except
Susan. She got up and left.
EVERYBODY EXCEPT SUSAN WAS
AMUSED. THEY ALL FOUND THE FILM
AMUSING. SUSAN WASN'T AMUSED.
SHE DID NOT THINK IT WAS AMUSING.

1. Ask what Susan saw and what happened.
2. What did everybody do when the man slipped
3. What did everybody think about the film?
4. How did they feel?
5. Make two sentences about Susan with
   "amused" and "amusing".

1. The audience in the cinema is laughing. Tell
me about the film and the people.
2. We can say I FIND . . . VERY AMUSING.
Ask the person next to you about:
(a) Frankenstein films (b) stories like this
(c) English jokes (d) Mickey Mouse cartoons

3. Use AMUSED or AMUSING for these words
the play/the audience
the TV programme/I
the novel/all the readers
the circus clown/the children

61 Embarrass/ING/ED

Catherine saw a man at the bus stop. His back was turned but she was sure it was her brother, so she tapped him on the shoulder with her umbrella and shouted "Look out! The police are after you!" The man turned around. He was a complete stranger.
SHE WAS TERRIBLY EMBARRASSED. IT WAS A VERY EMBARRASSING EXPERIENCE.

1. Who did she think the man was?
2. Why didn't she see it was not her brother?
3. What did she do?
4. How did she feel?
5. What kind of experience was it?

Variations

1. Tim's brother got drunk at a party and spilled wine all over a woman. Tell me about his brother's behaviour! How do you think Tim felt?
2. You started telling a story about someone and that person came in in the middle of it. How did you feel? What can you say about the incident?

3. Mary is a very shy girl. Yesterday she had to speak in public. How do you think she felt? What did she say about it later?
4. Ask the person next to you if he is when he has to speak in public!
5. Make examples of your own with I GET EMBARRASSED WHEN I HAVE TO.

62 Disgust/ING/ED

An American traveller in China in 1930 went into a restaurant. He could not make himself understood so he pointed to the first thing on the menu. The waiter seemed surprised, but he bowed slightly. He came back with a huge, dead rat.
THE AMERICAN WAS DISGUSTED.
A DEAD RAT IS A DISGUSTING THING.

1. Why did the American point to the first thing on the menu?
2. What was the waiter's reaction?
3. What did he come back with?
4. What was the American's reaction?
5. Ask why he felt this way! (answer)

Variations

1. In some countries people eat ants and other insects. What do most Europeans think of such food? How do many people feel about this?
2. A drunken soldier went into an art gallery and threw ink all over a picture. What did people say about (a) the soldier (b) his action (c) themselves.

3. Make sentences with DISGUSTED or DISGUSTING with these words: (the meal/the film/the audience/his behaviour) (what you did/ such language/people who say such things)

63 New ING/ED adjectives

Look at these new words and do with them in examples of your own what is done here with AMUSED and AMUSING

amusing = IT WAS A VERY AMUSING FILM.
or = I FOUND THE FILM VERY AMUSING.
amused = EVERYONE WAS VERY AMUSED WHEN THEY HEARD THE STORY.

1. shocked
2. shocking
3. exciting (a film)
4. excited
5. horrifying (vampires, Frankenstein, etc)
6. horrified
7. exhausting (work)
8. exhausted
9. thrilling
10. irritating (a fly)
11. irritated

64 NATIONAL STEREOTYPES

The programme "Radio Investigator" recently looked into the ideas many people have of typical foreigners. This is part of that programme.

Reporter: Most of us, in this age of mass tourism and travel, would probably be shocked to hear someone talking like this.

Woman: I've never left England and I don't want to. I mean, once you cross the Channel you meet a lot of disgusting foreigners, don't you. Disgusting habits! Shocking food! They eat rats and snakes and things like that, you know. I've heard that most foreigners hardly ever wash.

Reporter: Such ignorance and prejudice is very shocking, but many of us have very strange ideas, even today. This Dutch girl, who now speaks English with hardly any accent at all, had a very amusing experience when she first came. Only, she was not very amused by it and who can blame her?

Girl: My first job was as an "au pair" girl with an English family. When they met me, they could hardly believe I was Dutch. "Where are your wooden shoes?" they asked me.

Reporter: I asked one man what he thought Americans were like.

Man: All Americans are the same. They all drive huge cars and talk fast. When they visit a country they never really see it. They hardly see anything at all except through a camera!

Reporter: I asked the man whether he knew any Americans personally.

Man: No, I've never known any Americans personally, but I've seen lots of them!

Reporter: And they were all the same?

Man: That's right! All the same.

Reporter: But tell me, how do you know you haven't met and seen Americans who you've never noticed, simply because they didn't look like your idea of a typical American?

Man: Well, uh . . .

Reporter: I mean, how do you know some Americans don't look just like me?

Man: Like you? Impossible.

Reporter: Is it? As it happens, I am American. I was born in New York but I've lost my accent.

1. What does the first woman say about foreigners?
2. What does the reporter think of such ignorance and prejudice?
3. Describe the experience the Dutch girl had.
4. Ask and answer questions about this girl's accent.
5. Ask two more questions about this story. Use the words "amused" and "amusing" in the questions.
6. What does the man say about Americans?

65 SPECIAL EXERCISES

Study these participles

i. I've never left England. I almost left it last year but I fell ill.
ii. I've met lots of foreigners. I met some last summer.
iii. I've known lots of Americans. I knew a lot when I was at school.
iv. The reporter has lost his American accent. He lost it when he came to England.

Now cover the examples and reproduce them from these prompts.

i. never/England. almost/last year.
ii. lots of foreigners. some last summer.
iii. lots of Americans. at school.
iv. The reporter/his accent. came to England.

UNIT B SIX

HAS/HAVE BEEN vs. WAS/WERE
HAVE YOU EVER DONE? vs. WHEN DID YOU DO?
HAVE YOU DONE THAT YET?
DID IT FOR vs. HAS BEEN DOING IT FOR

66 HAS/HAVE BEEN vs. WAS/WERE

Problem Situations

i. Ask someone else if he or she has ever been to
(a) Paris (b) Rome (c) Berlin (d) Stockholm
(e) Oxford (f) Prague

ii. Suppose the answer is "Yes" in each case. Ask
and answer questions about:
(a) When? (b) the weather? (c) Which hotel?
(d) How much money?

67 GRAPHIC EXPOSITION

Notice the examples. They all start in some way
in the Past and come into the Present.

WHERE HAVE YOU BEEN? (up to now or
a second ago)
HAVE YOU EVER BEEN IN AMERICA?
(in all your life)
HOW LONG HAVE YOU BEEN HERE?
(from the time you came to now)
HAVE YOU SEEN THE MANAGER? (I do
not know WHEN or even IF. This is the only
possible form.)
Did you notice the form?

Now notice what happens as soon as we can
put things into the Past circle or if we want to
find out WHEN.

Notice the form!

I SAW THE FILM YESTERDAY.
I CAME HERE A WEEK AGO.
WHEN DID YOUR HAIR TURN GREY?
I WAS IN DALLAS IN NOVEMBER, 1963.

Think of Two Circles

One circle is
The Past

The other is
The Present

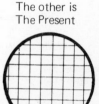

Now think of
a Third Circle
It is part of both
The Past and The Present

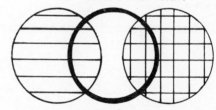

The Past

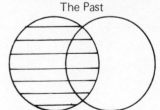

68 HAVE YOU EVER....?

Illustrative Situation

Patricia Riley is an Irish girl. She is trying to get a job as a shorthand-typist. At interviews people ask her questions like these.

"HAVE YOU EVER DONE THIS SORT OF WORK BEFORE?"
"WHERE DID YOU WORK LAST?"
"HOW LONG DID YOU WORK THERE?"
"HOW LONG HAVE YOU BEEN OUT OF WORK?"

1. What is Patricia trying to do?
2. Ask the same questions people ask her at interviews.
   (a)   this sort of work before?
   (b)   last
   (c)   How long/there?
   (d)   out of work

Variations

1. Arthur Docker has a different car every year. He has a Rolls Royce this year.
Ask a question with "ever/a Mercedes?"
He says 'Yes'; ask WHEN
His answer is '2 years ago; ask questions with:
(a) satisfied? (b) a good car? (c) fast?
(d) How long

2. You ask someone: 'Have you ever been to Rome?' and the answer is 'Yes'.
Ask WHEN? Ask about the weather. Ask WHICH HOTEL?
expensive? a lot of tourists? happy there?

69 Invention Exercise

Study the prompt and the model conversation that results from it. Then make conversations of your own on the same model. Ask WHEN and other things like this

Prompt: to Paris

A: HAVE YOU EVER BEEN TO PARIS?
B: YES, I HAVE.
A: WHEN WERE YOU THERE?
B: LAST SPRING
A: WHAT DID YOU THINK OF IT?
B: IT WAS VERY BEAUTIFUL.
    etc.

1. Chinese food
2. English lamb
3. on an English train
4. on the London Underground
5. Spanish wine
6. Irish coffee
7. in a London hotel
8. at the Hilton
9. a Fellini film
10. a Japanese film
11. a lesson with Mr. X.
12. an argument with your parents

70 Illustrative Situation

Notice what happens when Richard does not know WHEN.

Then notice what happens when he does know WHEN or wants to find out WHEN

Richard never believes what the critics say about a film. He always asks his friends instead. He wants to know if the new Fellini film is any good. He is talking to a friend now. His first question is:
HAVE YOU SEEN THE NEW FELLINI FILM?
The answer is YES, I HAVE
Richard then asks different questions, like:
WHEN DID YOU SEE IT? WHERE DID YOU SEE IT? WHAT DID YOU THINK OF IT? WAS IT GOOD?

1. Why doesn't Richard simply read the reviews in the paper?
2. What does he want to know now?
3. What is the first thing he asks?
4. What is the answer?
5. Ask the same questions with these words:
   (a) good   (b) think
   (c) where   (d) when

Variations

1. You never believe what the travel brochures say. You want to know about Leningrad. Perhaps your friends know.
What do you ask your friends first? Ask WHEN? Ask: 'very cold?' any other tourists? the ballet? by train or plane? caviar vodka think

2. You want to go to a language school in Bournemouth, England. You want to know about the town, the weather, etc. You have a friend who has travelled a lot. Ask questions with these words.
   (a) ever/Bournemouth   (b) When
   (c) weather like?   (d) How long/there?
   (e) a lot of English?   (f) prices very high?

71 HAVE YOU DONE THAT YET?

Illustrative Situations

i. Mr. Collins gave his secretary some letters to type an hour ago. He is going home soon and he wants to sign the letters before he leaves. He has just picked up the phone and asked his secretary this question.
"HAVE YOU DONE THOSE LETTERS YET?"

1. When did he give his secretary the letters?
2. Why does he want to sign them now?
3. What has he just done?
4. What is his question?

ii. Mrs. Mavis is in a phone kiosk. She is phoning a friend. She has been talking for twenty minutes now and a man outside the kiosk is tapping on the window.
"I HAVEN'T FINISHED MY CALL YET!" Mrs. Mavis says.

1. Where is Mrs. Mavis and what is she doing?
2. Ask how long.
3. What is the man outside doing and why?
4. What does she tell him?

72 FLUENCY PRACTICE

Progressive Substitution

Model: HAS JANE DONE THOSE LETTERS
        YET?

you = HAVE YOU DONE THOSE
       LETTERS YET?

read = HAVE YOU READ THOSE
       LETTERS YET?

HAS JANE DONE THOSE LETTERS YET?

1. you	7. his lunch
2. your homework	8. eaten
3. this test	9. the sandwiches
4. taken	10. you
5. they	11. made
6. Robert	12. bought

73 He DID it for . . . vs. HE HAS BEEN DOING it FOR . . .

Problem Situation

Patricia Riley has lived in only two places all
her life. She was born in Dublin but left when
she was twenty. She went to London. She is
thirty now and is still living there.

1. Where has Patricia lived?
2. When did she leave Dublin?
3. Where did she go?
4. How old is she now.
5. Now do this
   Ask two questions with "How long". Ask
   the first about Dublin and the second about
   London.

74 Illustrative Situations

i. Patrick Connor was also born in Dublin. He lived
there until he was 18. He went to India for five
years. Then he spent another five years in
Canada. Five years ago he came to London,
where he is living now.
HE LIVED IN DUBLIN FOR 18 YEARS.
THEN HE LIVED IN INDIA FOR FIVE
YEARS AND IN CANADA FOR FIVE
YEARS. HE HAS BEEN LIVING IN
LONDON FOR THE LAST FIVE YEARS.

1. Where was Patrick born?
2. How long did he live there?
3. Ask the same questions about India and
   Canada.
4. Where is he now?
5. Ask "How long".
6. Give full sentences with each place. Say how
   long he lived or has been living there.
   (a) Dublin (b) India (c) Canada (d) London.

ii. Two people are waiting at the bus stop. It is
9.30. They are waiting for the 9.10 bus. One
person is very angry. "This bus is never on
time!" he says.
"I'VE BEEN WAITING FOR IT FOR
TWENTY MINUTES NOW. YESTERDAY I
WAITED HALF AN HOUR FOR IT!"

1. What are the two people doing?
2. How late is the bus?
3. What does one of the people say?
4. Ask two questions with "How long". Use
   these two words: (a) today (b) yesterday.

iii. The English are having a terrible summer again. It is August. The rain started in May and has not stopped since then. The same thing happened last year. Everybody says the same thing.
"IT HAS BEEN RAINING ALL THIS SUMMER."
"IT RAINED ALL LAST SUMMER, TOO."

1. What month is it?
2. What sort of summer are the English having?
3. When did the rain start?
4. What does everybody say about this summer?
5. What do they say about last summer?

75 Practice Situations

Notice the change in form as the situation changes

Situation: Mary got to the station at 9. The train came at 10.
SHE WAITED FOR AN HOUR.

Situation: Peter got to the station at 9. It is 12 now and the train hasn't come yet.
HE HAS BEEN WAITING FOR 3 HOURS.

1. Mary got a job in the bank 5 years ago. She left the job last week.
2. Tom got a job in the bank 10 years ago. He's still there.
3. I started teaching 6 years ago. As you can see, I'm still a teacher.
4. My grandfather became a teacher at 20. He was still one when he died 40 years later.
5. 'Stonehead' Mackey started his boxing career when he was 15. He is still a boxer today, 30 years later.
6. British architecture was the best in Europe from 1700 until 1800.
7. Mr. Collins should be a good driver! He got his first car 30 years ago.
8. Mrs. Mavis started gossiping at 10. It's 12 now and she hasn't stopped yet.
9. One woman listened to her when she met her at 10, and then went home at 11.
10. John Graine became a printer when he was 20. He retired 45 years later.
11. Laura Pitt acted in her first film 5 years ago. She's still an actress.
12. You sat down more than 30 minutes ago and you're still here.
13. That student started complaining a week ago and he hasn't stopped yet.
14. That man started looking at me 5 minutes ago and he hasn't stopped yet.
15. Betty opened the book at 6. She put it down again at 12.
16. Peter opened that book 6 hours ago and he hasn't closed it yet!
17. My brother started coughing at this time last year. He still has the cough.
18. The baby started crying and stopped an hour later.

76 Text (*taken from a newspaper report in a popular Sunday paper*)

The judge said: It's the strangest case I've ever handled!'
He was referring to Mrs. Thelma Ogden's divorce action against her husband, Jack, 32. Mrs. Ogden, a pretty 29-year-old brunette told the judge this: 'He was very clean and nice when I first met him. Then, as soon as we got home from the church, he changed. He hasn't taken a bath since then. He hasn't even talked to me since he put the ring on my finger. I've been asking him to cut his nails and wash his hair for three years. I don't think he has even washed his hands once in all that time!'
'I've been living in a pig-sty for 3 years now! I've been trying to keep the house clean, but it has been impossible. He comes home in his dirty overalls and sits down on the best chair. Once, when I asked him to sit in the kitchen instead he got very angry and almost bit me. I've had 3 years of misery. I don't believe in divorce. I think it's immoral, but this has been too much for me!'
The judge gave her the divorce on the grounds of mental cruelty. Mr. Ogden, a mechanic, was not present.

1. What was Mrs. Ogden's husband like when she first met him?
2. When did he change?
3. What are some of the things he has not done since he married her?
   Prompts: (a) a bath (b) talk (c) his nails (d) his hair (e) hands
4. Without looking at the text, reproduce what Mrs. Ogden said. Use these prompts.
   (a) pig-sty/three years.
   (b) the house clean but/impossible
   (c) home/dirty overalls/best chair
   (d) Once/kitchen instead/angry.
   (e) three years of misery.
   (f) divorce/immoral but/too much.

77 Special Practice

Make the same type of exaggeration about

1. The judge says IT'S THE STRANGEST CASE I'VE EVER HANDLED (he is exaggerating)

a very funny film/a very very hot curry/a very very tall girl/a very hard test/a very good meal/a man who is a very big fool/a very bad book/a very kind person/a very bad cold/an extremely fine sweater/a very nice gift/

UNIT B SEVEN

"WHAT are you looking AT?" type questions
"WHAT did you do that FOR?"
"WHO DID THAT?" type questions
EXPLAIN SOMETHING TO SOMEONE

78 "WHAT are you looking AT?" type questions

Problem Situation

Bert Johnson took his girl-friend, Jill, to a dance last night. He left her at a table with some other friends and went to the bar for an hour or so. When he came back, Jill wasn't there. "Where is she? What's she doing" he asked someone else. "She's dancing" was the answer. Bert wanted to know who with.

1. Where did Bert and Jill go last night?
2. What did he do?
3. What happened when he came back?
4. What did he want to know?
5. What was the question Bert asked to find out who she was dancing with?

79 Illustrative Situations

i. Jill's father does not like any of her boy-friends. She told him she was going out last night.
"WHO ARE YOU GOING OUT WITH?" he asked.

1. What does Jill's father think of her boy-friends?
2. What did she tell him last night?
3. What was his exact question?

ii. One day last week Jill was talking to someone on the phone when her father came home.
"WHO ARE YOU TALKING TO?" he asked.

1. What was she doing when her father came home?
2. What was his question?

iii. Susan dropped something on the floor yesterday. It was a coin and she got down on her hands and knees and looked for it. Just then, Tony came in.
"WHAT ARE YOU LOOKING FOR?" he asked.

1. What did Susan do?
2. What was she doing when Tony came in?
3. What was his question?

H

80 Progressive Substitution

Model: WHO IS JILL THINKING ABOUT?
What = WHAT IS JILL THINKING ABOUT?
you = WHAT ARE YOU THINKING ABOUT?

Prompts
WHAT ARE YOU THINKING ABOUT
1. talking
2. who
3. to
4. Jill
5. writing
6. speaking
7. with
8. dancing
9. going out
10. you
11. looking for
12. what

81 Transformation Exercise (with Tense Variations)

Use WHO or WHAT in these situations.

Prompt: Jill went out with someone yesterday.
Question: WHO DID SHE GO OUT WITH?

1. When I saw Larry he was waiting for someone.
2. Do you know what the students did yesterday? They threw paint at someone.
3. When Tony came in, Susan was looking for something.
4. I want to talk to someone at the police station.
5. I want to talk about something very important.
6. Mrs. Hobden shouted at someone.
7. Nimbo the clown danced with some sort of animal.
8. Jane Martin doesn't work for us anymore. She works for someone else.

82 "WHAT did you do that FOR?"

i. It was very hot in the office yesterday. One of the other secretaries got up and closed the window. Jane could not understand it.
WHAT DID YOU DO THAT FOR? she asked.

1. What kind of day was it like yesterday?
2. What did one of the secretaries do?
3. What was Jane's question?

ii. Burt and Jill were in London yesterday. She wanted to see the British Museum but he wanted to go to the car show.
"WHAT DO YOU WANT TO GO TO A MUSEUM FOR?" he asked.

1. Where did Jill want to go?
2. Ask about Burt!
3. What was his question?

iii. The police have found out that the person who killed Rex Conway, the famous actor, was a secretary. She did not even know him. The police cannot understand it.
"WHAT DID YOU KILL HIM FOR?" they asked her.

1. Why cannot the police understand why the girl killed Rex Conway?
2. What exactly do they ask her?

83 "WHO DID THAT?" type questions

i. Carla Morass, the famous opera singer was singing last night when someone in the audience suddenly threw a rotten egg. She got very angry and stopped singing.
"WHO THREW THAT EGG?" she shouted.

1. What was the singer doing?
2. What did someone do?
3. What did she do?
4. What did she shout?

ii. Richard West is going to get a new job. He wants to keep it secret for a time but yesterday one of the secretaries told him she knew he was leaving.
"WHO TOLD YOU?" he asked her.

1. What is Richard going to do?
2. What did one of the secretaries tell him?
3. What was his question?

iii. Mary thinks sweets are very bad for children's teeth. She never gives her son any. Yesterday her son came home with some chocolate.
"Where did you get that?" she asked. "Someone gave it to me" he answered.
"WHO GAVE IT TO YOU?" she asked!

1. Ask why Mary never gives her child sweets!
2. What happened yesterday?
3. How did her son say he got the chocolate?
4. What was her question?

84 Invention Exercise

Prompt: you/those diamonds?
Response: WHO GAVE YOU THOSE DIAMONDS

1. this window
2. the radio off
3. you/that black eye
4. the door
5. this terrible word on the blackboard
6. dirt all over the carpet
7. all those Swiss watches in my bag
8. my chair away

85 Transformation Exercise

Study the situations here What question do you ask?

1. Someone gave me a copy of all the examination questions. The examination is going to take place next week.
2. Someone threw red paint all over a diplomat during a debate at the university.
3. The teacher was giving a lesson when something flew in through the window.
4. Someone said Peter and Jane got married yesterday.
5. Someone saw you in that rich playboy's car yesterday.
6. Someone got into your car a moment ago and drove it away.
7. Someone gave Jill a beautiful diamond ring.
8. Someone ate your sandwiches while you were away.

86 EXPLAIN SOMETHING TO SOMEONE

Problem Situation

It is the first lesson for a class of adults in a Language Institute. Some of the teaching methods are quite new and the teacher wants the class to understand them. He is explaining them now.

1. How many lessons has the class had?
2. Ask what the teacher wants the class to do?
3. Now do this:
(a) What does "them" in "He's explaining them" mean?
(b) Ask what he is explaining! (answer)
(c) Ask who he is explaining them to! (answer)
(d) Put all of this in one sentence!

87 Illustrative Situation

Notice the position of the words like HIM here.

Two students were both reading the same article in a foreign language yesterday. One knew the language far better than the other did. Whenever they came to a difficult word, he explained it to the other student.
HE EXPLAINED ALL THE DIFFICULT WORDS
HE EXPLAINED THEM TO THE OTHER STUDENT

1. What were the two students doing?
2. How often did one of the students explain things?
3. Ask why he did this! (answer)
4. Ask what he explained!
5. Ask who to!
6. The other student asked the first one to do this; what did he ask him to do?
7. Ask someone else if he or she ever does this when English people use difficult words!

88 Progressive Substitution

Model: HE EXPLAINED ALL THE DIFFICULT WORDS TO HIM
her =   HE EXPLAINED ALL THE DIFFICULT WORDS TO HER
the problem = HE EXPLAINED THE PROBLEM TO HER

HE EXPLAINED ALL THE DIFFICULT WORDS TO HIM
1. she
2. us
3. her plan
4. me
5. the difficulty
6. they
7. the new machine
8. the purpose of the lesson
9. us
10. the rules
11. her
12. the problem

89 Progressive + Variations

Model: HE EXPLAINED THE DIFFICULTY TO ME
I asked him to = I ASKED HIM TO EXPLAIN THE DIFFICULTY TO ME
Would you = WOULD YOU EXPLAIN THE DIFFICULTY TO ME?
your problem = WOULD YOU EXPLAIN YOUR PROBLEM TO ME?

HE EXPLAINED THE DIFFICULTY TO ME
1. Can you
2. Why didn't you
3. your problem
4. us
5. to the engineer
6. the plan
7. We should
8. to the others
9. them
10. When are we going to
11. the new pay-structure
12. I don't know how to

90 CONVERSATION

(a man is walking down a street. Suddenly a car pulls up beside him. There is a young man in the car and also a young woman. The young man is terribly nervous)

Young man: Excuse me . . . Could you tell me the way to the maternity hospital?

Man: The maternity hospital? You mean . . . where mothers have babies?

Young man: Yes. Where is it? We're . . . we're in a terrible hurry.

Man: But . . . but there isn't a maternity hospital anywhere nearby.

Young woman: (groaning) Oh, John! What did you come this way for? I told you it wasn't here! I knew it was north of the river and not south! What are we going to do now?

Young man: Just a second! Who told me to come this way? It was your brother, don't you remember? It's not my fault.

Young woman: (groaning again) I can't argue now. There just isn't any time. The baby's on its way.

Man: Good Lord. You mean, you're wife's having a baby now?

Young man: Yes. That's why we're in such a hurry.

Man: You're lucky you stopped me. I'll help you. I'm a doctor.

Young man: What are you getting in the car for? Stop!

Man: Don't be silly. Now just let me examine you, madam.

Young woman: Take your hands off me!

Man: What are you shouting for? Don't you realise I'm a doctor.

Young woman: And what gave you the idea I needed a doctor?

Man: What gave me the idea? You mean who gave me the idea! He did. This young man told me your baby was on its way! He's your husband, isn't he? He should know!

Young man: Who said I was her husband. I didn't! What are you talking about?

Young woman: I'm not his wife. I'm his wife's sister.

Young man: And it's my wife who's having the baby. She's in the maternity hospital. The doctor rang us a few minutes ago and told us to hurry.

Young woman: That's what he's been trying to explain to you!

1. Explain how the doctor got the impression that the young woman in the car was having a baby.
2. What are the questions asked here with the patterns "Who . . . .?" and "What . . . . . . for?"? See how many you can remember without looking at the text.
3. What does the young woman say when the man says "Don't you realise I'm a doctor?"?
4. At one point the young man thinks the other man is talking nonsense. What exactly does he say at this point?

UNIT B EIGHT

WANT SOMEONE TO DO
DON'T/DIDN'T WANT SOMEONE TO DO
MUSTN'T vs. DON'T/DOESN'T HAVE TO DO
DON'T YOU THINK YOU SHOULD . . . .?

91 WANT SOMEONE TO DO

Problem Situation

Richard West is worried about his young son. He is going to school now but he does not study very hard. Richard often tells his son that a good education is a very important thing. "YOU MUST GET A GOOD EDUCATION! STUDY HARD!" he often says.

1. Why is Richard worried about his son?
2. What does he often tell his son?
3. What are the exact words he uses?
4. Now do this
   What does Richard West want?

92 Illustrative Situations

Notice that we use words like HIM/HER etc. after WANT

i. Jill Burton is 18. Her father is sending her to a Secretarial College. He often says: "Get a good, practical education. Then get a good job. Perhaps you'll find a millionaire someday, too, and marry him!"
JILL'S FATHER WANTS HER TO GET A PRACTICAL EDUCATION. HE WANTS HER TO GET A GOOD JOB. HE ALSO WANTS HER TO FIND A MILLIONAIRE. HE WANTS HER TO MARRY ONE.

1. What sort of school is Jill going to and who is sending her there?
2. What does Jill's father often say to her?
3. What are some of the things he wants?

ii. Richard West has a new job. He has only one suit, an old grey one. His wife thinks he should buy a new one. "After all" she says: "You must make a good impression in your new job!"
SHE WANTS HIM TO BUY A NEW SUIT. SHE WANTS HIM TO MAKE A GOOD IMPRESSION IN HIS NEW JOB.

1. How many suits has Richard?
2. What does his wife think he should do?
3. What does she say?
4. What does she want and why?

iii. A number of foreign students are going to take an important oral examination in a few seconds. The examiner wants to read some important instructions first, but all the students are talking. None of them is paying attention. The examiner says these things. "PLEASE BE QUIET NOW. I WANT YOU ALL TO PAY ATTENTION. I WANT YOU TO LISTEN VERY CARE-FULLY. I WANT YOU TO UNDERSTAND EVERY WORD I SAY. IF YOU DON'T UNDERSTAND ME I WANT YOU TO TELL ME. I DON'T WANT ANY OF YOU TO FAIL SIMPLY BECAUSE YOU DON'T UNDERSTAND WHAT TO DO!

1. What are the students going to do in a few seconds?
2. What does the examiner want to read first?
3. What does he say to the students?
4. Now make as many sentences as you can with: "He wants them to . . ."

93 FLUENCY PRACTICE

Progressive Substitution

See if you can do these quickly, observe the form and position of words like THEM

Model: I WANT YOU TO PAY ATTEN-TION

he = HE WANTS YOU TO PAY ATTEN-TION

them = HE WANTS THEM TO PAY ATTENTION

listen = HE WANTS THEM TO LISTEN

I WANT YOU TO PAY ATTENTION
1. be quiet
2. He
3. them
4. listen
5. us
6. understand
7. come
8. she
9. him
10. buy a new suit
11. get a good job
12. her

94 Invention Exercise

Make your own sentences

Situation: Paula is a language student in England. She is a long way away from home. Her family want her to do a lot of things.

perfect English = THEY WANT HER TO LEARN PERFECT ENGLISH

1. a letter home every week
2. three good meals a day
3. good marks in her tests
4. good clothes
5. with a good English family
6. home for Christmas
7. lots of English people
8. a good job later

103

95 Practice Situations

Make sentences with WANT SOMEONE TO DO

1. Richard thinks everyone should understand science. Why does he often buy his son books on science?
2. The soldiers do not want to attack. Why is the General shouting at them?
3. It is 5 o'clock and Jane's boss has a lot of letters to be typed this evening. Why is he phoning Jane?
4. When Jill was 8, she still could not read. Why did her father get a special teacher for her?

5. Two students in a language class do not understand a word in the text. Why are they holding up their hands?
6. Lady Ottoway has a young daughter, Caroline. Lady Ottoway always invites rich, young men to dinner. Why?
7. Richard never used to be on time in his job. Why did his wife buy him an alarm clock when he got a new job?
8. Richard's son cannot go to sleep. Why is his mother singing to him?

96 DON'T/DIDN'T WANT him/her TO DO

Problem Situation

Paul and Jean have been married for 3 years. A few days ago, Paul bought a Finnish flower vase as an anniversary gift for Jean. He hid it in a drawer, but she found it by accident. Paul was disappointed. It was no longer a surprise. Their anniversary isn't until tomorrow.

1. Are Paul and Jean married?
2. Ask HOW LONG! (answer)
3. What did Paul do after he bought the vase?
4. What happened then?
5. Why was he disappointed?
6. Now answer this
   Why do you think he hid the vase?
   She found it; ask if he wanted her to (answer)
   Make 2 sentences with HE WANTED or HE DIDN'T WANT with (a) surprise (b) find

97 Illustrative Situations

i. Two doctors have just finished examining a patient. The patient is a very nervous man who gets worried very easily. The doctors want to discuss his case and have just gone outside his room.
   THEY DON'T WANT HIM TO HEAR
   THEY DON'T WANT HIM TO GET WORRIED

ii. The patient, however, is convinced they have gone outside for a different reason. He says this to himself:
   THEY DON'T WANT ME TO KNOW HOW ILL I AM!

1. Where are the doctors now?
2. What were they doing only a minute ago?
3. Ask if they still are
4. What do they want to do?
5. Why have they gone outside?
6. Ask and answer questions with DO THEY WANT + hear/worried!
7. Ask and answer what the patient thinks!
8. A few minutes later, when they come back, they'll explain why they went out; what will they say?

98 Progressive Substitution

Do these at speed! Follow the model!

THEY DON'T WANT HIM TO HEAR
1. We
2. He
3. me
4. us
5. know
6. find out
7. them
8. her
9. see it
10. have it

Now: (a) change to questions
     (b) change to DIDN'T

99 MUSTN'T vs. DON'T/DOESN'T HAVE TO

Illustrative Situations

Observe the difference in meaning between MUSTN'T and DON'T/DOESN'T HAVE TO.

i. Charles Gripp, the ex-bank robber, is in prison now. He has to get up early every morning. He has to wear a blue uniform and work hard all day. Then, at ten o'clock every evening, he has to turn off the light in his cell and go to bed. Charles often thinks of his friends outside. They can do what they want. It is not necessary for them to do these things.
HE HAS TO GET UP EARLY EVERY MORNING. HIS FRIENDS DON'T HAVE TO GET UP EARLY. THEY DON'T HAVE TO WEAR A BLUE UNIFORM. THEY DON'T HAVE TO GO TO BED AT TEN, EITHER.

1. Where is Charles now?
2. What are some of the things he has to do?
3. Why does he think his friends are so lucky?
   Prompts:
   (a) early (b) uniform (c) bed at ten.

ii. Jill's father had a very hard childhood. He had to work ten hours a day when he was 18. He had to save every penny. He had to get up at six every morning. He often tells Jill how much better her life is than his was at her age "YOU DON'T HAVE TO WORK TEN HOURS EVERY DAY!" he often tells her. "YOU DON'T HAVE TO SAVE EVERY PENNY!"

1. What did Jill's father have to do when he was her age?
2. What does he often tell Jill?
3. Make sentences with "had to" and "doesn't have to" with these words:
   (a) ten hours (b) every penny

iii. Jill is going out with Bert Johnson. Her father thinks Bert is no good. A few days ago he told her "YOU MUSTN'T GO OUT WITH THAT FELLOW BERT ANY MORE!" Jill and Bert are in his sports car now. They are in front of Jill's house. "WE MUSTN'T MAKE ANY NOISE!" Jill says "MY FATHER MUSTN'T FIND OUT WE'RE OUT HERE!"

1. Why doesn't Jill want her father to know what she is doing?
2. What exactly did he say to her a few days ago?
3. Where is Jill now?
4. What does she say to Bert?

100 Practice Situations

Make sentences with either MUSTN'T or DON'T/ DOESN'T HAVE TO for these situations

1. Richard always got to work late in his old job. Tomorrow is the first day in his new one What does his wife say to him?
2. Tony's wife thinks Tony has been working too hard. What does she say to him?
3. Paula usually has to get up very early but tomorrow is a holiday. Why is she so happy?
4. Jill and Bert are in the front room of her house. Her father is asleep upstairs. What does Jill say when she sees Bert is going to turn the radio on?

5. An old man is shouting at you. He isn't angry but he thinks you are deaf, too. What do you say to him?
6. Jill's mother knows she was out with Bert yesterday but hasn't told her father yet. What does Jill say to her?
7. Mr. Collins often travels abroad. Why does he always take non-iron shirts with him?
8. Tony is on a diet because he weighs too much. His doctor said "No potatoes, no sweets and no beer!" How else can you say this?

101 DON'T YOU THINK YOU SHOULD . . . ?

Illustrative Situation

Bert Johnson is in his fast sports car with Jill, his girl-friend. She wants to tell him she thinks he is going too fast. She does not want him to lose his temper so she has to say it very politely. This is what she says:
BERT? DON'T YOU THINK YOU SHOULD SLOW DOWN A BIT?

1. Where are Bert and Jill?
2. What does she want to tell him?
3. What doesn't she want him to do?
4. What does she say?

Practice Situations

Use DON'T YOU THINK YOU SHOULD . . . ? in these situations.

1. Your friend is going for an important interview. His hair is very long and his shoes are dirty.
2. Your friend wants another pint of beer. He has to drive home and he has already had too much to drink.
3. He has a very bad cough. He is going to light another cigarette.

4. Max, a foreign student, has a very important exam tomorrow. He wants to see a film this evening.
5. Your friend wants to use Max's bike without asking him.
6. Your boss is writing out a cheque. He is using a pencil.

Bert and Jill are in Bert's sports car. He is driving very fast.

Jill: Bert . . . uh . . . don't you think you should slow down a bit?

Bert: Slow down? What do you want me to do that for?

Jill: But the speed limit is 70 and you're doing at least 80 and . . .

Bert: Look! I've told you before that you mustn't talk to me while I'm driving. I can't concentrate!

Jill: But the speed limit . . .

Bert: And you don't have to tell me what the speed limit is, either. I know all about it!

Jill: I only want you to slow down a bit. And there's something else. There's a pol . . .

Bert: When I'm in my car, I'm the boss! So if you don't want me to lose my temper, keep quiet.

Jill: All right, Bert.

Bert: I don't want you or anyone to tell me how to drive.

Jill: No, Bert. (a pause. Suddenly there is the sound of a police car horn).

Bert: Good Lord! What's that?

Jill: A police car, Bert. They're following you. I think they want you to stop.

Bert: A police car! Why didn't you tell me? Do you want me to lose my driving-licence?

Jill: But that's why I wanted you to slow down before, Bert. I saw the car behind us and tried to tell you, but you said I mustn't talk to you while you're driving.

1. How does Jill suggest that Bert should slow down?
2. What does Bert say when he hears the suggestion?
3. What is the speed limit and how fast is Bert going?
4. What has Bert told Jill before, and why?
5. What does Bert say when Jill tries to say something about the speed limit?
6. What exactly does Jill want Bert to do?
7. What are some of the things he says with "Don't want"?
8. What does the police car want Bert to do?
9. What does Bert say when Jill tells him this?
10. What is Jill's answer?

UNIT B NINE

STOP/REMEMBER DOING vs. STOP/REMEMBER TO DO
DO something BY DOING
APOLOGISE to/THANK someone FOR DOING
THINK/DREAM OF DOING

103 STOP TO DO vs. STOP DOING

Problem Situation

Lawrence is a writer. He was writing yesterday when the phone rang. He had to stop and answer it.

1. What was Lawrence doing yesterday when the phone rang?
2. What did he do when it rang?
3. Now do this
   What did he stop doing and what did he stop to do?

104 Illustrative Situation

i. It was 3 o'clock in the morning. Lawrence Morrel was still typing. He began the first sentence of the last chapter of the novel, but then his eyes began to feel very heavy. He couldn't go on. He had to go to bed.
HE STOPPED TYPING. HE STOPPED TO GO TO BED.

1. What time was it?
2. What was he still doing?
3. What happened after he began the last chapter of his novel?
4. Could he go on?
5. Where did he go?
6. What did he stop doing?
7. What did he stop to do?

ii. Everybody was working in Jane's office yesterday when suddenly they heard a band playing music in the street outside. Then they saw a lot of soldiers marching. It was a parade. Everybody in the office stopped and watched.
THEY ALL STOPPED WORKING. THEY ALL STOPPED TO WATCH THE PARADE.

1. What was everybody doing when they heard the band?
2. What did they all do?
3. What did they stop doing?
4. What did they stop to do?

105 Practice Situations

Make sentences with both STOP DOING and STOP TO DO for each situation like, this.

Lawrence Morrel was typing when his wife came in. "You must eat something" she said. He stopped and ate a sandwich.
HE STOPPED TYPING. HE STOPPED TO EAT.

1. Everybody was working in the office. Then the tea-woman came in.
2. The painter finished a detail in the picture. Then he had a cigarette.
3. The gardener cut some more grass. Then he looked at the lawn.
4. Peter and his wife were arguing. Then the doorbell rang.
5. The speaker's throat became very dry. He drank some water.

6. Just before the final movement in the concerto, the pianist stopped. He wiped his face.
7. The director, in the middle of a sentence, lit his cigar.
8. The student threw his books down and went for a walk.
9. The librarian put her book down and answered my question.
10. In the middle of the lesson, the teacher went over to the window and closed it.

106 REMEMBER DOING vs. REMEMBER TO DO

Illustrative Situations

i. Richard has a very poor memory. He once stayed in a town called "Dover-on-Sea". His wife asked him the other day if he remembered this. "DO YOU REMEMBER STAYING THERE?" she asked. Richard said he did not. "BUT YOU MUST REMEMBER STAYING THERE!" she said. "It was on our honeymoon." RICHARD'S WIFE REMEMBERED STAYING THERE BUT HE DIDN'T.

1. Where did Richard once stay?
2. Exactly what did his wife ask him?
3. What did she say when he said he did not remember?
4. What was it that she remembered and he didn't?

ii. Richard wanted to buy his wife some flowers the other day, but he forgot all about it. Then he passed a flower shop on his way home, and he remembered. He went in and bought some.
HE REMEMBERED TO BUY THE FLOWERS SHEN HE PASSED THE SHOP.

1. What did Richard forget?
2. What happened when he passed the shop?
3. What did he remember to do?

Special Comment
Use REMEMBER TO DO only when you are talking about what you do or did after you remember. Use REMEMBER DOING when you are talking about something you have done and which you look back on when you remember it.

107 Practice Situations

Now make one sentence for each situation. Use either REMEMBER TO DO or REMEMBER DOING.

Richard often forgets to set his alarm but he did not yesterday.
HE REMEMBERED TO SET IT YESTERDAY.

1. Richard often forgets to lock his car but he didn't today.
2. Ask Richard a question with DID YOU REMEMBER . . . .
3. The picture of his hand putting the key in the lock is quite clear in Richard's mind. What does he remember?
4. Jill can't find any money in her green purse, but then she remembers: she put it in her red purse.
5. Ask Jill if she definitely remembers this!
6. David's mother is always telling him to close the door. He went out a minute ago and it is still open.

7. Somebody tells you "Now listen to this new joke." You heard it 5 years ago. What do you remember?
8. It is Richard's wedding anniversary today, but he has just come home without any flowers.
9. "Let's go to the film at the Odeon." your friend says. When you get there, you realise you've seen it. What do you remember?
10. Why did you go to the cinema at all if you had already seen it?
11. "I'd like you to meet Mr. Grey." your host says; but you remember the man. It was in Paris a year ago.
12. Mrs. Mavis was just about to leave the shop when she said, "Oh, yes. Salt!"

108 DOING after BY/FOR/OF

Problem Situation

Max is a foreign student. When he arrived in England his English was very bad. However it is very good now. While Max was in England, he studied hard and spoke English all the time. That is how he learned it.

1. Ask about Max's English when he first arrived?
2. Ask about it now!
3. What did he do while he was in England?
4. How did he learn English, then?

109 Illustrative Situations

Notice the form after BY

Fred Mulley was born poor but he is a rich man now. He often says this is only because he has worked hard all his life. He has a big house, a swimming pool, four cars, a beautiful blonde wife, and also a stomach ulcer.
HE GOT ALL THESE THINGS BY WORKING HARD.

1. What has Fred done all his life?
2. What does he often say?
3. Ask and answer how he got these things:
   (a) all his money (b) four cars (c) beautiful wife (d) ulcer

110 Make sentences with BY ... ING

Practice Situations

1. Children learn how to speak without teachers. They listen and they practise.
2. David learned how to play chess without a teacher. He watched his father play.
3. When Hugo was in England he listened carefully and always spoke English. As a result he learned perfect English.
4. Susan wanted to lose weight and she did. She ate less.
5. Fred lost a lot of weight, too. He took more exercise.
6. Bob simply took pills. He lost a stone. (14 lbs.)
7. Fred went out and looked for his first job and got it.
8. Bob's first job was very good. He advertised for it in the paper.
9. Fred worked 16 hours a day and got rich.
10. Bob got rich too. He married a rich woman.
11. Richard often helps his brother. He gives him money and advice.
12. The film-star killed herself. She took a bottle of sleeping pills.

111 Illustrative Situations

i. Fred is rather angry with his wife. He gives her expensive things, sends her to Florida or Bermuda in the winter (they live in London) and often takes her with him on business trips, but she never thanks him.
SHE NEVER THANKS HIM FOR DOING THINGS.

1. Who is Fred angry with?
2. What kind of things does he give her?
3. Ask if she ever thanks him!
4. Where does he send her in the winter?
5. Ask if she thanks him!
6. Does he ever take her with him on business trips?
7. Ask if she thanks him!
8. Ask why he is angry with her!

ii. The lecture was due to begin at 3. The hall was crowded. The lecturer came ten minutes late. The first thing he said was "I'm sorry I'm late."
HE APOLOGISED FOR BEING LATE.
HE APOLOGISED TO THE AUDIENCE FOR BEING LATE.

1. When was the lecture due to begin?
2. Ask when the lecturer came! (answer)
3. Ask what the first thing he said was!
4. So, what was the first thing he did?

Make sentences with THANK ... FOR/ APOLOGISE (to ...) FOR

112 Practice Situations with Variations

1. Fred gave his wife 2 beautiful diamonds. She didn't say anything. Ask if she thanked him for it! Ask if she ever does!
2. Paul was late for an appointment yesterday. What did he apologise for? We often begin our apologies by saying; "I really must ..."; what did Paul say?
3. Betty was in hospital and all her friends sent her flowers. What did she say in her letters to them?
4. Mrs. B. wants her son to have perfect manners; What does she always say to him when people give him things?
5. A student was late this morning. What did he do when he came into the class? Ask someone else if they always do this.
6. Make at least 8 sentences of your own with THANK/APOLOGISE FOR ... (Say things like: I ALWAYS/YOU SHOULD.)

113

i. Lady Caroline Ottoway is 22. She leads a very independent life in London where she lives and works. She enjoys it very much. Her mother, however, is worried because she hasn't got married yet and is not even thinking of it. Last week she introduced Caroline to the 30th Earl of Mountebank, no chin, very little hair, and interested only in hunting pheasants and collecting butterflies.
Caroline's mother wants her to marry him but CAROLINE WOULDN'T DREAM OF DOING SUCH A THING.

ii. Lawrence Morris hasn't bought a car yet or even learned to drive. Everybody tells him he ought to. He took two important steps yesterday. He looked at a car and even said he might buy it. He also went to a driving-school and asked about lessons. He said he might take a full course.
HE IS THINKING OF DOING THESE THINGS.

1. What kind of life does Caroline lead?
2. Ask if she enjoys it!
3. What does she do in London?
4. Ask if she enjoys it!
5. Has she got married yet?
6. Ask if she is thinking of it!
7. What happened last week?
8. What does Caroline's mother want her to do?
9. Ask if she would even dream of it! What exactly wouldn't she dream of?

1. Has Lawrence bought a car yet?
2. Ask if he is thinking of it!
3. What else is he thinking of doing?
4. Has he looked at a car yet?
5. Ask WHEN!
6. What did he say about the car?
7. Has he been to a driving-school yet?
8. Ask WHEN!
9. Did he promise to take a full course?

114 **Progressive and Variations**

Model: ARE YOU THINKING OF DOING IT?

1. When
2. going there
3. buying it
4. Are you really
5. emigrating
6. How long have you been
7. they
8. When are they
9. you
10. eating
11. What
12. doing

Conversation and Invention

A: Now Herbert is a very nice boy. I'm sure he'd make a very good husband for you.
B: What! I WOULDN'T EVEN DREAM OF MARRYING HIM.

1. This bike has 3 wheels, sir. It's much safer for older people.
2. We have some excellent crocodile steak on the menu, sir.
3. I'm sorry that your room has been taken, sir. We have a bed in the basement.
4. There's a new film on in town. It's all about brutality and killing.

Mr. Bashford thinks he is an important man. He is sitting in an aeroplane that is still on the ground at London airport. There is a loud noise coming from outside the window he is sitting at.

Mr. Bashford: Stewardess! Stewardess!

Stewardess: Yes, sir?

Mr. Bashford: What is that dreadful noise? Tell the men outside to stop making it at once!

Stewardess: Dreadful noise? Oh! You mean the machine the men are using. It's all the snow and ice, sir, and . . .

Mr. Bashford: I don't care what it is! Tell them I'm tired of listening to it!

Stewardess: But . . . but . . . sir . . .

Mr. Bashford: And when you do that, remember to give the pilot a message!

Stewardess: The pilot? A message?

Mr. Bashford: Yes. Tell him I'm thinking of complaining to the head of this airline. We've been on the ground for an hour now and the pilot has not even apologised for keeping us here.

Stewardess: (beginning to lose her temper and raising her voice) Sir! I don't think you realise just what is happening. We're in the middle of a snowstorm and . . .

Mr. Bashford: I beg your pardon, young lady! You'll make things very bad for yourself by shouting at me. I am a very important person and I have a very important position!

Stewardess: And the machine that's making that noise is a very important machine! It's a de-icing machine!

Mr. Bashford: A what?

Stewardess: A de-icing machine. It gets ice off the wings. A plane can't fly with ice on its wings. That's why we've been on the ground so long!

1. What does Mr. Bashford want the stewardess to tell the men outside?
2. What does he say he is tired of doing?
3. What does he want the stewardess to remember to do?
4. What does he say he is thinking of doing?
5. Ask why!
6. What does he say when the stewardess begins to shout at him?
7. What kind of machine is it that the men are using?

T

UNIT B TEN

WOULD/WOULDN'T DO IF I WERE YOU
WOULD DO IF DID/DIDN'T DO
WOULD/COULD/MIGHT DO
WISH WOULD DO and WISH HAD/WERE/DID

116 WOULD IF WERE

Illustrative Situation

Notice the form of the word after IF in these situations

Richard is thinking of buying a car. The car he has in mind is a used car. It is over ten years old and rather expensive. His friend does not think the car is a very good buy. Richard has just asked him for his advice. His friend says:
I WOULDN'T BUY THAT CAR IF I WERE YOU.

1. Ask and answer what Richard is thinking of doing!
2. Is it a new car?
3. What does his friend think of the car?
4. What exactly does he say?

117 Variations

Use WOULDN'T DO IF I WERE YOU for what you or someone else might say in these situations.

1. A third person has asked Richard for some money. The friend knows that person will never pay it back.
2. Your friend wants to wear a pair of white shoes. It is winter and the streets are very dirty.
3. Tony is overweight. His friend thinks he eats too much.

4. Your friend is thinking of staying at a hotel. You know it is not very good.
5. Tony is thinking of taking another job. His friend does not think it as good as his present one.
6. It is raining. Your friend has a very bad cold, and he says he'd like to go out.

Special Comment
Notice that usually the form used after IF in this type of situation is exactly the same as the Past (DID/WORKED/HAD). Only WERE is different, although some people say WAS for I/HE, SHE, IT/ exactly as in the ordinary past form.

John's friend has to say WERE (or WAS) because, of course, he isn't John. It is a theoretical situation.

We can also use I'D DO and not only I WOULDN'T DO for advice in such a situation.

118 Invention

an aspirin = I'D TAKE AN ASPIRIN IF I WERE YOU (Your friend has a headache)

1. this umbrella
2. to the doctor's
3. in bed
4. warmer clothes
5. another car
6. the manager about it
7. some heavy shoes

119 WOULD IF DID

Illustrative Situation

Some people are rather fat because they eat too much and take no exercise.
THEY WOULD BE THINNER IF THEY ATE LESS AND TOOK MORE EXERCISE.

1. Ask and answer why these people are fat!
2. Suppose one of them starts complaining to you; what do you say to him?

Practice Situation

Use the patterns for these situations

1. Ted is an intelligent person but he never studies. He never learns anything either.
2. Your car looks awful. It's only because you never clean it.
3. People never speak to Frank because he never speaks to them.
4. You never read the papers and you never know what's happening.

5. Jill never saves any money. That's why she never has any.
6. Betty never looks nice. She needs some nice clothes, that's all.
7. Max isn't happy. He hasn't any money.
8. The manager isn't popular. He never talks with his employees.
9. That's why he doesn't know anything about them.

Invention Exercise

Make your own examples

(Situation: You are talking about something that is not satisfactory. You are saying what would make it satisfactory.)
happy/a car = I'D BE HAPPY IF I HAD A CAR

1. the cinema more often/more time
2. a lot of weight/less sugar
3. a card to her/her address
4. a walk today/warmer

5. a better job/more languages
6. the beach every day/so many people
7. better marks/homework every evening
8. more cars in that factory/American methods

120 WOULDN'T IF DIDN'T

Illustrative Situation

Mr. James Black is an important British politician. He often loses his temper in public. As a result, journalists follow him everywhere. He frequently complains about this.
THEY WOULDN'T FOLLOW HIM EVERYWHERE IF HE DIDN'T LOSE HIS TEMPER SO OFTEN.

1. Who is James Black?
2. What does he often do in public?
3. What happens as a result?
4. Ask if he ever complains about this!
5. So, what might someone say to Mr. James Black if he said
"These . . . journalists follow me everywhere!"

Make sentences with WOULDN'T DO IF DIDN'T DO (or WEREN'T)

Practice Situations

1. Patrick Connor loses his temper a lot, too. It's because he drinks too much.
2. Paula hates her professor. He often says sarcastic things to her.
3. I carry an umbrella all the time. It rains so often.
4. Detectives follow Max all the time. They think he's a spy.

5. The Americans sell a lot of goods here. They know what we want.
6. The workers there lose a lot of time. They drink tea all the time.
7. Some athletes win everything. They train all the time.
8. Susan always buys 'Jardin' perfume. She thinks it's the best.

121 Short Exposition WOULD/COULD/MIGHT

A is not the same as B
but they do meet

In language, as in all living things, an idea, concept or definition can be very clear but perhaps not always clearly distinguishable from other ideas, concepts or definitions.

For instance, some money is paper, and some paper is money, but that does not mean that all money and all paper are the same.

This happens with words. For instance we can say IT IS DANGEROUS TO RUN INTO THE STREET.
and we can also say IT IS FOOLISH TO RUN INTO THE STREET because what is danger-ous is very often foolish, as well.

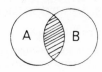

However, there is still a clear difference. For instance HEART OPERATIONS ARE ALWAYS DANGEROUS. Few would deny this. But few would also say they were foolish, particularly if that operation is the only chance someone has to live.

This also applies to WOULD/COULD/MIGHT. Obviously there are times when you could use all three in a situation. There are also times when you could use only one. A lot depends not on the situation but on exactly what you want to say.
It is really like this.

A is not the same as B but they do meet.

122 Short Review of WOULD/COULD/MIGHT

Illustrative Situations

i. There are plenty of jobs around and Tom White has very good qualifications. He hasn't found a job yet simply because he hasn't looked.
Study the difference in meaning. HE WOULD (He'd) FIND A JOB IF HE LOOKED.

1. Are there plenty of jobs around?
2. Ask about Tom's qualifications!
3. Why hasn't he found a job yet?
4. What would you say to Tom if he told you "I'm sure I'll never find a job"?

ii. Richard says he cannot learn how to dance. He says he simply hasn't got the talent. You think it is simply because he doesn't try hard enough. HE COULD LEARN IF HE TRIED HARDER.

1. Ask if Richard has learned how to dance! (answer)
2. What does Richard say?
3. What do you think?
4. What do you say to Richard each time he tells you "I can't learn, really I can't!"

123 Practice Situations

Use WOULD/ COULD/or MIGHT for these situations Tony never gets any exercise. He can't lose any weight.
HE WOULD LOSE SOME WEIGHT IF HE TOOK SOME EXERCISE.

1. You know your friend has a talent for languages. However, you think the school he is going to is very bad. He isn't learning anything.
2. Tom wants to get a particular job., So do a hundred others with good qualifications, but Tom hasn't even applied yet.
3. Susan wants a particular job. She is the only person with the right qualifications. She hasn't applied yet.
4. Tony never writes to his mother. She never knows how he is.
5. Joseph cannot tell wine from coca-cola. He never drinks them.
6. Frank is a stupid, prejudiced man. He doesn't understand foreigners but he never talks to them, either.
7. It is always difficult to learn Chinese but you never even study.
8. You can't see the river from this window. It is possible from the other window.

9. You never know what's on the notice-board. You never look.
10. One student can't read the words on the board. She never wears her glasses.
11. You can't hear the professor. You're not near enough.
12. Your friend says he can't learn English because it's too hard. You think it's because he never studies.
13. Your friend wants to get to Paris in an hour. There is a good plane-service there.
14. It is always difficult to get a seat at the opera. You haven't tried.
15. Paula is looking in her purse but can't find her money. It's in her pocket.
16. You can't find any Continental coffee but you don't go to the right shops.
17. You want to get to Paris quickly. There is an express train.

124 WISHES he/she HAD/WERE/DID

Problem Situation

Prisoner Z 3030 hates prison. He isn't in London but he often dreams of it. Another thing he dreams of is his own private bathroom. Naturally he hasn't got one in prison.

1. Ask if he ever dreams of London!
2. Is he there now?
3. What else does he dream of?
4. Ask if he has one!
5. Now do this
   He isn't in London. What does he wish?
   He hasn't got a private bathroom. What does he wish?

125 Illustrative Situation

Study the form used after WISH in the Illustrative Situation Jake is a young man from the North of England. He lives in London now. He knows very few people, lives in a very small room, and sometimes gets homesick.
HE WISHES HE KNEW MORE PEOPLE. HE WISHES HE LIVED IN A LARGER ROOM. SOMETIMES HE WISHES HE WERE BACK HOME.

1. Ask where Jake comes from!
2. Where does he live now?
3. What does he wish sometimes?
4. What kind of room does he live in?
5. What does he wish?
6. Ask and answer how many people he knows!
7. What does he wish?

126 WISHES WOULD DO vs. WISHES HAD/WERE/
DID

Illustrative situations

i. Prisoner Z 3030 is a very clean and tidy man.
He is in an old and dirty prison and he knows it
will always be like this.
HE WISHES THE PRISON WERE CLEAN
AND MODERN.

1. Is the prison clean and modern?
2. Will it ever be?
3. What does he wish?

ii. The Government might tear the prison down
someday. No one really knows, but Prisoner
Z3030 sometimes thinks about it and what he
wants them to do to the prison in the future.
HE WISHES THEY WOULD TEAR THE
PRISON DOWN.

1. What might the Government do some day?
2. Does anybody really know if they will?
3. Is this in the future or is it now?
4. What does Prisoner Z 3030 wish?

iii. Mrs. Mavis hates flats. One reason is that she can
hear the people around her all the time. The
people upstairs are singing now. She wants them
to stop. Of course she does not know if they
will.
SHE WISHES SHE HAD A HOUSE. SHE
WISHES SHE LIVED SOMEWHERE ELSE.
SHE WISHES THE PEOPLE UPSTAIRS
WOULD STOP SINGING.

1. Where does she wish she were NOW?
2. Ask and answer WHY!
3. What are the people upstairs doing?
4. What does she want them to do as soon as
possible IN THE FUTURE?
5. So, what might she say to herself about them
as she looks up at the ceiling and hears the
noise?
6. Where does she wish she lived?

127 Study the practice situations. If a situation is
like Situation (i) HE WISHES THE PRISON
WERE CLEAN AND MODERN. Use the
pattern with DID or HAD or WERE.

If it is like Situation (ii) HE WISHES THEY
WOULD TEAR DOWN THE PRISON. Use
the pattern with WOULD DO.

Practice Situations

1. Mrs. Green lives in a small house. She often
looks at pictures of larger houses in the magazines.
2. You are trying to explain something to your
boss. He is not listening.
3. It is raining. You cannot go out until it stops.
4. Phil has an old car. All his friends have new
ones.
5. The lesson seems very long. You do not know
when the bell is going to ring.
6. It is night. You are alone at a bus stop on a
dark road. The bus hasn't come yet.

7. No one knows when the war is going to end.
They are all tired of it.
8. Mrs. Butler's husband is never polite to her.
9. Tom hates the town he lives in. London is
his dream.
10. Prisoner Z 3030 wants his wife to write but
she never does.
11. Tim is not tall enough to look through the
keyhole.
12. Tom is not rich enough to do all the thing.
he wants to do.
13. Susan hates black hair. She thinks red hair
is beautiful. Her hair is black.

Barbara and Janet are two women who live in London. They were both born in small towns. Barbara is talking about "home" now.

Barbara:	Don't you ever get homesick?
Janet:	Homesick? You mean . . . do I ever wish I were back home? Never!
Barbara:	I do. Life would be far easier if I lived at home. I'd have a lot more money, for instance.
Janet:	How? You wouldn't earn as much as you do here in London.
Barbara:	Yes, but I wouldn't pay so much in rent. I'd live with my family.
Janet:	Well I wouldn't go back home even if you gave me all the tea in China! If I lived there, I'd be . . . a vegetable! A cabbage!
Barbara:	What do you mean?
Janet:	Well, there's nothing to do there! Nothing to talk about! All the men in the town ever think about is football and beer. They wouldn't know what to do with themselves if you took those things away from them!
Barbara:	But just think what life would be like if you lived in a suburb here! What if you were a housewife and had three children and a husband who worked in the city and thought only about his work!
Janet:	But I don't live in a suburb! I live in the centre of London. And I'm not a housewife, either!
Barbara:	That's the trouble. It's mine, at least.
Janet:	What do you mean?
Barbara:	We're both nearly 35 and neither of us has a husband yet. And we're not getting any younger, are we?

1. If people are homesick, what do they wish?
2. What does Barbara say about "life" and "Money" if she were at home?
3. Ask why she'd have more money!
4. What does Janet say about home? ("all the tea in china")
5. Ask why she wouldn't go back home! ("cabbage")
6. What does she say would happen if you took football and beer away from the men in her hometown?
7. What is Barbara's answer ("life . . . like . . . housewife . . . suburb" etc.)
8. What does Barbara say both their trouble is?

UNIT B ELEVEN

HAS/HAVE BEEN DONE
HAVE SOMETHING DONE (with tense variations)
HAS BEEN DONE vs. WAS DONE

129 Has/Have Been Done

Problem Situation

Richard's son got a bike for Christmas. This morning he took it to school and left it outside. He forgot to lock it. He has just come out of school and the bike is not there. People often steal bikes when they are not locked.

1. What did Richard's son do this morning?
2. What did he forget to do?
3. What has he just done and why is he worried?
4. Now do this
   What do you think has happened to the bike?

130 Illustrative Situations

i. Peter and Jane are in their sitting room. A terrible storm is blowing outside. They have both just heard a very loud crash outside. Peter is looking through the window. He can see a huge tree on the ground.
"A TREE HAS BEEN ('s been) BLOWN DOWN" he says.

1. Where are Peter and Jane and what is happening outside?
2. What have they both just heard?
3. What can Peter see through the window?
4. What does he say?

ii. Patric Connor has gone back to Ireland for a few days. Dublin has changed a lot. Patric is talking to an old friend now. "A LOT OF FINE OLD BUILDINGS HAVE BEEN PULLED DOWN!" he says.

1. What has Patric done?
2. Is Dublin the same as when he left?
3. Why is it so different?

iii. Richard's wife saw some very good alarm clocks at special prices in a department store last week. She has gone back there today, but all the clocks are gone. "I'm sorry, Madam" the salesgirl is saying. "ALL THOSE CLOCKS HAVE BEEN SOLD".

1. When did Richard's wife see the clocks?
2. What has she done today?
3. What does the salesgirl tell her?

131 Model: MY CAR HAS BEEN STOLEN.

Now study the 'models'. DO NOT simply look at them. Use them to generate your own examples. For instance
Make more examples yourself. Use HAS BEEN STOLEN with all the words you can think of in the position of MY CAR.

Models
1. THE WINDOW HAS BEEN BROKEN.
2. THE MANAGER HAS BEEN SACKED!
3. Look at that dog there. IT HAS BEEN RUN OVER.
4. ALL THE CHAIRS HAVE BEEN TAKEN AWAY.
5. THIS CAR HASN'T BEEN CLEANED FOR YEARS.
6. I'm afraid THAT CAR HAS ALREADY BEEN SOLD, Sir.
7. THE DIVORCE LAW HAS BEEN REFORMED RECENTLY.
8. THREE NEW SCHOOLS HAVE BEEN BUILT HERE.

132 Practice Situations

1. You look down at the floor and see that the mirror is in pieces.
2. When you left your room this morning it was very dusty. Now, when you come back, it isn't
3. When you were last in London, there wasn't a theatre by the river. Now there is.
4. You are in the garden. You notice a bird on the ground with its feet in the air.
5. There was a telephone in Mr. Hunt's office when he left last night. There isn't one now.
6. Only a week ago Mr. Holmes had a good job in a very large firm. Now he's looking for another job.
7. You left your bike in front of the cinema and went in. You've just come out and it isn't there.
8. You have just paid for your bottle of yoghourt. You notice that the top is loose.
9. You are on your way to work after a terrible storm. One house has no roof.
10. There is a dead cat in the middle of the road.
11. There was a beautiful antique vase in that shop yesterday. It isn't there now.
12. The firm made 300 special sports cars. There isn't one left.

133 Progressive Substitution

Notice some of the new words like SOLD here
Model: THIS ROOM HAS JUST BEEN REDECORATED.

All the flats = ALL THE FLATS HAVE JUST BEEN REDECORATED.

sold = ALL THE FLATS HAVE JUST BEEN SOLD.

THIS ROOM HAS JUST BEEN REDECORATED

1. these rooms	7. all the seats
2. cleaned	8. reserved
3. my jacket	9. all our rooms
4. stolen	10. broken into
5. my last penny	11. the safe
6. taken	12. blown open

134 (Have Just Had)
(Going to Have) **Something Done**
(Had (etc)   )

Problem Situation

Last month you noticed that your light grey coat was dark with dirt. You took it to the cleaner's and now it is light grey again. You've put it on again for the first time today and a friend says: 'That coat looks like new!'

1. What did you notice last month?
2. What did you do then?
3. What is it like now?
4. Have you put it on for the first time?
5. Now do this
   You cannot say you have cleaned the coat yourself: However you can say you have done something. What?

135 Illustrative Situations

i. Ronnie is very proud of his clothes. He is very particular about them. He never buys clothes ready-made. He always goes to a tailor who makes all his suits for him. Ronnie is just putting a new suit on for the first time. The tailor is standing there with him. The suit has just been finished. Ronnie Always HAS His Suits MADE
He HAS Just HAD A Suit MADE

1. Will Ronnie wear any old thing?
2. Where does he go when he wants a new suit?
3. Where is he now?
4. What is he doing?
5. Is the suit ready now?
6. Does Ronnie make his own suits?
7. What does he do when he wants one?
8. What has just happened?

ii. Lady Agatha would not dream of decorating the flat herself. Her husband is absolutely useless, too. Every year the decorators come and she watches them carefully.
She HAS Her Flat DECORATED EVERY YEAR.
She HAD Her Flat DECORATED LAST YEAR.
She IS GOING TO HAVE Her Flat DECORATED NEXT YEAR.

1. What is it that Lady Agatha would not dream of doing?
2. Does her husband ever do such things?
3. Who comes every year?
4. So, what can we say she does every year?
5. Tell me about last year!
6. Ask about next year!

136 Exposition

Notice also that the basic order is rigid! II and III always come in the order shown.	I	II	III
	I often have	the car	serviced
	I'm going to have	this radio	seen to
	Have you had	your hair	cut yet?
	He had	the whole house	rebuilt
	You should have	your shoes	mended
	When did you have	the engine	repaired?

137 Progressive + Variations

Do these at speed. Pay attention to the position of HAIR etc. and CUT etc.

Model = done the garden

I'VE JUST HAD MY HAIR CUT
I'VE JUST HAD MY HAIR DONE
I'VE JUST HAD THE GARDEN DONE
(Somebody came and did all the garden work)

I'M GOING TO HAVE MY HAIR CUT

1. done
2. the garden
3. Are you going to have
4. all the decorating
5. She's just had
6. When did you have
7. He's rich enough to have
8. all his suits made
9. I can't have another suit
10. all my clothes
11. cleaned
12. this coat
13. I think I'll have
14. repaired
15. the radio
16. When did you
17. Where
18. your car

138 Invention Exercise

Think of words to go with the prompt.

her hair every week =

SHE HAS HER HAIR DONE EVERY WEEK

her hair last week =

SHE HAD HER HAIR DONE LAST WEEK

1. the engine last month
2. my summer dress before July
3. her hair at Antoines's
4. a new suit very soon
5. all my suitcases and bags when I came
6. the brakes only last week
7. her last tooth yesterday
8. all her clothes every spring

139 Practice Situations with Variations

Make sentences with the pattern for these situations

1. There's something wrong with my television set. I've just phoned the repair-man.
2. This happened only last week, too.
3. Paula didn't carry all her luggage. A shipping-firm did all the work.
4. Ask the person next to you if he or she is going to do this!
5. I couldn't mend the puncture in my tyre. A mechanic did it.
6. Ask someone else how much this costs in his or her country.
7. Richard's hair is very long. He's going to the hairdresser's.
8. Ask how much this costs in England.
9. The telephone repair man came some time ago. It's all right now.
10. Ask me exactly WHEN!
11. Lord Girth wants a new suit. He's going to his tailor's now.
12. Ask 'how many suits/last year'
13. June Dobson, the millionaire's daughter has tiny feet. There is a special shoemaker's in Florence and all her shoes come from there.
14. Alf Fleming, the novelist, can't type. A girl types his novels.
15. Bill's tooth is rotten and it is hurting now. He's going to the dentist's.
16. Ask how much this costs in England!

140 HAS BEEN DONE vs. WAS DONE

Problem Situation

Lady Agatha Jollicks thinks she is just about the last aristocrat left. She tries very hard to live in style. Her small flat is always redecorated every year.

A friend has come to tea. She notices that the room is different. The decorators, in fact, have only just left.

The friend says: 'This room is different'

1. What does Lady Agatha try to do?
2. Can you give an example of this?
3. What does the friend say?
4. Are the decorators still there?
5. Now do these
   What does Lady Agatha say about the flat?
   Ask her WHEN

141 TEXTS (Radio News Items)

i. Good evening, here is the six o'clock news. The President of Santa Sierra has been assassinated. He was stabbed late last night at the Presidential Palace. The assassin was shot dead by police only a few moments later. The President was rushed to hospital and was given blood transfusions, but he died early this morning. The small Latin American republic is in a state of wild disorder. There is fighting in the streets of the capital, San Sabrosa, and it has been reported that at least 100 people have been killed. Most of them were killed immediately after the assassination. The radio station there was cut off early this morning, and no more news has been received.

1. Who has been assassinated?
2. Ask WHEN! Ask HOW!
3. What happened to the assassin?
4. Ask WHEN!
5. What happened to the President immediately after the assassination?
6. What was done in the hospital?
7. Has anyone been killed in the fighting?
8. Ask HOW MANY! Ask WHEN!
9. How do we know this?
10. Has the radio station been cut off?
11. Ask WHEN!
12. Ask a question with: 'Any More News?'

ii. Another atomic bomb has been exploded in China. The news was announced yesterday by the Chinese Government. A bright flash was seen over 200 miles away. An official note of protest from the Japanese Government has already been given to the Chinese Government. The note was handed to them late last night.

1. What has been exploded in China?
2. Ask WHEN!
3. Ask when the news was announced!
4. Tell me about the bright flash!
5. Ask if a note of protest has been given to the Chinese Government!
6. Ask WHEN!
7. Who was the note from?

iii. Richard Grantchester, on his round-the-world voyage alone on his yacht, Reckless, is now only 50 miles away from Plymouth. He was seen early this morning by an R.A.F. helicopter. This is Mr. Grantchester's seventh round-the-world voyage alone. A month ago he was almost drowned near Cape Horn when a giant wave hit his yacht, which almost capsized.

1. How do we know Grantchester is only 50 miles from Plymouth?
2. What happened last month?

UNIT C ONE

ALWAYS DOES vs. IS/ARE ALWAYS DOING
SHOULD/CAN/MUST DO vs. SHOULD/CAN/MUST BE DOING

1 Always Does vs. Is/Are Always Doing

Illustrative Situations

i. Lawrence Morrel, the writer, gets up at 7 every morning and says the same thing to himself: "I must write at least a thousand words today!" He starts work at 8 every morning and never stops before he has written those 1,000 words. HE ALWAYS DOES THESE THINGS. HE ALWAYS GETS UP AT 7 AND HE ALWAYS STARTS WORK AT 8. HE ALWAYS WORKS UNTIL HE HAS WRITTEN A THOUSAND WORDS. HE ALWAYS WRITES A THOUSAND WORDS EVERY DAY.

1. How often does Lawrence get up at 7?
2. What does he say to himself every morning?
3. Now ask questions with "always" and these words: (a) up at 7? (b) work at 8? (c) 1,000 words
4. Now make some sentences with "always" about yourself.
   Prompts: breakfast   work
              to bed   up

ii. Fred Mullins thinks that there are certain things his wife does far too often. For instance she buys new clothes far too often. He is also tired of hearing her say "You never give me enough money." The last time she said that, he got angry and shouted "YOU'RE ALWAYS SAYING THAT. YOU'RE ALWAYS ASKING FOR MORE MONEY! YOU'RE ALWAYS SPENDING IT ON NEW CLOTHES. YOU'RE ALWAYS COMPLAINING!"

1. Ask questions about Fred's wife with "How often . . . . .?"
   (a) new clothes (b) more money (c) complain
2. What is he tired of hearing her say?
3. Ask what he did the last time she said that!
4. Make as many sentences as you can about Fred's wife with "always"
5. What are some of the other things men often say their wives are always doing?

iii. Richard West works in London. He catches a train at 8.05 every morning and another one at 5.55 every evening. At least once or twice a month he leaves his umbrella on the train. Richard's wife says he loses things far too often. HE ALWAYS TAKES THE 8.05 TO WORK AND ALWAYS CATCHES THE 5.55 HOME. HE IS ALWAYS LEAVING HIS UMBRELLA ON THE TRAIN. HE IS ALWAYS LOSING THINGS.

1. Ask questions about Richard with "How often . . . . .?"
   (a) the 8.05 (b) the 5.55 (c) his umbrella (d) things
2. Now make as many sentences as you can about Richard with "always"

2 Invention Exercise

Do these prompt words suggest AL-WAYS DOING or ALWAYS DOES? Make sentences with either one form or the other, like this

The secretary/late = THE SECRETARY IS ALWAYS COMING TO WORK LATE

tea-break/10.30 = WE ALWAYS HAVE A TEA-BREAK AT 10.30

1. The neighbours/noise at night
2. Richard/an egg for breakfast
3. two lumps of sugar in my coffee
4. The 8.30 bus/at 8.30
5. That cat/birds
6. That man/stupid jokes
7. Paula/a bath in the morning
8. I/the cinema on Friday
9. Mrs. Mavis/fish on Friday
10. Bert/trouble with his car
11. Jill/arguments with her father
12. Mr. Collins/to work at 8.

3 Practice Situations

Use either IS/ARE ALWAYS DOING or AL-WAYS DOES/DO for each situation. Use IS/ARE AL-WAYS DOING when "always" really means "far too often" and you want to express anger or irritation.

Situation: The bus came late again today. That is the third time this month!

Response: IT IS (It's) ALWAYS COMING LATE.

Situation: As usual, Jane caught the 8.20 bus this morning.

Response: SHE ALWAYS CATCHES THE 8.20 BUS.

1. My radio broke down again this week. It seems to do this every month.
2. When Carla Morass, the singer, comes to London, there is only one place she stays; The Ritz Hotel, of course.
3. We know when the lesson ends because a bell rings.
4. Richard left his hat in the office again today. He does this at least once a week.
5. It is 7 o'clock and Mrs. Mavis is eating dinner. She never eats dinner at any other time.
6. General Jollicks gets up at exactly 6.30, every morning.

7. Mrs. Mavis is very religious. It is Sunday. She is going to church, of course.
8. Look at that rain! It seems to rain every day in this terrible place!
9. Richard sees his mother every Sunday.
10. Tony is putting on a white shirt. This is the only colour he ever wears.
11. Mr. Collins is flying to Paris again next week. As usual, he is going to fly BEA.
12. Fred's wife says she hasn't enough clothes. Fred is tired of hearing her say that.

4 Remedial Fluency Practice

Observe the position of AL-WAYS and words like ON SUNDAY. Do these quickly!

Model: HE ALWAYS SEES HIS MOTHER ON SUNDAY

Friday = HE ALWAYS SEES HIS MOTHER ON FRIDAY

goes out = HE ALWAYS GOES OUT ON FRIDAY

We = WE ALWAYS GO OUT ON FRIDAY

HE ALWAYS SEES HIS MOTHER ON SUNDAY

1. phones her
2. Saturday
3. I
4. do the shopping
5. We
6. Friday
7. go dancing
8. she
9. They
10. eat fish
11. Monday
12. never

5 SHOULD DO vs. SHOULD BE DOING

Problem Situation

Mr. Howe is an old man. The doctor told him last week to sit in the sun as much as possible. It's a beautiful day but Mr. Howe is in his tiny, dark sitting-room.

1. Ask what the doctor told Mr. Howe last week! (and answer)
2. Is he following the doctor's advice?
3. Now do this
   The doctor has just come and found Mr. Howe in the sitting-room. He is very angry; what does he say to him with the word SHOULD?

6 Illustrative Situations

i. Young Dr. Pildare is drunk. Everyone is shocked. The worst thing is that he has just come into the operating theatre without a mask on. There is also a dirty black cigar in his mouth. He knows all this is strictly forbidden.
   HE SHOULD BE WEARING A MASK
   HE SHOULDN'T BE SMOKING

1. Why is everyone shocked?
2. Where is Dr. Pildare now?
3. Is he wearing a mask?
4. Ask if he should! (answer)
5. What is he doing that is forbidden?
6. Ask if he should. (answer)

ii. Tony is typical of many young men today. He is overweight and he never gets any exercise. He drives everywhere. Even when he wants a packet of cigarettes from the corner-shop, he drives there. The doctor has told him to get more exercise and to walk as much as possible.
   HE SHOULD GET MORE EXERCISE
   HE SHOULD WALK WHEN HE GOES TO THE CORNER SHOP
   PERHAPS HE SHOULD TAKE UP TENNIS OR GOLF

1. Is Tony overweight?
2. Ask why!
3. What does he do when he wants a packet of cigarettes from the corner-shop?
4. What has the doctor told him to do?
5. Has he taken up tennis or golf yet?
6. Now ask and answer questions with SHOULD
   Practice Questions
   (a) more exercise?　　(d) tennis or golf?
   (b) How much　　　　(e) less food?
   　　exercise?　　　　(f) along the beach in
   (c) to the corner-　　　　fine weather?
   　　shop in his car?

7 Practice Situations

Make sentences with SHOULD BE DOING and SHOULD NOT BE DOING for each situation

1. Max has an important exam tomorrow and he has hardly studied for it. He's watching television now.
2. The lorry is travelling at more than 60 miles an hour but the driver's eyes are on the pretty girl next to him.
3. The teacher is talking. One of the students has just started a letter to his mother.
4. The great military parade has just started. One of the soldiers has sandals on.
5. The music for the soprano's great aria has just begun. She is shouting at the conductor.
6. It is raining. The little girl is in the street with only a cotton dress on.

8 CAN'T DO vs. CAN'T BE DOING

Illustrative Situations

i. Only an hour ago the director of a large firm was found dead in his office with a bullet in his head. The police have established that he was murdered at 2.35. They are questioning his secretary now.
"I was in the canteen having lunch at that time." she has just said.
The office manager is listening. "SHE CAN'T BE TELLING THE TRUTH" he tells one of the detectives. "The canteen was closed at 2.35."

1. What have the police established?
2. Ask what they are doing now!
3. What has she just said?
4. What does the office manager say when he hears this?
5. Ask why he says this! (answer)

ii. Malcolm is a pathological liar. He is always confusing his fantasies with reality. That is why he says things like: "When I was last at the White House . . .", or "We secret agents . . .", and things like that.
When people talk about Malcolm they often say: "HE SIMPLY CAN'T TELL THE TRUTH"

1. What is Malcolm always doing?
2. What do you call such a person?
3. What are some of the things he says?
4. What do people often say about Malcolm?

9 Practice Situations

Make sentences only with CAN'T BE DOING

1. Someone says "Richard's sitting in the park". You saw him in the office a second ago.
2. You hear piano music and see Jane at the piano. You know she has never played before.
3. Your uncle has something that looks like a cigarette in his mouth. He is the head of the Anti-Tobacco League.
4. You understand Russian but you do not understand the two foreigners at the next table.
5. The six-month-old child has a book open in front of it.
6. "Bill's playing tennis", someone says. You know Bill has a broken leg.

10 Practice Situation

Make sentences with CAN'T DO

1. You have an invitation to a party tomorrow. You'll be somewhere else.
2. The teacher asks you to read a word on the board. It is too small.
3. The ship is sinking. There is a lifeboat only a few yards away in the water. There is something you've never learned.
4. Someone asks: "How about a game of chess?" You don't know the rules.
5. The train is leaving in 5 minutes. The station is miles away.
6. A foreigner is trying to say something. You don't know his language.

11 MUST DO vs. MUST BE DOING

Conversation

i. 9.30 in the office.
Two men are talking about another man in their office.

A: George has a black eye again.
B: What? Another one?
A: Yes.
B: He had one last month, didn't he?
A: That's right. They say his wife has a terrible temper.
B: She must have. How does he get all those black eyes?
A: I don't know. She must throw things at him.
B: Yes, that must be it.

1. Has George had any other black eyes?
2. Ask WHEN?
3. What does one of the men say about George's wife and her temper?
4. What does the other man say?
5. When he says "She must have," is he talking from direct experience?
6. How does the first man say George gets all his black eyes?
7. What does the second man say then?

ii. 9 p.m. the evening before.
The married couple in the flat below George and his wife are talking. They have just heard a scream. Someone is shouting upstairs.

Man: What on earth could that be?
Woman: It's that couple upstairs. They must be having another argument.
Man: An argument? They must be having a battle.
(A cry of "HELP" is heard.)
Woman: That must be the man shouting now!
Man: The man? You mean . . . .
(Now the sound of a vase breaking is heard.)
Woman: Yes, she must be throwing things at him again.

1. What were the different sounds the couple in the flat below heard the night before?
2. What did the woman think when she heard the first scream? What did the man think?
3. What did they both hear breaking and what did the woman say at that point?

12

Make sentences with MUST DO or MUST BE DOING for these situations.

1. A man's breath always smells of whisky. He is sitting in the office now.
2. You have just come into a room. Cigarette smoke is hanging over your young son's head. His hands are behind his back.
3. You hear a strange language behind you. Two Chinese are there and you hear the words "Mao Tse Tung" several times.
4. You can hear a typewriter upstairs. You know a writer lives there.
5. In his library he has books in 6 different languages.
6. The only kinds of bottles in his dustbin are always empty champagne bottles.
7. You go to bed rather late every evening, but when you do there is always a light on in the man's house across the street.
8. You can see the man now. It is midnight and he is just turning that light off!
9. A priest is walking down the road. There is a small book in his hands and his lips are moving.
10. The beautiful woman in the airport lounge is holding a Pan Am ticket to Los Angeles.
11. Max is asleep but his lips are moving and you can hear a few words.
12. You mentioned the President's name. The man you were talking to called him by his first name.
13. The man in the bus is wearing blue overalls with the word "Ford" on them.
14. The man you are talking to in church has a pipe sticking out of his pocket.
15. The girl on the beach has her ear next to the radio.
16. Tom knows all about French politics and there are lots of French newspapers in his room.

K

129

UNIT C TWO

WINE/WOMEN/HORSES etc (concrete words)
vs. THE WINE/THE WOMEN etc
MATHEMATICS/DEATH/INDUSTRY etc (abstract words)
vs. THE MATHEMATICS/THE INDUSTRY etc
NEWS/TASTE/WEATHER etc (words that never take "a")

13 **Concrete Words with and without THE**

Problem Situation

Do these simple Problem Situations. They are a General Intro-duction to the problem of THE and no

George is a connoisseur of wine. He loves it. Yesterday he went to a restaurant and had a meal. Naturally he had some wine with it. He took one sip from the glass and then motioned to the waiter. "Take this back" he said. "It's terrible!"

1. What is George a connoisseur of?
2. Ask where he went yesterday! (answer)
3. Ask what he had there! (answer)
4. How much did he drink?
5. What happened then?
6. What did he say?
7. Now do this
   What is it that George loves?
   What didn't he like in the restaurant?

14 Special Comment

Study the next four pages. Notice when we say THE and when we do not. To grasp and master the problem one needs observation and a few guiding concepts rather than a mass of rules. Above all, observe when THE is used and when it is not when you are outside the classroom as well as inside it. This, of course, is something you should do with all aspects of English.

Illustrative Situation

Lord Kippner, the famous British General, hated women. He once said;
WOMEN ARE MORE DANGEROUS THAN ENEMY BULLETS and also:
SOCIETY WOULD BE PERFECT IF THERE WERE NO WOMEN
Once, in Egypt during a war, he had to save some women from the enemy. They were in a village on the Nile and he went there in a small boat. When he got there he found five Army horses there, too. The boat was not big enough for both the horses and the women
HE TOOK THE HORSES AND LEFT THE WOMEN

1. How did Lord K. feel about women?
2. What did he once say about them and enemy bullets?
3. What did he say about society?
4. Ask someone else if he or she agrees!
5. Where were the women he had to save?
6. How did he get there?
7. Ask what else he found there!
8. Was the boat big enough?
9. Ask and answer what he took and what he left!

15 EXTRACTS FROM A GREAT MAN'S AUTOBIOGRAPHY

Bernard Howell was born in 1870 and is still alive today. He is a famous thinker and mathematician. Some people say he is a very great man. Others regard him as a devil. These are some of the things found in his autobiography.

About War in General and the First World War in Particular

I have hated war all my life. It is wasteful and it always creates far more problems than it solves. The First World War was the most meaningless of them all. People say suicide is wrong and yet hardly anyone tried to stop the suicide of a whole civilisation then. When I and a few others protested against the war we were sent to prison. Men rarely have much respect for life, particularly the lives of others. The men responsible for that war had respect for nothing at all except their own authority.

1. What has he hated all his life?
2. Ask WHY! (and answer)
3. What do people say is wrong? Ask someone else if he or she thinks this!
4. What does Howell say about the First World War?
5. What did hardly anyone try to stop?
6. What did Howell and a few others protest against? Were they protesting against all wars?
7. Ask what happened to those who protested!
8. What does he say men have little respect for?
9. Who had respect for nothing except their own authority?

Make sentences of your own with these words

death = **ALL OF US ARE AFRAID OF DEATH**
the death = **THE DEATH OF SO MANY YOUNG MEN WAS A TRAGIC THING**

(a) war
(b) the war
(c) suicide
(d) the suicide
(e) prison
(f) the prison
(g) life
(h) the life (or lives)

16 About Mathematics

Mathematical problems should be based on reality. I discovered when I was still a very young boy that most of the mathematical problems in the books I was given were not. Mathematics is a precise and useful science. It can help us all. What a pity this cannot be said about the mathematics so often taught to us in school!

1. What does he say should be based on reality?
2. What did he discover when he was still very young? Ask someone else if he or she agrees!
3. What does he say is a precise and useful science? Ask someone else if he or she agrees!
4. What does he say is often not very useful?

Again, make examples of your own with these words

(a) Mathematics/the mathematics I learned
(b) Algebra/the algebra taught in schools
(c) Politics/the politics of this Government
(d) Architecture/the architecture of this building
(e) Medicine/the medicine in this bottle
(f) Grammar/the grammar of the . . . language/ etc.

17 About Marriage

I believe that marriage in its present form may be impossible for many of us. Many of the marriages I have seen have been based on a lie. Ten or twenty years after the marriage first started, the two partners have to pretend that they are still the same people. Often, however, one has completely outgrown the other.

1. What does he say may be impossible for many of us?
2. Ask someone else if he or she thinks it is!
3. What does he say has often been based on a lie?
4. When is it that the two partners have to pretend they are the same people?
5. What has often happened by this time (in Howell's opinion)?

18 About Ideals

Some of the ideals I have had in my life have been very silly. None of them, however, has been brutalising. Ideals can make us better human beings but they can also degrade us. The ideals a lot of people had in the 1930's, for instance, must have been some of the very lowest in history.

1. What does he say about the ideals he has had in his life?
2. Ask if he thinks they always make us better human beings! (answer)
3. What does he say about the 1930's?

Invention

Now do this with the words in the box

science = MORE OF US SHOULD STUDY SCIENCE

or = SCIENCE IS A VERY INTEREST-ING SUBJECT

or = I HAVE NEVER BEEN INTEREST-ED IN SCIENCE

etc.

1. Commerce
2. Art
3. Modern Art
4. The Art of this Century
5. Medical Science
6. The Science of the Greeks
7. The destruction of Dresden/Hiroshima/Lidice
8. Destruction for its own sake
9. Education
10. The education of children
11. Work
12. The work most of us do
13. Murder
14. The murder of so many people
15. Freedom/Freedom of Speech
16. The Freedom to say what one wants to say.

19 EXPOSITION THROUGH EXAMPLES

Note:

We all learn the 'rules' of our language through experience of using the language. None of us learns our language through verbal rules.

Whenever someone tries to put these rules into ordinary or even semi-technical language, a particular problem occurs. The problem is that different people have entirely different ideas of what the words used in the definition mean.

Study the Basic Situations here, but remember that the examples are more important.

Remember that the examples will help you understand the rule, and not the other way around!

Basic Situation I

You are thinking of things in general. You are not thinking only of some of these things in a particular place at a particular time in a particular situation.

You do not use THE

MEN ARE ARROGANT CREATURES

PEOPLE INTEREST ME MORE THAN THINGS

POTATOES ARE EXPENSIVE AT THE MOMENT

CHILDREN AND PARENTS ARE OFTEN ENEMIES

FILM STARS EARN MORE THAN PRIME MINISTERS

OPERA SINGERS ARE BAD ENOUGH. CONDUCTORS ARE EVEN WORSE

POLITICIANS ARE JUST ORDINARY PEOPLE WHO SOMETIMES FORGET THAT THEY ARE

Basic Situation II

You are thinking of some of the things or thing in a particular place at a particular time in a particular situation.

You do use THE

THE MEN IN THIS FACTORY HAVE DONE A FINE JOB

THE PEOPLE I HAVE MET HAVE ALL BEEN VERY HELPFUL

I BOUGHT THE ONIONS FOR THE STEW BUT I FORGOT THE POTATOES

40 YEARS AGO, THE CHILDREN IN THIS TOWN WERE ALL HUNGRY AND BADLY-CLOTHED

"THE FILM STARS I HAVE KNOWN"
(Title of a recent book by a gossip-columnist)

Now Compare

SHE GAVE ME MEAT AND POTATOES FOR SUPPER. I ATE THE MEAT BUT LEFT THE POTATOES

WE HAD WINE AND CHEESE AT THE PARTY
THE CHEESE WAS ALL RIGHT BUT THE WINE WAS TOO SWEET

He is studying POLITICAL ECONOMY and PHILOSOPHY

THE ECONOMY is in trouble again!
(Not the subject but the real thing!)

There are plenty of good jobs in INDUSTRY

THE CAR INDUSTRY has had no more strikes than any other industry.

Notice now how the same word can change its meaning simply because it has THE or hasn't THE before it. Without THE it can be a kind of general idea of the thing. With THE it can be a definite example of it.

20 NEWS/WORK/AIR/WEATHER/FURNITURE etc
(words that never take "a")

Illustrative Situations

i. Richard listens to the news every morning. Sometimes it is good, but usually it is bad and often it is terrible. These were three of the things Richard heard this morning. "The cost of living has risen by 3% this month." "125 people were killed in an air crash yesterday." "British exports have risen by 10% this month." When Richard heard the first thing, he said "THAT'S BAD NEWS!"

1. What does Richard do every morning?
2. What was said about the cost of living this morning?
3. What else was said about an air crash and then about British exports?
4. What did Richard say about the first thing?
5. Reproduce the other two items again and then say what you think Richard said about each.
   (a) 125 people   (b) British exports/10%

ii. Bill Rawlings thinks he was born unlucky. He works in a factory and hates it. "IT'S VERY BORING WORK!" he often says. The air in the factory is very dirty. "YOU'VE NEVER BREATHED SUCH DIRTY AIR!" he told his wife yesterday. Last year he and his wife went to the seaside and it rained every day. "WHAT TERRIBLE WEATHER!" he said. "NOBODY HAS SUCH TERRIBLE LUCK AS I DO!" Bill often says to himself.

1. Where does Bill work and what does he say about it?
2. What is the air like and what did he tell his wife about it?
3. What sort of weather did he and his wife have on their last holiday?
4. What did he say about the weather?
5. What does he often say about his luck?

iii. Mrs. Ottoway is very rich. Yesterday she bought a very expensive, very large table. "THIS IS VERY GOOD FURNITURE" she said. Her daughter, Caroline, thought it was terrible. "MY MOTHER HAS TERRIBLE TASTE!" she said.

1. What did Mrs. Ottoway buy yesterday?
2. What did she say about the table?
3. Did Caroline like it?
4. What did she say about her mother?

21 FLUENCY PRACTICE

Substitution with Variations

Do this at speed.

Model: WHAT TERRIBLE NEWS
weather =   WHAT TERRIBLE WEATHER
awful =   WHAT AWFUL WEATHER
Have you ever seen such = HAVE YOU EVER
                         SEEN SUCH
                         AWFUL WEATHER?

WHAT TERRIBLE NEWS
1. furniture
2. expensive
3. good
4. taste
5. news
6. food
7. bad
8. We get such
9. weather
10. I've never had
11. luck
12. Bill always has

22 TEXTS
Items from various Radio Programmes

i. From a programme called "This Week's Football"

East Ham is a club that believes in attack and not in defence. When they are on the top of their form, the attack East Ham can put up is truly magnificent. Unfortunately, today was not one for such excellence.
Time and time again we saw the East Ham attack come to nothing just as it reached the Manchester goal. To make matters worse, the Manchester forwards soon found holes in the East Ham defence. The result was a bad defeat for a club capable of much better things.

1. What is it that East Ham believes in?
2. Ask what they don't believe in!
3. Ask if the East Ham attack was good today!
4. What can happen when they are on the top of their form?
5. What happened time and time again in front of the Manchester goal?
6. What did the Manchester forwards soon do?

ii. A critic in a programme called "This Week's Music" talks about a concert given by the Youth Orchestra

Until recently Britain was thought to be a country very short of musical talent. Britain was "The Land Without Music". Today, however, it can truly be said that the musical talent in these islands, and particularly the musical talent of some of our youngest musicians, is outstanding. Both the music and the orchestral playing we heard last night in the Festival Hall demonstrated this. The musicians were all under 18 but they played with the assurance of experienced craftsmen. The music itself was all by composers under 30. The composers, too, were British.

1. What was Britain thought to be short of?
2. Ask if it still is!
3. What was the title given to Britain?
4. Ask if Germany or Italy is or ever was!
5. What does the reviewer say is outstanding today?
6. What demonstrated this?
7. Ask about the age of the musicians!
8. How did they play?
9. Who was the music by?
10. Ask if they were: (a) under 30 (b) British

iii. From a women's programme called "Shopping Around This Week"

Fruit, vegetables and eggs are still rather expensive this weekend. Meat, on the other hand, particularly beef and pork, is beginning to come down in price. Lamb is not yet a good buy and will not be so until the New Zealand imports arrive in greater quantity.
Almost all the fruit in the main London markets is below the usual standard for this time of year. Growers blame this on the late Spring. They say that the fruit we shall be getting in a few weeks will be both cheaper and better. All the vegetables I saw were definitely second-grade, too.

1. What is still rather expensive?
2. Ask someone else if these things (name them) are expensive on the Continent!
3. What does the report say is beginning to come down in price?
4. Ask if lamb is a good buy!
5. Now ask the same thing about beef and pork!
6. How long will it be before lamb is a good buy?
7. What is below the usual standard?
8. What do growers blame it on?
9. What do they say will happen soon?
10. What does the reporter say were second-grade?

UNIT C THREE

WILL DO UNTIL vs. WILL HAVE DONE BY
WILL DO vs. WILL BE DOING
MIGHT DO vs. MIGHT BE DOING

23 Will Do Until vs. Will Have Done By

Illustrative Situations

i. Bill Rawlings and all the other men in the factory have just had their last tea break. It is 2.30. They are all working again. They will go on working and then, at 4 o'clock a whistle will blow and they will all stop. Most of them will run out immediately. A few will stay for a few minutes but the last one will be out before 4.10. THEY WILL ALL WORK UNTIL 4. THE LAST ONE WILL HAVE LEFT BY 4.10.

1. What have all the men just done?
2. What are they doing now?
3. When will the whistle blow?
4. When will the last one be out of the factory?
5. Make two sentences, one with UNTIL and the other with BY

ii. Lawrence Morrel, the writer, is trying to finish a story. He must get it in this evening's post. The post is collected at 5.30. "I'LL GO ON WRITING UNTIL I FINISH THIS!" he says to himself. "I'LL WRITE UNTIL 5.30 BUT I MUST FINISH IT BY THEN. I HOPE I'LL HAVE FINISHED IT BY THEN!"

1. What is Lawrence trying to do?
2. When must he finish it and why?
3. How long will

iii. Paula is taking her final examination at the Language Institute. It is 2 o'clock, and a teacher is handing out the papers now. "You have exactly three hours and no more!" he says. "I shall collect all your papers at exactly five. YOU CAN GO ON WRITING UNTIL 5 BUT YOU MUST ALL FINISH BY THAT TIME!" It is a very difficult exam and Paula will need every minute.

1. What is Paula doing?
2. What is a teacher doing at the moment?
3. Ask questions with these words.
   (a) How much time?
   (b) When/collect?
   (c) When/finish?
   (d) How long/go on?
4. What do you think Paula hopes she will have done by 5?
5. What will Paula do until 5?

Special Comment

Use UNTIL when you want to say how long an action will go on and identify the point at which it will stop.
Use BY when you want to identify the last possible point at which an action can finish.

24 FLUENCY PRACTICE

Substitution with Variations

Observe the
construction of
WILL HAVE
DONE. Ob-
serve that the
form is the
same for all
persons

Model: THEY WILL (They'll) HAVE
        FINISHED BY 5.
left = THEY WILL HAVE LEFT BY 5.
he =   HE WILL HAVE LEFT BY 5.
6 =   HE WILL HAVE LEFT BY 6.

THEY WILL HAVE FINISHED BY 5.
1. Bill   7. Will you
2. gone home   8. done everything
3. 6   9. Jane
4. eaten   10. left here
5. I   11. the train
6. typed the letters 12. we

25 Practice Situations

Make one sen-
tence with
either BY or
UNTIL for
each situation,
like this

All the men in the factory are working. The whistle blows at 4.
THEY WILL (They'll) WORK UNTIL 4.

Sometimes the boss goes home at 5.30, but he never goes home later than 6.
HE WILL (He'll) HAVE GONE HOME BY 6.

1. Richard is watching a programme that ends at 9. He wants to go to bed then.
2. The latest possible time Richard can get up is 7.30.
3. That bus never leaves later than 8.
4. Old Mr. Howe is reading a very good book in the library. It closes in a few minutes, at 9.
5. Mr. Collins is staying in a hotel. He will leave on Friday.

6. Some students are sitting in the language lab at the Institute. The lesson ends at 3 o'clock.
7. The professor sometimes comes at 9.15 and never later than 9.30.
8. It is the middle of the morning and Lawrence Morrel is writing. He always has lunch at 12.
9. Lawrence may finish today at 4, certainly not later than 4.30.
10. Lawrence is waiting for some money from his publisher. The publisher has told him that it will arrive not later than Tuesday.

26 Invention Exercise

Some of these
prompts
suggest sen-
tences with BY.
Others suggest
sentences with
UNTIL. Make
your own sen-
tences, like this

stay here/Monday = WE'LL STAY HERE
                   UNTIL MONDAY
lunch/2 =   I'LL HAVE EATEN
                   LUNCH BY 2

1. sleep/8
2. up/8.30
3. study/12

4. Jane/all her boss's letters/5.30
5. all the dirty dishes/7 o'clock

27 WILL BE DOING vs. WILL DO

Problem Situation

Bill Rawlings always gets a lift to work in his friend's car. Every morning, at 6.30, he goes to the corner and stands there. A few minutes later, his friend comes by and stops. Bill gets into the car and they drive off.

1. What does Bill do every morning at 6.30?
2. What happens a few minutes later?
3. What does Bill do for the few minutes before the car comes?
4. Now do this
   Bill is going to do all these things tomorrow
   What will he be doing when the car comes and what will he do?

28 Illustrative Situations

i. Lord Kane, an important British diplomat, must fly to Washington immediately on an emergency mission. A government car is taking him to London airport now. A special plane is already waiting. Everything is ready for an immediate take-off.
   THE PLANE WILL BE WAITING FOR HIM WHEN HE GET THERE
   IT WILL TAKE OFF WHEN HE GETS THERE

1. Who is Lord Kane?
2. What is happening now?
3. Why is there all this rush?
4. What is the crew of the plane doing now?
5. Ask what they'll be doing when he gets there!
6. Ask what they'll do!

ii. 3 police cars are speeding through the night. They have just received information that a notorious criminal is playing roulette at this very moment in a gambling club.
   HE'LL BE PLAYING ROULETTE WHEN THEY GET THERE
   HE'LL RUN AWAY WHEN THEY GET THERE

1. Why are the police cars in such a hurry?
2. What is the criminal doing at this moment?
3. Ask 2 questions about him with
   WILL BE DOING and
   WILL DO WHEN THEY GET THERE!

iii. It is only a few seconds before 4 o'clock in the factory where Bill works. All the men are working hard but they know that the whistle always blows at exactly 4 o'clock. They always stop then and rush home.
   THEY WILL ALL BE WORKING WHEN THE WHISTLE BLOWS. THEY WILL ALL STOP WHEN IT BLOWS.

1. What time is it?
2. What always happens at 4?
3. What are the men doing now?
4. What will they be doing when the whistle blows?
5. What will they do?

iv. Bill Rawlings is having dinner. His wife is in the kitchen, washing a few cups. Bill does not know it but in a few seconds a man from the Football Pools will knock on his door and tell him he has won £60,000.

BILL WILL BE HAVING DINNER WHEN THE MAN KNOCKS. HE WILL ANSWER THE DOOR WHEN HE KNOCKS.

1. Ask and answer what Bill and his wife are doing now?
2. What will happen in a few seconds?
3. Ask and answer what Bill will do and what he will be doing.
4. Ask the same two questions about Bill's wife.

29 Practice Situations

Say what the people in these situations WILL BE DOING and also what they WILL DO. (2 sentences for each situation)

Bill's mother is watching television. He is going to phone her in a minute.

SHE WILL (She'll) BE WATCHING TELEVISION WHEN HE PHONES. SHE'LL ANSWER THE PHONE WHEN IT RINGS.

1. Richard is standing on the platform. The train will come in a minute.
2. Janet is playing tennis but it is going to rain in a few minutes.
3. Paula is trying to finish her exam. She is writing furiously, but the teacher is going to shout "Stop!" in a second.

4. Mrs. Collins is standing outside Gate 10 at London airport. Her husband will come out soon.
5. It is 9.30 in the factory and all the men are working. The whistle for the tea-break will blow in a few seconds.
6. The students always listen to the teacher until the bell rings. Then they all rush out. All this will happen tomorrow.

30 Invention Exercise

Basic Situation: You have already planned your evening. A friend has just told you he wants to see you at 8. He asks what you will be doing then. Make the answers with these words.

1. some homework
2. the radio
3. a letter home
4. a new book I got today
5. a party with some friends
6. a play on television
7. dinner in the new Chinese restaurant
8. my suitcases before I go away

31 Might Do vs. Might Be Doing

Illustrative Situations

i. Mrs. Collins usually has a driving-lesson every afternoon. Her instructor isn't sure if he can give her one tomorrow.
SHE MIGHT HAVE ONE TOMORROW

1. What usually happens every afternoon?
2. Ask about tomorrow! (answer)

ii If she has a driving-lesson at all tomorrow it will be from 2 to 3 o'clock. One of Mrs. Collins's friends has just rung up and has said she wants to come over at 2.30. "Don't come over then." Mrs. Collins says:
"I MIGHT BE HAVING A DRIVING LESSON"

1. Is there any chance she will have a lesson tomorrow?
2. Ask when! (answer)
3. When does her friend want to come over?
4. What exactly does she say?

32 Practice and Expansion

A young married couple want to have a party soon. They have to get the landlord's permission first. He lives in the flat downstairs. If he gives it they are going to do all the usual things. They have a good collection of jazz records and some dance music as well. There is a piano in their flat. They are also going to get in some wine, beer and a lot of cheese. Some of the people they are going to invite will probably want to do nothing but talk.

1. What do the married couple want to do?
2. Is it definite yet?
3. Why not?
4. Tell me some of the things they are going to do if the landlord gives his permission! (records. dance music. wine. cheese. the piano. jokes)
5. Will everyone want to dance or listen to music?

Expansion

(a) What are some of the things that might be happening around 9.30 on the evening they will be giving the party?

(b) What are some of the things you might be doing at these times:
  i.   7.30 tomorrow morning
  ii. 6.15 tomorrow evening
  iii. 10.25 next Sunday morning
  iv. 11 o'clock in the morning on a warm day next summer
  v.   this time next year

33 CONVERSATION

Two spies are arranging a meeting by telephone. They have never seen each other before.

A: (strong and aggressive) Now, have you understood everything?

B: (weak and nervous) Yes, I think so.

A: You think so! What do you mean? Everything must go according to plan! Tell me when we will meet, where I'll be standing, and what I'll say to you!

B: Uh . . . . we'll meet at . . at 8 o'clock tomorrow morning and . . .

A: No, no, you fool! At 9 o'clock tomorrow morning! At 9!

B: Of course. At 9. That was just a slip of the tongue. I meant 9.

A: Now, where will I be standing and what will I say to you?

B: You'll be standing in front of the Bank of England, and you'll say . . . . you'll say . . . uh . . . .

A: (very angry) I'll say "What terrible weather!" Do you understand, you fool!

B: Yes, but don't you think that might sound strange. I mean, the sun might be shining tomorrow, and someone might overhear us. Perhaps the Secret Service will be watching us and . . and . . .

A: Never mind about that. Just remember to be there at 9, tomorrow morning. I shall wait only until then! I'll have left by 9.05! Remember!

B: Yes, I'll remember. I won't forget.

A: Now, there's still one thing we haven't settled. How will I recognise you?

B: Oh, that's easy, I'll be wearing a bowler hat and carrying an umbrella.

A: What! In the centre of London! That won't help me at all! Don't you realise that a thousand other people might be doing the same thing on the same street!

B: Oh, dear. I suppose you're right. You see, I thought the police might be following me, and I wanted to look like everyone else. I know! I'll wave to you. Will that help you?

A: All right. But wave to me, and not to someone else!

B: Yes, of course. But . . . oh, dear . . . . how will I recognise you?

A: That's easy. I'll be wearing a grey raincoat and carrying a black briefcase.

1. Ask and answer these questions about the first spy (the strong, aggressive one)
   (a) Where/stand (b) What/say
2. Why does the other spy think "What terrible weather!" might sound strange?
3. Who is he afraid will be watching them?
4. How long will the first spy wait and when will he have left?
5. How does the weak, nervous spy say he can be recognised?
6. What does the first spy say when he hears this?
7. What will the weak, nervous spy do when he sees the other spy?
8. What is the problem that the weak spy suddenly realises, and how does the other spy say he can be recognised?
9. Why did the weak spy want to look like everyone else?
10. Ask your own questions with these words about this conversation.
    (a) How many other people/grey raincoats?
    (b) Why/difficult/recognise each other?

UNIT C FOUR

HAD DONE vs. DID
HAD NO IDEA
DIDN'T KNOW/THINK   WAS GOING TO HAPPEN

34 HAD DONE vs. DID

Problem Situations

The police received a phone call telling them that a certain notorious criminal was in a hotel-room with a woman. They rushed there immediately. When they burst into the room the woman was still there and so were the criminal's shoes. Unfortunately he wasn't.

1. What did the police learn from the phone call?
2. Ask what they did!
3. What did they find in the hotel room?
4. Now answer this.
   Why were the police too late?

35 Illustrative Situations

i. The ship was 50 miles off the English coast when there was an explosion in the engine room. An S.O.S. message was sent and a helicopter and two life-boats set out. The ship sank before they got there.
IT HAD SUNK WHEN THEY ARRIVED

1. Why was an S.O.S. message sent?
2. What happened as soon as it was received?
3. What happened before they got there?
4. So, why didn't they find anything when they arrived?

ii. Richard went home a few minutes early yesterday. A few minutes after he had left, his boss phoned and asked to see him urgently. He was very angry when Richard's secretary told him he had gone.
HE HAD ALREADY GONE WHEN HIS BOSS PHONED

1. Ask how early Richard went home!
2. Ask when his boss phoned!
3. What did his boss want?
4. What did Ted's secretary tell him?
5. So, why couldn't his boss speak to him?

Practice and Expansion

The meal was very good and they completely forgot about the time. It was only when Richard looked at his watch that he realised how late it was. He and his wife dashed out of the restaurant and got to the theatre a few minutes later, but the doors were already closed and they could hear the actors' voices inside the auditorium.
THE PLAY HAD STARTED WHEN THEY GOT THERE

1. Where did they go before the theatre?
2. Ask about the meal!
3. When did Richard realise the time?
4. Ask what they did then!
5. When did they get to the theatre?
6. Ask about: (a) the doors
             (b) actors' voices
             (c) the play
7. Why didn't they see all the play?
8. What else had happened before they got there? (the curtain. the lights. the audience. the actors.)

36 Practice Situations

Make your own examples with WHEN (DID) HAD DONE

The plane was already in the air and was flying overhead when you got to the airport.
WHEN YOU GOT THERE, THE PLANE HAD TAKEN OFF.

1. It was raining when I went inside. I looked out later and the sun was shining.
2. I got out of the train to get a paper. When I came back the train wasn't there.
3. The waiters were clearing away all the dishes when I got to the banquet.

4. When the police got to the scene of the robbery, all they found was an empty safe.
5. The war ended in 1945. Paul went into the Army in 1946.
6. The students were all in class when I got to **school.**

37 A FEW FREQUENTLY USED IRREGULAR PARTICIPLES

Do not take these examples too seriously. They are a memory aid if you have difficulty remembering participles (DONE/GONE etc.). Study the examples at home or in class. Then cover them and look at or listen to only the recall prompts.

When the police got there, the spy HAD

BROKEN OPEN THE SAFE
STOLEN ALL THE MONEY
TAKEN OFF IN A CHINESE JET
DRIVEN AWAY IN A FAST CAR
RUN DOWN A DARK ALLEY
DRUNK THE LAST BOTTLE OF
CHAMPAGNE
EATEN ALL THE CAVIAR

Recall Prompts (table covered):
  i. the safe
  ii. the money
  iii. a Chinese jet
  iv. in a fast car
  v. down a dark alley
  vi. the last bottle of champagne
  vii. all the caviar

38 LISTENING PRACTICE

Another problem associated with HAD DONE occurs when the DONE form (participle) is the same as the DID form (Past)

In such cases students often think they have heard DID when they have really heard HAD DONE

This is because English speakers often give weak stress to HAD. Foreigners often do not hear it at all when this happens

Listen to the sentences.
The teacher will pronounce HAD with weak stress ('d).
Say YES when there is a HAD in the sentence.
Say NO when there isn't.

The train had ('d) left when we got there
YES

The train left when we got there
NO

1. The trouble had ('d) started when the police got there.
2. The guests walked out when he said that.
3. The match ended when the rain began.
4. The match had ('d) ended when the rain began.
5. The trouble started when someone threw a bottle.
6. Everyone had walked out when I got there.
7. He stopped speaking when he saw me.
8. He had stopped speaking when I came.
9. She had killed herself when the police broke in.
10. She killed herself when the police broke in.

39 Had No Idea
Didn't Know something Was Going to Happen

Problem Situation

Nora Elliot's husband is a young advertising executive. Yesterday at 5.30 he brought an important customer home for dinner. Nora was astounded. She had absolutely no warning. The house was in a terrible state and she was in her old clothes.

1. What does Nora's husband do?
2. What happened at 5.30 yesterday?
3. What was Nora's reaction?
4. Ask why!
5. Ask about the house and Nora herself!
6. Now do this
   Nora's husband brought the guest home at 5.30; what had she absolutely no idea of at 5?

40 Illustrative Situations

i. Last Monday, at 5 p.m. Bill Rawlings was feeling very sorry for himself. "I'm never going to have any money. I'm going to be a factory worker for the rest of my life." he said to himself. An hour later, at 6 o'clock, a man from the Football Pools came and gave him a cheque for £60,000.
BILL HAD NO IDEA THIS WAS GOING TO HAPPEN. HE THOUGHT HE WAS GOING TO BE A FACTORY WORKER FOR THE REST OF HIS LIFE.

1. What was Bill doing last Monday at 5 p.m?
2. What did he say to himself?
3. What happened an hour later at 6?
4. Ask (and answer) if Bill knew any of these things at 5 p.m?
   (a) so much money?
   (b) a cheque for £60,000?
   (c) rich?
5. A lot of things have happened since then. Ask if Bill knew about them a week ago
   (a) All sorts of people have asked him for money.
   (b) He has bought a new house.
   (c) His wife has spent £600 on clothes.
   (d) The neighbours have become jealous.

ii. Two years ago, another man won £100,000 on the Football Pools. "Life's going to be easy from now on" he said at the time. He now says the money has brought him all sorts of trouble. His wife has left him. He had a bad accident in a new car he bought, and he is bored most of the time.
HE THOUGHT LIFE WAS GOING TO BE EASY. HE HAD NO IDEA HE WAS GOING TO HAVE SUCH A LOT OF TROUBLE.

1. Ask how much the other man won! (and answer)
2. Ask a question with "When"
3. What did he say at the time?
4. What does he say now?
5. What are some of the things that have happened?
6. Ask if he knew these things were going to happen
   (a) his wife (b) accident (c) bored
7. What did he think at the time?
8. What didn't he know then?

41 Progressive + Variations

Do these at speed

Model   SHE DIDN'T KNOW HE WAS GOING TO GIVE HER DIAMONDS

buy her a car = SHE DIDN'T KNOW HE WAS GOING TO BUY HER A CAR

did she = DID SHE KNOW HE WAS GOING TO BUY HER A CAR?

SHE DIDN'T KNOW HE WAS GOING TO GIVE HER DIAMONDS

1. Had she any idea
2. to come early
3. Did he tell her
4. to work late
5. She was sure
6. to propose marriage
7. I never realised
8. to get so angry
9. No-one thought
10. to win
11. that horse was going to
12. How was I to know

Comment

Notice that we can also say   WOULD DO *instead of* WAS GOING TO DO

42 Invention Exercise

Now make your own examples. Notice that each word can produce a number of sentences!

the test = THE CLASS HAD NO IDEA THE TEST WAS GOING TO BE SO HARD

or = THEY DIDN'T KNOW HE WAS GOING TO GIVE THEM THE TEST THEN

1. the train
2. the peace talks
3. the football team
4. the operation
5. the guerrillas
6. the fire
7. the toast
8. her husband
9. the bill

43 Practice Situations

Make at least one sentence for each situation. Use HAD NO IDEA/WAS GOING TO or THOUGHT WAS GOING TO etc.

Richard's son, David has been afraid of dogs ever since he put his hand out and petted one a year ago. It looked friendly but it bit him. HE HAD NO IDEA THE DOG WAS GOING TO BITE HIM. HE THOUGHT THE DOG WAS GOING TO BE FRIENDLY.

1. Bill thought the weather was always good in Spain so he went there last summer. It rained all the time.
2. Bill looked at the ocean. "The water must be very warm" he said, and jumped in. It was very, very cold.
3. Everybody thought the horse hadn't a chance, but it won the race.
4. "The price of gas will go down" the advertisement said, so Richard got gas central heating. Then the price of gas went up.

5. Richard's son was terrified yesterday when he saw two dogs running towards him. They only wanted to play.
6. The teacher gave the class a test yesterday. They were all surprised.
7. A lot of tourists went to Cam Pong for the "Flowers for Peace" festival. While they were there, a war broke out.
8. All the passengers were looking forward to a "summer cruise of sun and fun". The weather was stormy all the time.

L

Mrs. Grace Hume is one of the few living survivors of the S.S. Tyrone disaster. The ship sailed from Liverpool for New York on the 7th of April 1926. 500 passengers were aboard. Only 85 of them survived. Mrs. Hume described the voyage recently for a BBC radio programme.

"The morning we left Liverpool the weather was very pleasant and we were all sure we were going to have a very pleasant voyage. The captain told us it would be warm and calm all the way to New York. I still remember some of the passengers. There was an old lady who was going to visit her son in Boston. Then there was a man who was going to start a new life in Canada. They both went down with the ship. The first and second days were very nice. I thought I would soon have a fine suntan. Then, on the second evening, the captain told us that the weather the next day was going to be a bit worse than expected but that it wouldn't last long.

It turned very nasty on the third day. I remember someone saying "Oh, well, it'll soon be over." None of us had any idea how bad it was going to get. By the time it was evening, it was really terrible.

Everybody stayed in their cabins on the fourth day. The storm was impossible to describe by then. Suddenly I felt a jolt. Then someone started screaming something about a huge leak in the engine room. We all ran up on to the deck. I was sure I would never be able to get in one of the lifeboats! There were too many people fighting over them. I also knew that I would go down with the ship if I stayed any longer because it was going to sink any minute. When I jumped into the water I sank so deep that I was sure I was never going to come up again. Somehow I did and there was a lifeboat in the water near me, only half full. Someone pulled me in.

During the night I often thought we were going to sink again or at least die of the cold, but the next morning the storm died down. Then a ship came into sight and we and some people in another lifeboat were rescued."

1. What was the weather like at the beginning?
2. What did the captain say about the weather?
3. What did the passengers think at that point?
4. Did Mrs. Hume ever get her fine suntan?
5. What was the old lady going to do in Boston? Ask if she did!
6. What was one man going to do in Canada? Ask if he did!
7. What did the captain say about the weather on the second day?
8. Did he say how long it would last?
9. What happened on the third day? (nasty)
10. What does Mrs. Hume remember someone saying?
11. So, what did that person think?
12. What did she do when someone started screaming about a leak in the engine room?
13. Why didn't she try to get into a lifeboat?
14. Why exactly did she jump (any minute, down if.)
15. What did she often think would happen during the night? (sink. cold.)

Special Practice

Without looking at the text, retell some of it with these prompts:

(a) Liverpool/very pleasant
(b) all sure/lovely voyage
(c) the captain/warm and calm
(d) old lady/son in Boston
(e) man/new life in Canada
(f) I thought/suntan
(g) the captain/worse than expected
(h) sure/one of the lifeboats
(i) When/into the water/so deep
(j) the night/of the cold

45 MORE PATTERNS FROM THE TEXT

In all the texts in this book there are additional patterns worth learning. Perhaps your attention is not always drawn to them but you should learn to recognise them yourself.

The patterns below are just a few simple examples of how much there is in any piece of English you hear or see that is worth your attention and serious study.

Invention

Think of different words to replace LEFT/VERY PLEASANT', etc.

Model: THE MORNING WE LEFT LIVERPOOL THE WEATHER WAS VERY PLEASANT

evening/London/the fog = THE EVENING I ARRIVED IN LONDON THE FOG WAS VERY THICK

1. afternoon/friend in hospital/the weather
2. day/the market-place/the streets
3. morning/test/all the students
4. night/party/some of the guests
5. week/conference/ demonstrations
6. day/race/rain
7. day/picnic/snow
8. month/all those storms/ill

NOW THINK OF SOME EXAMPLES OF YOUR OWN!

Invention

Notice what happens in the example to the words HAS BEEN or HAD BEEN (they disappear)

Situation: Good weather HAD BEEN expected. We were told it was going to be a bit worse than that.
WE WERE TOLD THE WEATHER WAS GOING TO BE A BIT WORSE THAN EXPECTED

1. the voyage/longer/ anticipated
2. the weather/wetter/ forecast
3. the banquet/later/ planned
4. speed/slower/

Invention

Notice the meaning of ANY MINUTE here

Model: I was sure THE SHIP WAS GOING TO SINK ANY MINUTE
or   I'M sure it IS GOING TO SINK ANY MINUTE

1. the bus
2. the phone
3. the ammunition ship
4. all the lights
5. the enemy
6. the film

Invention

Model: I KNEW I WOULD GO DOWN WITH THE SHIP IF I STAYED ANY LONGER
Prompt: all my money
Response: I DIDN'T KNOW I WOULD LOSE ALL MY MONEY IF I INVESTED IT IN THAT FIRM

1. miss the bus
2. catch a bad cold
3. into trouble
4. my hands dirty
5. the glass vase
6. wet
7. a bad impression
8. an accident

UNIT C FIVE

LOOK/SOUND/SMELL/FEEL with Adjectives
LOOK/FEEL GOOD vs. LOOK/FEEL WELL
SHOULD HAVE DONE vs. SHOULD HAVE BEEN DOING

46 LOOK

Problem Situation

An insect is under a microscope. The effect is very strange. Anyone looking at it now might think it was enormous.

1. Where is the insect?
2. What might a person looking at it now think?
3. Is it really enormous?
4. What can you say about an insect or any small thing under a microscope?

47 Illustrative Situation

You have just painted a chair. You have used a new colour of off-white. You don't like the effect.
IT LOOKS DIRTY.

1. What colour have you painted the chair?
2. Is it really dirty?
3. What do you say about the effect?

48 Practice Situations

Make sentences with LOOK and words like BAD/OLD/ILL etc, to fit each situation

You look at Tony and think he should go to hospital.
HE LOOKS ILL

1. You can see all the big buildings and things from the airplane. You are high in the air.
2. You think Mr. Collins is 35. Someone tells you he is really 60.
3. Richard has been working very hard. You can see it in his face.

4. The car isn't really new. It has just been painted.
5. You think the vegetables are fresh but, of course, you can't be sure.
6. You can tell by looking at the refugees that some haven't eaten for days.

49 SOUND

Illustrative Situation

Jane was in the front office when her boss buzzed her on the intercom. She knew he was angry.
HE SOUNDED ANGRY.

1. Where was Jane?
2. Where was her boss?
3. What did she realise as soon as she heard him?
4. Ask how she knew he was angry!
5. Suppose you can actually hear him now; what do you say?

50 Practice Situations

Make sentences with SOUND and words like ANGRY/NERVOUS/GOOD etc to fit each situation You know there must be something wrong with the car. You can tell from the noise the engine is making.
IT SOUNDS TERRIBLE

1. There was something in your friend's voice over the phone that made you ask 'Are you worried?'
2. You didn't actually hear the joke. All you heard was the laughter afterwards.
3. When the man spoke, you thought you noticed a slight accent.

4. A foreign friend is learning your language. He asks if he can say something in a particular way. You think it's wrong. You don't know why.
5. A doctor is listening to a patient's heart. He is shaking his head.
6. The conductor is listening to the orchestra. He is nodding his head.

51 SMELL

Illustrative Situations

i. Susan is not sure whether she should use some meat she has had in the fridge for several days. She does not like the look of it and she has just smelt it. "THIS MEAT LOOKS BAD AND SMELLS EVEN WORSE!" she says.
THE MEAT LOOKS AND SMELLS BAD.

1. Ask how long she has had the meat! (and answer)
2. What doesn't she like and what has she just done?
3. What does she say?
4. How does the meat look and smell?

ii. Susan bought some very expensive perfume and put it on just before her husband, Tony, came home. "SOMETHING SMELLS STRANGE" he said when he came in. When she told him what it was, he said "What I really meant was that IT SMELLS WONDERFUL. IT CERTAINLY SMELLS EXPENSIVE!"

1. What kind of perfume did Susan buy?
2. When did she put it on?
3. What did Tony say at first?
4. What did he say later?

52 Invention Exercise

Make sentences with SMELL and words like WONDERFUL/BAD/STRANGE etc This meat = THIS MEAT SMELLS STRANGE.

1. These flowers
2. The air around the gasworks
3. Coffee early in the morning
4. The inside of a car that has just come from the factory
5. A room in which there was a party the night before

53 FLUENCY PRACTICE

Substitution with Variations

Do this at speed
Model: TONY LOOKS TIRED
Do I = DO I LOOK TIRED?
strange = DO I LOOK STRANGE?
the meat = DOES THE MEAT LOOK STRANGE?
smell = DOES THE MEAT SMELL STRANGE?

TONY LOOKS TIRED
1. better
2. feels
3. Do you
4. The engine sounds
5. strange
6. Your story
7. stupid
8. He
9. angry
10. looks
11. you
12. wonderful

54 FEEL/LOOK GOOD vs. FEEL/LOOK WELL

i. Illustrative Situations

Tony has bought Susan a fur coat. She has just put it on for the first time. She likes the feel of it very much. "THE COAT FEELS GOOD AND I LOOK GOOD IN IT" she says.

1. What has Susan just done?
2. What does she like?
3. What does she say about the coat?
4. What does she say about herself?

ii. Tony was in hospital for a month. He came out a week ago. His doctor is asking him how is feels. "I FEEL VERY WELL, NOW, THANK YOU. EVERYBODY SAYS I LOOK WELL, TOO. I CERTAINLY LOOK AND FEEL MUCH BETTER THAN I DID A MONTH AGO!"

1. What did Tony do a week ago?
2. What is his doctor doing now?
3. Ask and answer questions about Tony, using these words. (a) look now (b) feel now.
4. How does he look and feel now compared with a month ago?

Special Comment

Notice that WELL is not an adverb here. It is an adjective that describes how someone is. It is not an adverb that describes how someone does something.
Observe also that FEEL/SOUND/LOOK and SMELL are not verbs that describe what a person does. They describe what our senses tell us about the state a person is in. That is why we use adjectives with them.

55 Practice Situations

Make sentences with either FEEL and LOOK GOOD or FEEL and LOOK WELL to fit each situation

Susan has just put on a fine new dress. It suits her, and she likes the feel of it.
IT FEELS GOOD. SHE LOOKS GOOD IN IT.

Tony was ill about a month ago but he is much better now. Everyone notices it.
HE FEELS AND LOOKS WELL.

1. Richard has bought a new jacket. It is made of fine material and it suits him.
2. The ground on which a football match is going to be played soon is not too wet and not too dry. It is a fine colour, too.
3. Mrs. Mavis is feeling some tomatoes. They are a beautiful red and not too soft.

4. Susan's headache and stomach-ache have all gone now. You can see this when you look at her.
5. Susan is wearing her new fur coat. The fur is very soft. The coat is perfect for her.
6. The English football team have been training for a month. They are all in very good health, as you can see.

56 SHOULD(N'T) HAVE DONE
vs. SHOULD(N'T) HAVE BEEN DOING

Problem Situation

Bert was not looking at the traffic ahead when he ran over the dog. He had taken his eyes off the road to look at a pretty girl on the pavement. When he ran over the dog a policeman shouted "Stop!" but he didn't.

1. Was he looking at the traffic ahead when he had the accident?
2. Ask why not! (and answer)
3. What did a policeman do when he ran over the dog?
4. Ask if he did! (answer)
5. What should he have been doing when he ran over the dog?
6. What should he have done when he ran over it?

57 Illustrative Situations

i. You went out without your mac yesterday. When it started raining you didn't even shelter under a tree.
YOU SHOULD HAVE BEEN WEARING YOUR MAC
YOU SHOULD HAVE SHELTERED UNDER A TREE

1. What did you do yesterday?
2. What happened?
3. Did you shelter under a tree?
4. What should you have done?
5. Were you wearing your mac?
6. Should you have been?

ii. The supervisor was furious. It wasn't tea-time, yet when she went into the packing-department she found all the girls there were not working. They were having a cup of tea. They didn't go back to work when she came in. In fact, they laughed at her.
THEY SHOULDN'T HAVE BEEN DRINKING TEA
THEY SHOULDN'T HAVE LAUGHED AT HER

1. Was it tea-time when she went into the packing-department?
2. Ask what the girls were doing!
3. Ask if they should have been!
4. Did they go back to work when she came in?
5. Ask if they should have done!
6. What did they do when she came in?
7. Ask a question about the last with SHOULD!
8.· What should they have been doing?
9. Ask you own questions with SHOULD HAVE DONE or SHOULD HAVE BEEN DOING
   Use (a) tea   (b) her a cup of tea
        (c) laugh   (d) work
        (e) back to
            work

iii. The goal-keeper suddenly decided to have a rest. He sat down in front of the goal and didn't even bother to get up when the other team attacked. One of the forwards shot the ball into the net. He simply watched.
HE SHOULD HAVE BEEN STANDING UP
HE SHOULD HAVE STOPPED THE BALL

1. What did the goal-keeper do?
2. What didn't he bother to do?
3. What happened when one of the forwards shot into the net?
4. Ask if she should have!
5. Was he standing up?
6. Ask a question with SHOULD!

Five soldiers were put on a desert island. "Guard this island. Wear your uniform at all times. Always listen to your radio for messages. If an officer comes, first ask him who he is. Then salute him" they were told. They forgot all these things on the island, took off their uniforms, and did not listen to the radio. A message was sent to them "The Inspector General is coming!" it said, but nobody heard it. When the general came they were all either swimming or lying in the sun. Nobody asked him who he was and nobody saluted.

1. What were they told to do on the desert island?
2. Ask if they were doing or if they did these things when the general came.
   (a) uniforms   (b) guard
   (c) the radio   (d) ask
   (e) salute
3. What were they doing when the general came?
4. Now say all the things they should have been doing when he came!
5. What should they have done?
6. What shouldn't they have been doing?

59 FLUENCY PRACTICE

Progressive Substitution I

Do these short drills at speed. Compare the construction of the two forms

YOU SHOULD HAVE COME EARLIER
1. told me   5. Dick
2. They   6. got a better job
3. done that   7. I
4. years ago   8. bought another car

Progressive Substitution II

THEY SHOULD HAVE BEEN DOING SOME WORK
1. something useful   5. I
2. You   6. preparing for
3. the test   7. the party
4. studying for   8. She

60 Practice Situations

Make a sentence with either SHOULD HAVE DONE or SHOULD HAVE BEEN DOING for each situation.

The soldier had swimming-trunks on when the general came.
HE SHOULD HAVE BEEN WEARING HIS UNIFORM
The soldier looked at the general and did not do anything.
HE SHOULD HAVE SALUTED

1. "Type these letters at one!" Mr. Collins told his secretary. When he saw her a few minutes later, she was in the canteen.
2. It began to rain and the window was wide open, but Richard went on reading.
3. "Do you homework and don't stop until you've done it all!" David's mother told him. Five minutes later she saw him playing in the garden.
4. "Now you must all stand up when the Director of Education comes!" David's teacher told the class. They did not do anything when he came.

5. If a driver sees another driver in difficulty, he should stop. Bert saw one last week and drove on.
6. Drivers should pay attention to the traffic at all times. Bert's eyes were on a pretty girl when he drove his car into a bus.
7. "Watch that house from 9 till 12!" the inspector told the detective. He found him in a pub at 11.
8. "Sit down and eat your food!" David's mother told him. She came back a minute later and found him in front of the television.

61 A TELEVISION DISCUSSION

"The Question This Week" is a popular discussion programme. Each week, three different famous people discuss some question of interest.

Interviewer: Our guests this week are Mr. James Black, a minister in the present government, Mr. Spencer Beaumont, the opposition party's expert on economic matters, and Miss Mary Lovely, the famous young dress designer. Our question is "How can Britain improve her economic position?" What do you think, Mr. Black?

James
Black: We should have recognised years ago that we must export more. Now, why did things look so bad before we took power? Because we should have been exporting far more than we were! That's why my party has concentrated on raising exports and cutting imports, and that's why things look better now!

Interviewer: Mr. Beaumont, what are your views?

Spencer
Beaumont: Well, first of all, everything James Black says is nonsense! Things weren't half as bad as they looked when my party left power. When his party came to power, they talked too much about the problem. They should never have done that! Things sounded bad and people lost confidence. Now when we were in power, even on the very last day, we were doing exactly what we should have been doing. We were trying to keep people's confidence in the Pound!

James
Black: Nonsense! Things didn't only look or sound bad before we came to power! They were bad!

Interviewer: I really don't think this should be only a political discussion. Miss Lovely, what do you think as a dress-designer?

Miss
Lovely: The first thing we should do is to sell British goods abroad. It's also very important to buy British things whenever possible. Sell British and Buy British, as I do. I have designed lots of dresses that sell all over the world. I call them "export dresses". I sell British dresses and I buy British dresses.

Interviewer: I see. Sell British things and buy British things. Is that dress you're wearing now one of your famous export dresses?

Miss
Lovely: Well . . . uh . . . . actually . . . . this is something I bought in Paris last week.

1. What does Mr. Black say everyone should have done years ago?
2. What does he say about things before his party took power?
3. According to him, why were things so bad?
4. What has his party concentrated on and how do things look now?
5. What does Mr. Beaumont say about things when his party was in power?
6. What does he say Mr. Black's party shouldn't have done?
7. Why does he say people lost confidence?
8. What does Mr. Black say about all this?
9. What is Miss Lovely's advice and what do you think she shouldn't have done?

UNIT C SIX

HAS BEEN DOING vs. HAS DONE
HAD BEEN DOING vs. DID
Text with Revision of HAD DONE/HAD BEEN DOING
Also additional Patterns (Hear someone do/Let someone do)
Revision of HAS BEEN vs. DID

62 HAS BEEN DOING vs. HAS DONE

i. Problem Situation

When the Canadian lumberjack started work 3 hours ago, all the trees were still standing. Now there are already 3 trees lying on the ground, waiting to be taken away. He has just started on another tree.

1. When did he start work?
2. How many trees are there on the ground now?
3. Is he still working?
4. Ask a question with HOW LONG!
5. Now ask one with HOW MANY TREES!

Comment:

There is really only one type of situation in which it is essential to distinguish between HAS DONE and HAS BEEN DOING. This is when you want to talk about the Quantity of Things done in a time rather than How Long the Thing has been going on

63 Illustrative Situations

The baker has nearly finished now. There are now a thousand fresh loaves waiting to be sold. All he has to do now is to clean up and go home. He started work 8 hours ago.

1. Has he finished yet?
2. What else has he to do?
3. How many loaves are there in his bakery now?
4. When did he start working?
5. Ask a question with HOW LONG!
6. Ask one with HOW MANY LOAVES!

ii. Bill's wife is having a baby. She is in the delivery ward. Bill himself is waiting outside. He has just lit another cigarette. When he came in 4 hours ago, he had a full packet of 20. This is his last one.
HE HAS BEEN SMOKING CONSTANTLY FOR 4 HOURS
HE HAS SMOKED 20 CIGARETTES IN THAT TIME

1. Do you think Bill is nervous?
2. Where is his wife and what is she doing?
3. When did Bill get to the hospital?
4. What has he just done?
5. What has happened to the full packet of cigarettes he had?
6. Ask a question with HOW LONG and also with HOW MANY!

iii. Five hours ago Jane opened the book at the first page. She immediately became very absorbed in it and hasn't put it down since. She is now at page 300.
SHE HAS BEEN READING FOR FIVE HOURS
SHE HAS READ 300 PAGES

1. What exactly is Jane doing now?
2. Ask a question with HOW LONG AGO!
3. What happened as soon as she began reading it?
4. What page is she at now?
5. Ask a question with HOW LONG!
6. Ask a question with HOW MANY PAGES!

Practice and Expansion

iv. a Dr. Campbell came to the village of Lochbrae
when he was a young doctor 40 years ago. He
was, and still is, the only one for miles. He does
everything. He delivers babies, sets broken arms
and legs, and sometimes even pulls teeth. He
also performs operations in the small cottage
hospital. He probably sees a thousand patients
every month and prescribes hundreds of bottles
of medicine every week. There will be no other
doctor to take his place when he dies.

1. Where is he a doctor?
2. Ask HOW LONG!
3. Ask if he does these things: (babies. broken
arms. operations.)
4. What else does he sometimes do?
5. How many patients does he see every month?
6. Ask a question with 'medicine'!
7. What will happen when he dies?

b **Expansion**

Dr. Campbell has been a doctor for 40 years;
ask some questions with HOW LONG and HOW
MANY about him in that time. Think of possible answers (do not worry too much about
the facts.)

Prompts:
babies/arms and legs/bandages/operations/
patients/bottles of medicine/teeth/sick children/
black eyes/serious accidents

64 Practice Situations

*Make sentences
using both
HAS DONE
and HAS BEEN
DOING for
these situations*

Jane started on page 1 of the book three hours
ago. It is three hours later and she is now at
page 150.
SHE HAS BEEN READING FOR THREE
HOURS
SHE HAS READ 150 PAGES

1. Captain Hay is a 'million-mile' pilot. He
started flying 20 years ago.
2. It is a 3-mile walk from Bob's house to the
city-centre. He started an hour ago and has just
reached it.
3. There are now 90 novels with Dennis Oatley's
name on them. He wrote the first of them 30
years ago.
4. Laura started the washing-machine up an
hour ago. There are now 30 clean shirts in the
basket.

5. You are just finishing the 5th and last page
of homework. You sat down at the writing-desk
2 hours ago.
6. The whisky-bottle was full when Mike sat
down an hour ago. He is drinking the last of it
now.
7. The tourist came into the old town an hour
ago. He is leaving now with 60 new photographs.
8. The typist started an hour ago. Six letters
are ready now.

65 Invention

*Make your own
examples*

television all evening = HE HAS BEEN
WATCHING TELE-
VISION ALL EVEN-
ING

four programmes so
far =

HE HAS WATCHED
FOUR PROGRAMMES
SO FAR

1. English
2. a lot of new words
3. football for ten years
4. 600 matches
5. at the roulette table
6. at least £1,000
7. foreign students for
years
8. at least 2,000 of
them
9. all my cigars
10. this brand of cigar
11. 80 customers this
morning
12. customers all morn-
ing

155

66 HAD BEEN DOING vs. DID

Problem Situations

i. The Prime Minister held a press conference yesterday evening. He answered the first question at 7. The last one was not asked until 10. He was very tired by then.

1. What happened yesterday evening?
2. When did the P.M. answer the first question?
3. When was the last one asked?
4. Why was he so tired by then?

ii. The heart transplant operation began at 7 in the morning. It did not end until 7 that evening because it was an extremely complicated one. When it finally did, the members of the surgeon's team were utterly exhausted.

1. Ask when the operation began!
2. Ask when it ended!
3. Ask why!
4. How did all the people on the surgeon's team feel when it did?
5. Why?

67 Illustrative Situations

i. People say that Herbert von Kappel is a demon among conductors. He often drives his orchestra to the point of exhaustion. Yesterday, for instance, they began rehearsing Mozart's Jupiter Symphony at 9 in the morning and it wasn't until 9 in the evening that he finally let them go home.
THEY REHEARSED FOR 12 HOURS YESTERDAY
THEY HAD BEEN REHEARSING FOR 12 HOURS WHEN HE FINALLY LET THEM GO HOME

1. What do people say about von Kappel?
2. What does he often do?
3. What time did they begin rehearsing yesterday?
4. Ask when they finally finished?
5. So, why was yesterday a hard day for them?
6. Why were they so tired when he finally let them go home?

ii. The train was due any minute when Jane walked on to the platform. There was no place to sit down or keep out of the bitter wind. She tried to keep warm but it was very difficult. Suddenly there was an announcement over the loudspeaker: "The next train will be slightly delayed." It finally came an hour later.
SHE WAITED AN HOUR FOR THE TRAIN
SHE HAD BEEN WAITING AN HOUR WHEN IT CAME

1. How long did Jane think she would have to wait?
2. Why didn't she sit down?
3. Why was it hard to keep warm?
4. What was the announcement?
5. Ask what finally happened!
6. Do you think she was fed up when the train came? Why?
7. What else had she been doing for an hour when it came? (Remember! No place to sit, etc.)

iii. Mr. Collins had a nervous breakdown last year. The doctor said the cause was overwork. Three months before he had it, he began working 14 hours every day. He kept this up until he finally broke down.
HE WORKED 14 HOURS A DAY FOR 3 MONTHS
HE HAD BEEN WORKING 14 HOURS A DAY FOR THREE MONTHS WHEN HE BROKE DOWN

1. What happened to Mr. Collins last year?
2. Ask what the doctor said!
3. How many hours a day did he work?
4. Ask how long he kept this up!
5. Now ask 2 questions with HOW LONG!

Practice and Expansion

i. Charles Bigson, the famous train-robber,
    escaped from prison in 1964. Inspector Buller
    immediately began looking for him. He found
    him 3 years later in Canada.

    1. When did Bigson escape?
    2. What did Inspector Buller do immediately?
    3. Ask when and where he found him!
    4. Use FOR 3 YEARS for each of these
       situations
       i. What Buller said the day he caught
           Bigson.
       ii. What was said about Buller sometime
           later.
       iii. What was said together with the phrase
           'when he finally caught him!'

ii. a The sale was advertised as "The Greatest Ever".
       The department store was going to sell off all its
       stock "at absolutely bargain prices!" The sale
       began at 9 o'clock on Thursday morning. The
       first shoppers were already outside the main
       entrance at 9 o'clock on Wednesday evening.
       Most of them had picnic-stoves and tea-pots.
       Some had transistor-radios. One older woman
       and her husband had a chess-set. A young
       married couple actually brought their baby and
       a feeding-bottle.

       1. What was the sale advertised as?
       2. Ask why!
       3. When did the sale begin?
       4. When did the first shoppers come?
       5. What did they have with them?
       6. Ask about the older married couple!
       7. Ask about the young married couple!

   b Think of all the various things the people out-
      side had been doing when the doors opened!
      Think of a few questions with HOW LONG!
      What other things might they have been doing
      in order to pass the time?

      Prompts:
      tea/the radio/chess/cards/the baby/books/etc.

68 Practice Situations

Make your own sentences with HAD BEEN DOING WHEN ... for these situations

1. Hal Klein got his first job in the film industry
when he was 20. He made his first film when he
was 25.
2. Roy started studying for his doctorate when
he was 25. He got it when he was 30.
3. Mary started in the shop when she was 19.
When she was 29 she became the manageress.
4. It was 3 o'clock when Jill went out to look
for her son and 6 o'clock when she found him.

5. Miss Roach began her driving-lessons in
January 1967. She didn't pass her test until
January 1968.
6. You started the composition at 8 in the
evening. You gave up at midnight and went to
bed.
7. You went to the bus-stop at 7. It was 7.30
when the bus came.
8. You ordered the meal at 7 and the waiter
brought it at 8.

69 Invention

Think of examples with HAD BEEN ... ING FOR ... ... WHEN with these words

1. on the corner/
   my friend
2. the programme/
   the telephone
3. about the question/
   the answer
4. in the waiting-room

5. in Viet Nam/the war
6. in the park/the rain
7. the small print/my
   eyes
8. the problem/the
   solution

70 Fast Revision of HAS DONE vs. DID

i. **Problem Situation**

George Errol is a famous English writer. There is a brief biography of him on the back of one of his books. This is part of it.

1925–30	Colonial Police Officer in Burma
1930–33	Vagabond in London and Paris
1933–45	Journalist and broadcaster
1945–50	Farmer and novelist
1950–67	Television-director and writer
Since 1967	Guest Professor at Stafford University, California, U.S.A.

1. Who is George Errol?
2. Where is he now?
3. Ask HOW LONG? (answer)
4. Look at or listen to these facts and dates. Then ask questions with EVER and then with WHEN
5. Now ask questions with HOW LONG! (Look at the dates again.)

ii. **Invention**

Make variations of HAVE DONE (including HAS BEEN) and DID (including WAS/WERE) with these words

1. along the beach yesterday
2. three hours before the train came
3. three hours and it hasn't come yet
4. in Montreal in 1967
5. my brother/there/ since 1960
6. an accident yesterday
7. Kennedy/President/ 3 years
8. that film last week
9. very bad floods/ Florence/1966
10. this place/too long

Use this conversation as a model. Ask similar questions and give similar responses with the prompts. Then think of your own examples!

iii. **Model Conversation and Invention**

A: Have you ever eaten American cheese?
B: Yes, I have. I had some when I was in New York.
A: What did you think of it?
B: It tasted like soap. I didn't like it very much.

Prompts:
1. an electric type-writer
2. a pair of very cheap shoes
3. genuine pizza
4. English ice-cream
5. English cigarettes
6. a very fast sports-car

71 TEXT

(A country doctor recently told this story on the radio)

I had just gone to bed after a very hard day when the phone rang. It was an eccentric farmer. I had never met him before although I had often heard people talk about him. He seemed quite hysterical and he had been talking for a minute or so before I understood anything. Even then all I could make out was that someone called Milly had had a very bad accident. I hadn't the slightest idea who she was but I obviously had to go.

It had been snowing heavily that day and I didn't know the way. I had been driving for at least an hour when I finally found his place. He was standing there, waiting for me. It seemed Milly had already died. "She meant more to me than anyone . . . . even my own wife!" he said. I could see that he had been crying. I assumed a terrible tragedy had taken place with overtones of a possible scandal. I must admit I was even more shocked when he told me he had put her in the barn. "I wouldn't leave her out in the cold!" he said.

Milly had clearly been a secret sweetheart of his. I was about to tell him he could not expect me to cover anything up when he opened the barn door and pointed his torch at a motionless shape on the straw.

"She was such a good cow! I wouldn't let anyone but a doctor touch her!" he said, and burst into tears again.

1. What had the doctor just done when the phone rang?
2. Had he ever met the man?
3. How did he know anything about him?
4. Did the doctor understand him immediately?
5. What information was he able to get?
6. Ask about the weather that day!
7. Was it still snowing?
8. How long was it before he found the place?
9. What had happened?
10. What had the farmer been doing?
11. What did the doctor assume?
12. Why was he shocked?
13. What did the doctor assume then?
14. What was he about to tell the farmer?
15. What happened then?
16. What exactly did the farmer say?
17. What did he do after he had said this?

72 Study of Patterns from the Text

(i) I HAD OFTEN HEARD PEOPLE TALK ABOUT HIM
Think of other examples with this pattern! What can you hear people do or see them do?

(ii) Notice how FINALLY is used in I HAD BEEN . . . ING FOR . . . WHEN I FINALLY . . .
Give some examples of your own.
Prompts: a job/in the restaurant/at the bus stop/etc.

(iii) Contrast these 2 Patterns: SHE WAS SUCH A GOOD COW

THE COW WAS SO GOOD

Make your own examples with: (film/day/city book/suitcase/car/etc.)

(iv) I HADN'T THE SLIGHTEST IDEA WHO SHE WAS
Make your own examples using variations with HOW TO/WHEN TO/and WHAT TO . . . in place of WHO SHE WAS

(v) I WOULDN'T LET ANYONE BUT A DOCTOR TOUCH HER
Think of other examples. Change A DOCTOR and TOUCH HER.
Prompts: a very good mechanic/a good teacher/driver/etc.

159

UNIT C SEVEN

SUPPOSED TO DO/BE DOING/HAVE DONE
Questions like WHO KNOWS MARY?
contrasted with WHO DOES MARY KNOW?
Constructions like IT'S TOO HEAVY FOR HIM
TO CARRY and HE ISN'T TALL ENOUGH
FOR HER TO DANCE WITH

73 Introductory Situation

Someone asks you what the new film from
Czechoslovakia is like. You have not actually
seen it yourself but you have heard people talk-
ing about it and have also read the film reviews.
You answer: IT'S SUPPOSED TO BE VERY
GOOD

1. Have you actually seen the film?
2. Could you say 'It's very good'?
3. Why not?
4. How do you know about the film?
5. What do you say in such a situation?

74 Problem Situations

You have never been to California but you have
heard about the climate there. What can you say
about the climate?

Sir Arthur Travers was a famous explorer. In
1966 he disappeared somewhere in South
America. People say he died there. What can
you say about him?

Laura Gale was a famous film-star a few years
ago. People say she is singing in a cheap night-
club now. What can you say about her?

75 Illustrative Situations

i. John Griggs is the only member of the Great
Train Robbery gang who the police have not
caught yet. Nobody really knows for certain
what he did after the robbery or what he is doing now. However, certain well-informed people
in the underworld say that he went to Switzerland and that he is now living in a village there.
HE'S SUPPOSED TO HAVE GONE TO
SWITZERLAND
HE'S SUPPOSED TO BE LIVING IN A
VILLAGE THERE

1. Who is John Griggs?
2. What do people say about him?
3. Who really knows for certain?
4. Who exactly says these things about him?
5. Ask what he is supposed to have done!
6. Ask what he is supposed to be doing!

ii. There is another rumour about him. According
to it, he lost all his money in Monte Carlo and
is now working in a garage in Australia.
HE IS SUPPOSED TO HAVE LOST ALL
HIS MONEY IN MONTE CARLO
HE IS SUPPOSED TO BE WORKING IN A
GARAGE IN AUSTRALIA

1. What else do people say about him?
2. Ask if anyone really knows about:
   (a) his money (b) the garage!
3. Now ask what he is supposed to be doing
   and have done?

76 SUPPOSED TO HAVE DONE/HAVE BEEN DONE

Practice and Expansion

a There is an old woman who can often be seen in the park looking for things in the litter bins. She seems to live on pieces of bread meant only for the birds. People say she was once a famous dancer who fell in love with a musician. When the musician left her for another woman, so the story goes, she tried to poison him. They say she was sent to prison for several years. Naturally her career was ruined. As it happens, about 30 years ago there really was such a scandal. Who knows if the story is true?

1. Ask where this woman can often be seen! (answer)
2. Now ask what she can be seen doing!
3. As far as can be seen, how does she live?
4. What is she supposed to have been?
5. Ask who she is supposed to have fallen in love with!
6. What is supposed to have happened then?
7. What do people say she tried to do?
8. What is supposed to have happened to her?
9. Ask about her career!
10. Is it at all possible this is true?
11. Retell the story without looking at it. Use SUPPOSED TO HAVE
    Prompts: i. famous/dancer/musician
             ii. another woman/poison
            iii. prison/several years
             iv. career

b **Expansion**

Use SUPPOSED TO HAVE ... to tell what other people say about her life as a famous dancer.

Prompts: Kings and Queens
          all the capitals. champagne.
          big house. Rolls Royce.
          thousands of pounds a month
          etc.

77 Basic Situation: You cannot be sure if these things are true. However, other people say they are.

Study the Transform-ations for the 4 different types of sentences

That actress takes drugs
SHE IS SUPPOSED TO TAKE DRUGS

Those men are building a road
THEY ARE SUPPOSED TO BE BUILDING A ROAD

Scientists have found a cure for colds
THEY ARE SUPPOSED TO HAVE FOUND A CURE FOR COLDS

Another H-Bomb has been exploded
ANOTHER H-BOMB IS SUPPOSED TO HAVE BEEN EXPLODED

Now transform these sentences to show you are only saying what other people say is true

1. Chinese is a difficult language.
2. Whisky is bad for your liver.
3. She was a waitress before she married the King.
4. The police are looking for that man.
5. He is wanted by the police.
6. Oil has been found in Scotland.
7. That old style is coming back.
8. The Ancient Greeks saw flying saucers, too.

9. That old woman has a lot of money in the bank.
10. The English love animals more than children.
11. Beer was stronger before the war.
12. Butter is going up in price.
13. His son was in prison once.
14. We are all getting a rise next month.
15. These new Japanese cars are very good.
16. The secretary has had a terrible argument with the boss.

Now think of various things people say and transform them with variations of SUPPOSED TO

M

161

78 Questions like "WHO KNOWS MARY?"
contrasted with "WHO DOES MARY KNOW?"

Problem Situations

i. You know that Jill loves someone, but you do not know who. You are going to ask someone else who that "someone" is.

1. What is that you know and what is it that you do not know?
2. What are you going to do?
   What question do you ask?

ii. You know that someone loves Jill, but you do not know who. You are talking to another person who does.

1. What is it that you know and do not know?
2. Who are you talking to?
3. Now do this
   What question do you ask?

79 Illustrative Situations

i. The Secret Service are investigating a m an who they think is a spy. They want to find out everything they can about him. For instance, they know that someone phoned him at 6 yesterday evening and that he phoned someone else a few minutes later. They do not, however, know who that "someone" in both cases was.
"WHO PHONED HIM AT 6 AND WHO DID HE PHONE A FEW MINUTES LATER?" they ask.

1. Why are the Secret Service investigating the man?
2. What happened at 6?
3. What happened a few minutes later?
4. What is it that they do not know?
5. What questions do they ask?
6. Now do these
   (a) The police are now questioning the man. What do they ask him about yesterday evening?

ii. The director of a large chemical firm has just found out that a secretary in the firm gave important industrial secrets to someone outside the firm. The director cannot understand how the secretary got the secrets in the first place. He also wants to find out who she gave the secrets to afterwards. He is questioning her now. "WHO GAVE YOU THE SECRETS AND WHO DID YOU GIVE THE SECRETS TO?" he asks.

1. What has the director just found out.
2. What is it that he cannot understand?
3. What else does he want to find out?
4. He knows that someone gave her the secrets; what does he ask?
5. He knows that she gave the secrets to someone; what does he ask?

iii. The secretary is so hysterical that the director can understand only half what she is saying. "I gave them to a man! He loves me and I love him" she keeps saying.
"WHO DID YOU GIVE THEM TO? WHO LOVES YOU? WHO DO YOU LOVE?" he keeps asking.

1. Ask the questions and answer them.
   (a) How much/understand?
   (b) Why/only half?
   (c) the secretary keep saying
   (d) the director keep asking?

Practice and Expansion

iv. Jill Burton's father is very angry because Jill went out with someone yesterday evening and whoever it was kept her out very late.

1. Ask the questions and answer,
   (a) What/Jill/yesterday?
   (b) late or early?
2. Now do this
   (a) She went out with someone; what does her father ask?
   (b) He wants to know who that person was who kept her out so late; what does he ask?

80 FLUENCY PRACTICE

Transformation Exercise

Ask the correct type of question. Observe the position of words like WITH/TO/ AT (prepositions) in the WHO DID SHE GO OUT WITH?" type of question.

Jill went out with someone.
WHO DID SHE GO OUT WITH?

Someone kept her out very late.
WHO KEPT HER OUT VERY LATE?

Someone phones her every day.
WHO PHONES HER EVERY DAY?

She meets someone every evening.
WHO DOES SHE MEET EVERY EVENING?

1. Someone gives the secretary a lot of money.
2. Someone gave her a lot of money last month.
3. Someone sent her a lot of flowers.
4. She sent a lot of letters to someone.
5. She went out with someone last night.
6. She waited for someone.
7. Someone always waits for her every evening.
8. Someone saw her with a man.
9. She talked to someone this morning.
10. She went to dinner with someone.
11. Someone met her yesterday.
12. Someone talked to her this afternoon.

Special Comment

We use the "WHO KNOWS MARY?" or "WHO DID THAT?" type of question when we find out the person who does or did something.
We use the "WHO DOES MARY KNOW?" or "WHAT DID YOU DO?" type question when we know who does or did something and we want to find out something more. If there is a preposition with the verb in this type of question, it is natural to put it after the verb in the question.

81 Constructions like IT'S TOO HEAVY FOR HIM TO CARRY and HE ISN'T TALL ENOUGH FOR HER TO DANCE WITH

Problem Situations

i. Eight people want to get into a boat, but it is too small for them. The boat can carry really only four people.

1. How many people want to get into the boat?
2. How many people can the boat carry?
3. Now do this
   Make one sentence out of these two.
   (a) The boat is too small for eight people.
   (b) They cannot get into it.

ii. Peter and Jane live in a rather small flat. Peter's parents are staying with them for a few days and now Jane's parents want to come, too.

1. Ask the questions and answer them.
   (a) Where/Peter and Jane?
   (b) Who/staying
   (c) Jane's parents?
2. Now do this
   Make one sentence out of these two.
   (a) The flat is not big enough.
   (b) So many people cannot stay in it.

82 Illustrative Situations

i. Mrs. Bashford has always spent far more money than her husband really has. He has always been too afraid to tell her this. Once, for instance, she wanted him to buy a huge and very expensive dog for their son, Henry. Mr. Bashford said that Henry could not play with the dog because it was too big. Of course, the real reason was that it was too expensive.
HE SAID IT WAS TOO BIG FOR HENRY TO PLAY WITH.
IN FACT, THE DOG WAS TOO EXPENSIVE FOR HIM TO BUY.

1. What has Mrs. Bashford always done?
2. What has Mr. Bashford always been too afraid to do?
3. What did she want him to do once?
4. What did he say about the dog and what was the real reason he did not buy it?
5. Ask and answer these questions.
   (a) too big/play?
   (b) expensive/buy?

ii. Mr. Bashford wants to get a smaller house because his bank manager has told him he must stop spending so much. He and his wife are looking at a smaller house now. He likes it but she does not.
"IT'S FAR TOO SMALL FOR US TO LIVE IN!" she says

1. Ask and answer (a) Why/a smaller house?
2. What/now?
3. What does Mrs. Bashford say about the house?

iii. A very old professor is giving a lecture. He has been giving the same one for forty years and it is very boring. Most students simply cannot sit through it.

THE LECTURE IS TOO BORING FOR MOST STUDENTS TO SIT THROUGH

1. What is the professor doing now?
2. Ask and answer (a) How long/the same one?
                            (b) Most students/through?

83 FLUENCY PRACTICE

Transformation Exercise I

Observe that we do not say FOR SOMEONE if the person who does the thing in both sentences (the subject) is the same.

He is too afraid. He cannot tell her.
HE IS TOO AFRAID TO TELL HER.

These clothes are too shabby. I cannot wear them.
THEY ARE TOO SHABBY FOR ME TO WEAR.

1. He is not strong enough. He cannot lift it.
2. The table is too heavy. He cannot lift it.
3. The test is too difficult. I cannot do it.
4. I am too tired. I cannot do it.

5. You're too intelligent. You cannot believe that!
6. This work is too hard. Children cannot do it.
7. The film is too horrible. Children should not watch it.
8. The teacher spoke too fast. We could not understand him.

Transformation Exercise II

Observe what happens to any preposition that goes with the verb.

The dog was too big. Henry could not play with it.
IT WAS TOO BIG FOR HIM TO PLAY WITH.

1. The bus was too crowded. We could not get on it.
2. This bedroom is too cold. I don't think anybody should sleep in it.
3. The problem is too difficult. I cannot give a simple answer to it.
4. That man is too short. Caroline cannot dance with him.

5. The football team was too tough. We could not play against them.
6. This test is too difficult. The students cannot get through it.
7. This room is not big enough. They cannot take a test in it.
8. The subject was too horrible. She could not talk about it.

Agents 008 and 009 of the Secret Service are questioning some people who work in a government department. They know someone among them gave important secrets to a foreign country last month. They think they know who he is.

008: Who said the life of a secret agent is exciting? We've been in this office all day, asking one person after another the same questions.

009: There's only one more man left and he's waiting outside now. He's the spy! I'm sure of it.

008: Couldn't we eat something first? I'm too tired to go on. A man from the restaurant across the road is supposed to be coming any minute.

009: No! We can eat later. Look at all this information about the man who's coming in next. He's the one, I tell you. (There is a knock at the door) That's him now. Come in!

Man: Good evening. Someone said that . . .

009: Sit down. We have a lot of questions to ask you?

Man: Who? Me? What are you talking about?

009: Now don't pretend you don't know anything. Who do you think you're dealing with? A lot of amateurs? We're the Secret Service.

Man: (laughing) The Secret Service! Who are you trying to fool. You can't be the Secret Service. I'm not important enough for the Secret Service to bother with.

009: This is far too serious for you to laugh about. The sooner you realise that, the better! We have definite information that you are a spy.

Man: What do you mean? Who gave you that information? That's a lie!

009: Who gave you £1,000 on the 15th of last month?

Man: £1,000! You must be joking. Nobody has ever given me so much money in my life!

009: Who met you at Victoria Station on the 16th? Who did you give the secrets to? Tell us everything!

Man: Look here! Who do you think you're talking to? You can't order me about! I don't have to answer any of your questions!

009: Oh, yes, you do. You're a government employee!

Man: Who? Me? Who are you talking about? I work at the Capri restaurant across the road.

008: What did you say?

Man: I work at the Capri restaurant, and I'm not a spy!

009: Who sent you here?

Man: The manager did. He said someone here wanted something to eat. I've come to take your order.

1. Why does 008 want to eat first?
2. What does he say about a man from the restaurant across the road?
3. What does the man say when they tell him they are the Secret Service?
4. Why doesn't he think the Secret Service would bother with him?
5. What does 009 say when the man begins laughing?
6. What are some of the questions they ask him? (a) £1,000 (b) Victoria Station (c) the secrets
7. Why has the man really come and what do they say when they find out?

UNIT C EIGHT

**MAKE SOMEONE DO vs. LET SOMEONE DO
GET SOMEONE TO DO
WILL/WON'T BE ABLE TO DO and ILL HAVE TO DO**

85 MAKE SOMEONE DO

Problem Situation

Young David did not want to do his homework yesterday. His mother told him he had to before he went out to play. After he had done it, she said "All right. You can go out now"

1. What didn't David want to do yesterday?
2. What did his mother tell him?
3. What did she say after he had done it?
4. Now do this
   What did David's mother make him do and what did she let him do? (Two sentences)

86 Illustrative Situations

i. Mrs. Mavis saw a film yesterday. In the final scene a beautiful girl died in a handsome man's arms. Mrs. Mavis cried.
THE FILM MADE HER CRY.

1. Ask the questions and give the answers
   (a) What/yesterday?
   (b) in the final scene?
   (c) cry or laugh?
2. What can we say the film did to Mrs. Mavis?

ii. Max (a foreign student in England) is growing a beard. He hopes he will look older and more interesting with it.
HE HOPES IT WILL MAKE HIM LOOK OLDER AND MORE INTERESTING.

1. Ask what Max is doing and why! (and answer)
2. What does he think the beard will do to him?
3. Ask someone else if he or she thinks beards do this.

iii. Two Secret Service agents are talking to a spy they have caught. He has important information and the agents want it. The spy does not want to say anything and the agents have become very angry.
"WE'LL MAKE YOU TALK! WE'LL MAKE YOU TELL US EVERYTHING!" they have just told him.

1. Who are the agents talking to?
2. Ask why! (and answer)
3. Why have the agents become angry?
4. What have they just told him?
5. Do you think they are going to be very polite and gentle?
6. Make more sentences with "THEY ARE GOING TO MAKE HIM . . . . . ." with these words (a) all their questions
   (b) everything he knows

Practice and Expansion

iv. Three men robbed a post office last Friday. They made the people there do a number of things. First, one of the clerks had to lock the door. Then everybody had to lie down except the manager. He had to give them all the money. He had to put it in a black bag. When a woman became hysterical, one of the men shouted "Calm down, or I'll shoot you!" She did. THEY MADE THEM DO ALL THESE THINGS.

1. Ask the questions and give the answers.
   (a) What/last Friday?
   (b) a clerk have to do?
   (c) How many people/down?
   (d) Who/all the money?
   (e) What sort of bag?
   (f) Who/hysterical?
   (g) one of the men do?
2. Now make as many sentences as you can with THEY MADE . . . .
   (a) the door (b) down (c) all the money (d) black bag (e) calm down

Comment

Use MAKE SOMEONE DO when you want to express the idea of force or automatic effect.

87 LET SOMEONE DO

Illustrative Situations

i. Jill Burton is only seventeen. She still needs her father's permission to get married. She wants to marry Bert Johnson. "OH, PLEASE, DAD. LET ME MARRY HIM. LET ME DO WHAT I WANT!" she says.

1. What does Jill want to do?
2. Why is she talking to her father about it?
3. What does she say? (marry. what I want)

ii. Some eighteen year old students are having a discussion lesson. There is a teacher there but he refuses to say very much. He never interrupts, even when a student is saying something rather stupid. Occasionally he asks a few questions; that is all. HE ALWAYS LET THE STUDENTS GO ON. HE LETS THEM SAY WHAT THEY LIKE. HE BELIEVES IN LETTING PEOPLE SAY WHAT THEY FEEL.

1. Ask the questions and give the answers
   (a) What sort of lesson?
   (b) teacher there?
   (c) What/refuse?
   (d) every interrupt?
   (e) a lot of questions?
2. What does the teacher believe in?
3. What are the things he always lets the students do?
   (a) on (b) what they like (c) feel
4. Ask someone else if he or she believes in these things (3 questions)

iii. Bert Johnson had a bad accident in his car last month and the car is still in the garage. He wanted to use his father's car yesterday. "I WONDER IF YOU COULD LET ME USE YOUR CAR THIS EVENING?" he asked. "Of course" his father said.
HIS FATHER LET HIM USE HIS CAR

1. Ask and answer what Bert wanted to do yesterday and why?
2. What did he say to his father?
3. What did his father answer?
4. What did his father do?
5. Ask the person next to you if they would do this. ("Would you let . . . .?)

Practice and Expansion

iv. Richard does not believe in protecting his son, David, too much. There are often things on television that Richard's wife does not think David should see, but Richard usually says. "NO. LET HIM STAY. LET HIM WATCH. LET HIM LEARN WHAT LIFE IS REALLY LIKE"

1. What is it that Richard does not believe in?
2. When does Richard's wife want to send their son out of the room?
3. What does Richard usually say? (stay/watch/learn)
4. Ask the person next to you if they would let their children do these things
   (a) a lot of sweets   (e) anything they like
   (b) cigarettes   (f) all sorts of films
   (c) beer and wine   (g) all sorts of books
   (d) late at night

Comment

LET SOMEONE DO express the idea of giving permission or consent

88 Practice Situations

Make your own sentences with either MAKE SOMEONE DO or LET SOMEONE DO for each situation, like this (one sentence for each situation)

The photographer made funny faces at the little girl. Finally she laughed.
HE MADE HER LAUGH

David wanted to go out. His mother said he could.
SHE LET HIM GO OUT

1. There was an accident and a lot of people stopped to look. A policeman shouted "Move on" and they did.
2. Jane wanted to go home early one day. Her boss said it was all right.
3. David wanted to stay up late on Saturday. His mother said he could.
4. He wanted to do the same on Sunday. "No, go to bed" his mother said, and he did.

5. Jill's father said some very sarcastic things to her. She cried.
6. A student wanted to criticise a teacher's methods. The teacher did not stop him.
7. Grey is not a colour that suits Jane. She looks pale in it.
8. The comedian was very funny. The audience laughed.

89 GET SOMEONE TO DO

Problem Situation

Monica's car simply would not start yesterday morning. It was Sunday morning and all the garages were closed. However, this was no problem for Monica. All she did was phone her boy-friend, who happens to be a mechanic. She asked him to come over and put it right, and he did.

1. What was the matter with her car?
2. Why might this have been a problem?
3. Why wasn't it a problem?
4. What did Monica do?
5. What did her boy-friend do?
6. Now do this
   Monica asked him to do something and he did it; is there any shorter way of saying what happened?

90 Illustrative Situations

i. Anne's father is rich but Anne's husband isn't. Anne has very expensive tastes and she often wants to buy things her husband simply cannot afford. In such cases all Anne has to do is ask her father to buy them for her and he does.
SHE GETS HER FATHER TO BUY THEM FOR HER

1. Tell me about Anne's husband and also about her father!
2. Ask about Anne's tastes!
3. What kind of things does she often want?
4. What does she ask her father to do in such cases?
5. So, how is it that Anne has things which her husband cannot afford?

ii. The management of an Electrical Company wanted to introduce some labour-saving machines into their factory. The union was against the idea and threatened a strike. The management then promised a pay-rise in return for co-operation. Eventually the union agreed.
THE MANAGEMENT GOT THE UNION TO CO-OPERATE

1. What did the management want to do?
2. Ask about the union's reaction!
3. What did the management promise?
4. In return for what?
5. What did the union eventually do?
6. So, what can we say the management eventually did?

iii. When Nora went into her kitchen early yesterday morning, she smelt gas. She was sure there was a leak somewhere, so she immediately phoned the Gas Company's emergency service. A man came within an hour, found the leak and put it right.
SHE GOT A MAN TO COME IMMEDIATELY

1. Why did Nora become alarmed when she went into her kitchen?
2. What was she sure of?
3. Ask what she did then!
4. Then what happened?
5. So, what can we say Nora did?

91 Invention

Make your own sentences

a good mechanic = I GOT A GOOD MECHANIC TO REPAIR MY CAR

1. a good tailor
2. a good hairdresser
3. her rich uncle
4. his boss
5. the insurance company
6. the bank
7. the man who had caused the accident
8. an English teacher

92 WILL/WON'T HAVE TO / BE ABLE TO

Illustrative Situations

i. Mr. Bashford has been spending more than he earns. When a man does this he has to cut down on his spending. Mr. Bashford's bank manager is talking to him now. "YOU'LL HAVE TO SPEND LESS AND YOU'LL HAVE TO SAVE MORE!" he has told him. "How can I do that?" Mr. Bashford wants to know. "It's my wife who does most of the spending." "YOU'LL JUST HAVE TO MAKE HER SPEND LESS! YOU'LL HAVE TO MAKE HER REALISE HOW SERIOUS THINGS ARE!"

1. What does a man have to do when he spends too much?
2. Why is Mr. Bashford talking to his bank manager now?
3. What has his bank manager just told him?
4. What does Mr. Bashford want to know and why?
5. What are the two things he will have to do?

ii. Mr. Bashford has told his wife everything. They have always been able to go abroad for their holidays. This is very important to Mrs. Bashford because all their best friends can do this every year. "WILL WE BE ABLE TO GO ABROAD NEXT SUMMER?" she asks. Mr. Bashford's answer is not very encouraging. "NO, I'M AFRAID WE WON'T BE ABLE TO DO THINGS LIKE THAT ANY MORE. WE'LL JUST HAVE TO SPEND OUR HOLI-DAYS IN ENGLAND" he says.

1. What have they always been able to do?
2. Why is this so important to Mrs. Bashford?
3. What does she ask Mr. Bashford?
4. What is Mr. Bashford's answer?
5. What will they have to do?

iii. Bobby Greston, the famous footballer, is very ill. He has an important match in a few days, but his doctor won't let him play. "YOU WON'T BE ABLE TO PLAY ON SATUR-DAY. YOU'LL HAVE TO STAY IN BED!" he tells him.

1. Ask and answer the questions
   (a) wrong?
   (b) When/an important match?
   (c) play on Saturday?
   (d) stay in bed?

93 Invention Exercise

Make your own sentences with WILL HAVE TO DO and WILL/WON'T BE ABLE TO DO, like this

Mr. Bashford/such expensive suits
MR. BASHFORD WON'T BE ABLE TO BUY SUCH EXPENSIVE SUITS.

Mrs. Bashford/fewer clothes
MRS. BASHFORD WILL HAVE TO BUY FEWER CLOTHES

1. Bobby Greston/the doctor again
2. Mr. and Mrs. Bashford/a smaller car
3. Greston/football again next week
4. Mr. Bashford/champagne so often
5. Mrs. Bashford/1st class on the train
6. Greston/Saturday's match on television
7. Perhaps Greston/out of bed soon
8. Perhaps Mr. Bashford/a better job

Harry Evans, a factory worker, has just got a new job. He is in the factory canteen now, looking for somewhere to sit down. He has just seen a table with only one other man at it.

Harry: Do you mind if I sit down here?

Man: Not at all.

Harry: Thanks.

Man: You're new here, aren't you?

Harry: That's right. My first day. How long have you been here?

Man: Almost twenty years.

Harry: Really? That's very interesting. Do you mind if I ask you a few questions about the place?

Man: What sort of questions?

Harry: You know, the sort old hands like you always know the answers to. For instance, where can I go to have a little rest every hour?

Man: Every hour! I don't think you'll be able to do that here. You'll have to take your break when everybody else does; once in the morning and once in the afternoon.

Harry: Oh, no, I won't. You watch. In no time at all I'll be able to do what I like here. I can always make people believe I'm working when I'm not. The last place I worked in was typical. I never did more than four hours' work in eight hours.

Man: And you really think you'll be able to get away with that here?

Harry: I don't *think* I'll be able to. I know I will! They'll have to get a hundred policemen to watch me all the time to make me do an honest day's work!

Man: You sound almost proud of it.

Harry: I am proud of it. Why should I work hard for low wages?

Man: The wages aren't low here. They're very good.

Harry: Don't make me laugh. They're only paying you half what they should. Well, I won't let them rob me. I'll give them four hours' work for eight hours' pay.

Man: Really? Very interesting.

Harry: Tell me something else, will you? Is the canteen always this full at 12 o'clock?

Man: Yes, everybody eats here. Even the manager does. It's a very democratic factory.

Harry: Really. I've never worked in a place like this before. How do you recognise the manager and people like that?

Man: It's very hard. People who work in the offices wear white shirts, like the one I'm wearing, that's all.

Harry: I'll have to be more careful when I talk.

Man: Yes, you mustn't let the manager overhear you, must you?

Harry: No. Er . . . which office do you work in?

Man: In almost all of them. I'm the manager, you see.

Questions and Practice

1. What are some of the things Harry thinks he'll be able to do in his new job?
2. Ask if he'll be able to do these things. Give answers. (a) a break every hour
   (b) two hours for lunch
   (c) half a day's work
3. Ask if he'll have to do these things; give answers. (a) a full day's work
   (b) his break when everybody else does
   (c) harder
4. What does Harry say he won't let the factory do?
5. What does he say they will have to do to make him do an honest day's work?
6. Who was Harry talking to all the time and why didn't he realise it sooner?

Verb + Object + Preposition + Gerund Patterns
(Stop him from doing. Talk him into doing. etc.)
TRY DOING vs. TRY TO DO
Text revising gerund constructions and introducing
new ones.

95 Problem Situations

i. Max was at a cocktail-party last week. He
happened to lean against a table. There was a
beautiful vase on it and it fell off. Max saw it
toppling over and tried to stop it, but he
couldn't. The vase broke.

1. Where was he last week?
2. What did he happen to do?
3. Ask if there was anything on the table!
4. What happened?
5. What did Max try to do?
6. What couldn't he stop?

ii. The typewriter was almost worn out and **Jane**
wanted a new one. Unfortunately, her boss was
reluctant to buy it. However, she eventually
talked him into it.

1. What was wrong with the typewriter?
2. Ask what Jane wanted her boss to do!
3. How did he feel about buying a new one?
4. What happened eventually?
5. What did she talk him into?

iii. When Mr. Bashford left for the office yesterday,
he told his wife he would have to work late.
When he came home that evening, he was drunk.
Mrs. Bashford was sure he had lied and accused
him of it.

1. What did Mr. Bashford tell his wife yesterday
   morning?
2. Why was she sure he had lied when he came
   home?
3. What did she do?
4. What exactly did she accuse him of?

96 Key Examples

Study the key
examples.
Observe the
construction

1. How can we STOP ANOTHER WAR
FROM BREAKING OUT?
2. The salesman TALKED HIM INTO BUY-
ING a car he couldn't really afford.
3. They ACCUSED ME OF BEING lazy.
4. He often CRITICISES HER FOR SPEND-
ING too much money.
5. Her father OBJECTS TO ME GOING OUT
with her.
6. They sterilized everything and PREVENTED
THE DISEASE FROM SPREADING.

ii. Now cover the examples and use these
prompts as memory aids.

1. another war
2. the salesman/a car
3. lazy
4. too much money
5. Her father/me
6. sterilized everything/
   the disease

iii. Now do the problem situations again. Adapt
the patterns you have memorised to the situations

97 STOP SOMEONE / SOMETHING FROM DOING

Inventions

Use the patterns yourself with these prompts the vase = HE COULDN'T STOP THE VASE FROM BREAKING
or
HE TRIED TO STOP THE VASE FROM FALLING

1. the demonstrators
2. the thief
3. the drunken soldiers
4. the mad dictator
5. her little son
6. the cat
7. the mouse
8. that damned dog

98 These are also Inventions!

ACCUSE SOMEONE OF DOING

1. £200
2. the accident
3. during the exam
4. the war
5. brutal
6. disorder

TALK SOMEONE INTO DOING SOMETHING

1. a new suit
2. that film
3. a better mark
4. a rise
5. a lower price
6. all his money
7. the concert tomorrow
8. his beard off

Has anyone ever talked you into doing something?
What?

CRITICISE SOMEONE FOR DOING

Now think of your own examples with this pattern:
1. Has anyone ever criticised you for anything. What for?
2. What do people criticise the government for?
3. What do some nationalities criticise other nationalities for?

99 OBJECT TO PEOPLE DOING

Expansion

The Europa Export Company is not a very happy place to work in. People are constantly getting on each other's nerves. These are some of the things various people object to:

(i) One of the secretaries often uses the phone for private calls.
(ii) The manager criticises people in public.
(iii) One of the accountants smokes terrible-smelling cigars in the canteen.
(iv) Various people use Mary's typewriter.
(v) One of the secretaries is always spreading rumours about other people in the office.

What is it that people object to? Who in particular objects to what?

100 TRY DOING vs. TO DO

Problem Situation

A young teacher has just become tired of marking books, disciplining stupid and bored children, and pretending to know everything. He wants another job. He has advertised in the paper, registered with an employment agency, written letters to various firms, and even asked his friends if they know of anything. So far he has not been successful.

1. What has he become tired of doing?
2. What does he want to do?
3. Ask if he has done these things:
   (a) in the paper
   (b) an employment agency
   (c) letters to various firms
   (d) his friends
4. Has he been successful?
5. What has he tried to do?
6. What has he tried doing?

101 Illustration and Expansion

Study the difference between TRY DOING and TRY TO DO

An advertising-agency has just received a contract for a new type of soap. Somehow they have to make it well-known in a short time. The manufacturer wants people to think of the soap as very strong yet also "pleasant to use". The top executives of the advertising-agency are discussing ways of doing this now. Money is no object. Obviously they are going to advertise on television, but there must be other things they can do, as well.
THEY ARE GOING TO TRY TO MAKE THE SOAP WELL-KNOWN
THEY ARE GOING TO TRY ADVERTISING ON TELEVISION
WHAT ELSE ARE THEY GOING TO TRY DOING?

1. Who have they received the contract from?
2. What do they have to do?
3. So what are they going to try to do?
4. What does the manufacturer want people to think?
5. What are the advertising-executives doing now?
6. What is the first and most obvious idea?
7. So, what are they going to try doing first?

102 Invention I

Use the model for your own examples

Basic Situation: Someone wants to do something. You are not talking about what the person wants to do, but about ways in which it might be done.

Example: A friend knows you speak English well. He wants to improve his knowledge of English, too. You are making suggestions.

Models: HAVE YOU TRIED GOING TO A GOOD LANGUAGE SCHOOL?

or WHY DON'T YOU TRY GOING TO A GOOD LANGUAGE SCHOOL?

1. evening classes
2. English radio programmes
3. English films
4. some of the English people here
5. English pop songs
6. a holiday in England
7. English papers
8. the Anglo-European club

Invention II

Basic Situation: Something is difficult. You do not know if you can do it.

Model: I'LL TRY TO GET HERE EARLIER TOMORROW

1. the work by tomorrow
2. all this homework this evening
3. fewer cigarettes
4. a letter every week
5. a better job
6. this spot on my sweater
7. the war
8. the whole book today

This text introduces new gerund construction and revises old ones.

103 TEXT

For some reason Richard West has been having great difficulty in getting to sleep lately. Last night he thought it might help if he went to bed even earlier than usual, so at 9.30 he lay down, closed his eyes hopefully, and began counting sheep. Thinking of all those energetic little animals jumping over fences made him feel energetic himself, so he stopped, went downstairs, and found the most boring book he had. It was a book called "Home Rug-Making". At the end of an hour he had become quite interested in making rugs. He put the book down in desperation. Then he remembered someone telling him once that if you repeated "Sleep" often enough, it would finally come. 15 minutes later the people in the bedroom above him tapped angrily on the floor.
At 2 o'clock he took a sleeping-tablet. It had absolutely no effect.
At 3 he got up and walked around his room at least 20 times. At 4 he did a deep-breathing exercise. At 5 he stared at a spot on the ceiling until his eyes began to hurt.
At 6 his eyes began to feel heavy and, finally, he dropped off. His alarm-clock rang at 7.
This morning at work his boss looked at him gravely, shook his head, and said in a critical tone of voice: "See here, West, you have been looking very tired lately! Obviously, you haven't been getting enough sleep. I really think you ought to try going to bed earlier!"

PATTERNS FROM THE TEXT

HE HAS BEEN HAVING GREAT DIFFI-
CULTY IN GETTING TO SLEEP LATELY

Tell me some things you often have difficulty in doing!
Make sentences with the pattern + these words:
(a) up early
(b) the British Govern-
    ment
(c) the Americans in
    Viet Nam
(d) General de Gaulle
(e) when you speak fast
(f) money
(g) so many new words
(h) all these subtle
    differences

1. What did he try to do last night?
2. What did he try doing?

Question Practice:
1. Ask what he has been having difficulty in doing lately! (answer)
2. Ask why he went to bed at 9.30 yesterday!
3. What was the first thing he tried doing?
4. Ask if this helped him! Ask why not!
5. What was the next thing he tried doing (a boring book)?
6. What had happened after an hour? (interested)
7. What did he remember then? (someone/the word 'Sleep') Now ask if he tried this!
8. What did he try doing then? (a sleeping-tablet) Ask what happened!
9. What did he do when he got up at 2? Ask someone else if he has ever tried this!
10. What were the things he tried then? (deep-breathing exercise/a spot)
11. What finally happened around 6?
12. What did his boss say he had noticed this morning?
13. Had he any idea that Richard had been having difficulty in doing this?
14. What exactly was his suggestion?

DOING SOMETHING DOES SOMETHING
(Example: THINKING OF ALL THOSE . . .
lines 4—5)

Tell me what doing these things does or helps to
do.

(a) working hard
(b) smoking too much
(c) reading in a bad
   light
(d) getting up early
(e) listening to English
   radio programmes
(f) travelling around
   foreign countries
(g) reading the daily
   newspaper
(h) drinking coffee late
   at night

WOULD YOU BE INTERESTED IN . . . ING?
(line 8)

The director of an advertising agency is having
lunch with a very good graphic artist, who
works for another agency.

*Use WOULD
YOU BE IN-
TERESTED
IN . . . ING
with these
words*

Artist: Well, I must say, the way you des-
           cribe the job makes it sound very
           good.
Director: Yes. Would you be interested in
           taking it?

1. for our firm
2. this sort of work
3. the cinema this
   evening
4. my new house
5. another game of
   chess
6. tour of Italy
7. our new office in
   Brazil
8. the car over there, sir

HE REMEMBERED SOMEONE TELLING HIM THAT

Basic Situation: Someone did something. You
                  remember it.
                  YOU REMEMBER SOME-
                  ONE DOING SOMETHING

Examples: (i) The salesman said the car had a
               new engine. Max remembers it.
               MAX REMEMBERS THE
               SALESMAN SAYING THE
               CAR HAD A NEW ENGINE.

          (ii) Your friend put his book on the
               seat. You remember it.
               YOU REMEMBER YOUR
               FRIEND PUTTING HIS BOOK
               ON THE SEAT

This is what you remember:
The teacher said the dictation would be easy

*and this is what causes you to say you remem-
ber it:*
In fact it was hard, and he is denying that he
ever said it would be otherwise.

So you say
I REMEMBER YOU SAYING IT WOULD
BE EASY

1. The boss promised you the job. Now he is
saying he intended to give it to Harry.
2. Max came late on Monday. Now he is saying
that he has always come early.
3. The film star told the journalists she was 35
last week. Now she says she is 30.
4. Your teacher told you the examiner read the
dictation three times. Now the examiner says
twice is enough.
5. When you were in Sienna, it rained all week.
You are thinking about it now.
6. Mr. Empson got very nasty with you once.
Someone has just said he never does.

N

UNIT C TEN

It's TIME someone DID
WOULD/WOULDN'T HAVE DONE IF HAD/HADN'T DONE
Text 'A Series of Coincidences'
practising WOULD/WOULDN'T HAVE DONE IF HAD/
HADN'T DONE
and introducing HAPPENED TO DO/TO BE DOING
WISH HAD/HADN'T DONE

104 TIME someone DID

Problem Situation

You are in a jet that has been waiting at one
end of the runway for several minutes now. You
are getting impatient because it still has not
taken off. You think it's time this happened.

1. What is the jet doing?
2. Ask how long?
3. Why are you getting impatient?
4. Do you think it's time this happened
5. What do you think it's time happened?

105 Illustrative Situation

*Study the form
of the word like
DO (verb) after
IT'S TIME*

A large, powerful Western country has been
fighting a war in Asia for a long time and it has
still neither won the war nor even been able to
end it. A great many people in the country
think it would be a disaster if the war went on
any longer. They frequently say things like:
IT'S TIME WE ENDED THIS WAR
IT'S TIME WE PAID ATTENTION TO
OUR OWN PROBLEMS
IT'S TIME ALL THIS KILLING STOPPED

1. What is this country doing?
2. Ask how long!
3. What has it not yet been able to do?
4. What do many people think would be a
   disaster?
5. What are some of the things they say?

106 Progressive Substitution + Variations

Model	IT'S ABOUT TIME YOU CUT THE LAWN
went to bed =	IT'S ABOUT TIME YOU WENT TO BED
Don't you think =	DON'T YOU THINK IT'S ABOUT TIME YOU WENT TO BED?
Isn't it =	ISN'T IT ABOUT TIME YOU WENT TO BED?

IT'S ABOUT TIME YOU CUT THE LAWN
1. got a rise
2. we
3. asked for
4. Isn't it
5. went to the station
6. Don't you think
7. I really think
8. you wrote to your mother
9. bought a new suit
10. had those shoes mended

107 Practice and Expansion

Michael left university six months ago and is
still looking for a job. He is living at home. His
father thinks his hair is too long, that he should
buy a proper business suit, and that he hasn't
tried hard enough to find a job. They had an
argument about all these things yesterday.

1. Ask when Michael left university!
2. Where is he living now?
3. Has he found a job yet?
4. What do you think were some of the things
   Michael's father said yesterday with "IT'S
   TIME . . . ."?
   Prompts: hair/suit/job/advertisements/
   employment agency/white shirt

108 Practice Situations

What would Michael's father say in these situations?

1. It's 8 o'clock, Monday morning. Michael is still in bed.
2. Michael got a letter from one firm asking for information about himself a week ago. Michael hasn't answered yet.
3. Michael's father has just noticed that Michael's shoes are a bit shabby.
4. Michael also has a beard.
5. There is some work to do in the garden. Michael is still reading a book.

109 WOULD/WOULDN'T HAVE DONE IF HAD/HADN'T DONE

Problem Situation

The last train was at 11.30. At 11.10 Mrs. Robinson said "I really think it's time we left now." Her husband did not want to leave the party and did not listen. She did not get him to go until 11.20. Of course, by the time they got to the station, the train had left. "You see!" she said angrily. "I told you we should have left earlier!"

1. What did she say at 11.10?
2. Ask what her husband did and why!
3. When did she finally get him to leave?
4. What had happened by the time they got to the station?
5. What did she say?
6. Why?
7. Under what circumstances would they have caught the train?

110 Illustrative Situations

i. You liked the job but the pay was not any good. As a result you got another job.
YOU WOULD HAVE STAYED IF THE PAY HAD BEEN BETTER.
YOU WOULDN'T HAVE LEFT IF THE PAY HADN'T BEEN SO POOR.

1. Did you like the job?
2. Why did you leave, then?
3. So, under what circumstances would you have stayed?
4. The person next to you left a job for the same reason; ask him if he would have stayed!
5. What would you say if someone said to you: "It's a pity you left that job."

ii. The goal was wide open and the centre-forward was just about to shoot when someone tripped him.
HE WOULD HAVE SCORED IF SOMEONE HADN'T TRIPPED HIM.

1. What was the forward about to do?
2. Ask why he didn't!
3. Ask what would have happened if he had!

iii. A man had a serious accident on the motorway. He lost a great deal of blood. Luckily, he was near a hospital, and the accident surgeon was able to operate immediately.
THE MAN WOULD HAVE DIED IF HE HAD LOST ANY MORE BLOOD.
HE WOULD HAVE LOST MORE BLOOD IF THE SURGEON HADN'T OPERATED IMMEDIATELY.

1. Ask about the accident!
2. Ask how much blood the man lost?
3. Why was it lucky he was near a hospital?
4. What would have happened if the surgeon hadn't operated at once?
5. Ask what would have happened if he had lost more blood!

Practice and Expansion

i. Angus is a Scottish Nationalist. He loves
Scotland deeply. Two years ago he was offered
a good post in Nigeria at three times the salary
he was getting in Scotland. A house was also
included. His wife wanted him to take the post
and left him when he didn't. Angus did not
want to leave Scotland.

1. Ask about the salary he would have got in
Nigeria!
2. Would he have got anything else?
3. Ask how his wife felt about the post!
4. What happened?
5. What would and would not have happened if
he had taken the post?
6. What would have happened if he hadn't
loved Scotland so deeply?
There was a revolution in Nigeria afterwards;
houses were burnt down and people were
killed; what might have happened to Angus?

ii. Once, when Max was at school, he asked the
person next to him for a pen. It was during an
examination and the teacher thought he had
been cheating. Max tried to explain but the
teacher did not let him; he threw Max out.

1. What did Max ask the other student for?
2. What did the teacher think?
3. Why didn't Max explain?
4. What happened?
5. Ask what Max would have done if the
teacher had let him!
6. Ask what would have happened if the
teacher had listened!

111 ANALOGIES

*Observe the
two models
They illustrate
the same
pattern.*

You WOULD HAVE LIKED the film if you
HAD SEEN it.

She WOULDN'T HAVE LEFT him♦ if he
HADN'T BEEN so selfish.

*Now, to under-
stand the struc-
ture make
examples of
your own using
only the first
element*

YOU WOULD HAVE DONE/
SHE WOULDN'T HAVE DONE

*Use these
words*

that book/a better mark/a better job/a lot of
money
so wet/another car/all that meat/the sherry

*Now make
examples of the
second element*

IF YOU HAD DONE/IF YOU HADN'T
DONE

my advice/all your homework/an employment
agency
to the Casino/out in the rain/so hungry/thirsty

Invention Exercise

*Now make full
examples of
your own,
using these
words in the
first element*

such a bad mark = YOU WOULDN'T HAVE
GOT SUCH A BAD
MARK IF YOU HAD
STUDIED HARDER

1. such a headache
this morning
2. so tired this
morning
3. so wet yesterday
4. that accident
last year
5. that cold last week
6. to prison when he was
18
7. so much money these
last few years
8. such a good suntan last
summer

1. You went out and got terribly wet. Five minutes later the rain stopped.
2. You missed the 10 o'clock plane. It crashed.
3. You did not visit your friend. You did not know he was ill.
4. You were just about to get on the bus when you remembered your money was at home.
5. You studied very hard. You just managed to pass the test.
6. Alice married Bob. Then she found he snored. She can't bear people who snore.
7. You travelled second-class on the Channel ferry. Later you found out that first-class was only a bit dearer and much better.
8. Harry had all the right qualifications for the job, but the manager thought his hair was too long.
9. Jane wasn't interested in the old man at all. Then someone said he was a millionaire.
10. Tom happened to sit down in the park. There was a girl on the same bench. They got married later.
11. The famous heart surgeon did not want to become a doctor when he was young. His father persuaded him.
12. A film-director happened to see Lola in a night-club. She is a famous actress now.
13. The mountain-climber looked up when someone shouted. He slipped and fell.
14. Max thought the salesman was honest. That's why he bought the car.
15. The writer of this course banged on a type-writer for 6 months. The typewriter wore out.

113 HAPPEN TO DO/TO BE DOING (line 2)

We have seen how important tense variations of each pattern are. Now study this

I HAPPENED TO SEE JACK YESTERDAY (I did something by chance.)

I HAPPENED TO BE SITTING THERE WHEN HE CAME IN. (I was doing something by chance.)
or
I HAPPENED TO BE PASSING BY WHEN THE ACCIDENT HAPPENED.

114 Illustrative Situation

Jim went into the coffee-bar and ordered an espresso. He had just taken a sip from it when Martha came in.
HE HAPPENED TO BE DRINKING COFFE THERE WHEN SHE CAME IN.
SHE HAPPENED TO COME IN WHEN HE WAS THERE.

1. Was Him doing anything when she came in?
2. So, what can you say with HAPPENED TO BE DOING?
3. Did she intend to come in when he was there?
4. So, what can we say with HAPPEN TO DO?

Test Situations

i. You opened the paper and saw an article about heart-transplants. It was very interesting. Only a minute later you heard on the radio that some doctors had just done another one.

1. What had you just done when you heard the news?
2. What were you doing?
3. So, what did you happen to be doing when you heard the news?

ii. The reporter had just sat down and had ordered a drink in the bar when a famous film-star came in.

1. Where was he sitting when the film-star came in?
2. So, what did he happen to be doing?

iii. The people at the next table seemed to be talking about a very interesting person, so you listened. The person seemed to be familiar. Suddenly you heard your own name. They were talking about you!

1. What did you happen to be doing?
2. What did you happen to do?

Quite by chance Martha went into a coffee-bar one Saturday morning where she happened to meet an old friend of hers who was goint to the races. His girl-friend was ill and he did not fancy going alone, so he asked Martha to come. She had never been before.

She decided to bet 10 shillings on a horse called "Dublin Boy" simply because she had once spent a very pleasant holiday in that city. However, when she got to the betting-window, all she had in her purse was a £10 note. She did not realise she could ask for change and hesitated. The man behind her shouted "Hurry up!", Martha became nervous and confused and bet the whole £10.

The odds on the horse were 100—1. At the last fence it was running second. The leading horse suddenly stumbled and fell, and "Dublin Boy" won. When Martha went to collect her £1,000, a television-reporter happened to hear what had happened before.

That evening she was interviewed on a news programme. The regular interviewer was ill and his place was taken by a young man who fell in love with Martha. They got married shortly afterwards and now have three children.

(Do these either before or after the questions.)

1. What are all the things that wouldn't have happened if Martha had not gone into the coffee-bar that morning?

   Use IF . . . . HADN'T . . . . (DONE) . . . . WOULDN'T HAVE (DONE)

   + these words:
   (a) coffee-bar/her old friend
   (b) his girl-friend/ Martha
   (c) a holiday in Dublin/the horse
   (d) a ten-shilling note/£10
   (e) the man behind her/confused
   (f) confused/the whole £10
   (g) the whole £10/ £1,000
   (h) the leading horse
   (i) a television reporter/ the inverview
   (j) the regular inter- viewer

Practice Questions
1. Had Martha planned to meet her old friend?
2. Ask why he didn't go with his girl-friend!
3. Ask what would have happened if his girl-friend had been well!
4. Was there any other reason he asked Martha to come? (fancy)
5. Why was it lucky for her she had once been in Dublin?
6. Ask what happened when she got to the betting-window!
7. Ask why she became confused! Ask if this was lucky for her and why!
8. What were the odds? What was the horse doing at the second fence?
9. Ask about the leading horse at the second fence!
10. Why was this a lucky thing for Martha?
11. Was it also lucky for her that a television-reporter overheard her later? Why?
12. What happened that evening?
13. Ask if it was lucky the regular interviewer was ill and why!

116   **WERE (DID)**
　　　　WISH WOULD BE
　　　　　　　HAD DONE

In Part B we learned these two
I WISH THE WEATHER WERE NICER
(It isn't nice)
I WISH THIS RAIN WOULD STOP (I wonder
if it will stop)

Now study this
I WISH I HADN'T SAID THAT

Illustrative Situations

i. Nora's husband is away on business again. Their little boy has just fallen seriously ill. The doctor says an immediate operation is necessary. "I WISH MY HUSBAND WERE HERE" she says.

1. Where is Nora's husband?
2. What does she wish?
3. Ask why!

ii. He told Nora that she could always contact him at a certain number in Zurich. She is ringing now, but there is no answer yet. "I WISH HE WOULD ANSWER" she says.

1. What is Nora doing now?
2. Ask why!
3. What does she wish?

iii. A week has passed. Nora has had a terrible time all alone with her very sick son. Luckily he has survived the operation. Nora's husband is back, too. On the night she rang, he happened to go out to a film. "I WISH YOU HAD BEEN HERE" she says.
"I WISH I HADN'T GONE OUT THAT NIGHT" he answers.

1. How long ago did the first two things happen?
2. Ask what kind of time Nora has had!
3. Ask about her son!
4. Ask why Nora's husband did not answer that night!
5. What does Nora say when she remembers being all alone?
6. What does her husband say when he remembers going out to a film that night?

117 Practice Situations

1. You are trying to sleep. Two cats outside are wailing.
2. You have just caught the 10 o'clock train. Someone tells you that the 9.30 train was much faster.
3. You had a choice between two films. The one you went to wasn't very good. People say the other one was.
4. You had the money with you but even though the sweater was a real bargain, you did not buy it. Later, it was gone.

5. You are in England now, and it is July. People say the weather was better in May.
6. You are ill in bed. Some friends have just phoned. They are having a wonderful time at a party.
7. The car you have is too small.
8. You came late. The first part of the film was the best.
9. You did not watch the programme. Later, everybody said it had been extremely good.

118 Invention

Now make your own examples with only WISH HAD/HADN'T DONE + these words:

(a) in the sun so long yesterday
(b) that book in the sale last Thursday
(c) some more gold coins when I was in Zurich
(d) more time when I was in New York

Are there any other things you wish you had or hadn't done?

UNIT C ELEVEN

IS BEING DONE
MIGHT HAVE BEEN DONE
NEEDN'T HAVE BEEN DONE
SHOULD HAVE BEEN DONE
HAD (experienced) SOMETHING DONE

119 IS BEING DONE

Problem Situations

i. The Secret Security Agency believes that a certain government official is a spy. He has just left the Government Ministry now where he works. He does not know it but unseen eyes are watching him and unseen figures in the crowd are following him.

1. Who believes the man is a spy?
2. Ask what he has just done!
3. What is it that he does not know?
4. Do we know exactly who is watching and following him?
5. What can we say is happening to the man?

ii. Yesterday at this time he had just left the Ministry, too, and the same thing was happening.

1. What had he just done?

120 Illustrative Situations

i. Work has temporarily stopped on the jet planes in the factory. Everything has been finished except for the engines. They are lying around the planes. A few are already in place.
THE PLANES ARE BEING FITTED WITH ROLLS ROYCE ENGINES

1. Have the planes been finished yet?
2. What has to be done?
3. Are the workers actually doing anything at the moment?
4. Can you say anything is being done? What?

ii. You can see the clothes tumbling about in soap suds through a glass window in the washing-machine. It is all fully automatic.
THE CLOTHES ARE BEING WASHED NOW

1. How do you know what is happening?
2. What can you see?
3. What can you say?

iii. The huge, fully automatic printing presses are turning now. In a few minutes, the morning papers will be ready.
THEY ARE BEING PRINTED NOW

1. Are there a lot of printers working in the plant?
2. When will the papers be ready?
3. Is anything happening now?
4. What can you say is happening?

121 Practice and Expansion

i. There are at least a hundred cows in the huge milking-shed. The sound of the milking machines is very loud. Occasionally one sees a dairy worker measuring the milk being taken. Otherwise, there are no other people in the shed at all.

1. What kind of machines are making all the noise?
2. Are there any workers in the shed?
3. Are they milking the cows?
4. What kind of work are they doing then?
5. What can you say is happening?

122 Progressive + Variations

Do these at speed

	Model	HE IS BEING FOLLOWED	HE IS BEING FOLLOWED

Model   HE IS BEING FOLLOWED

He doesn't know = HE DOESN'T KNOW HE IS BEING FOLLOWED

watched = HE DOESN'T KNOW HE IS BEING WATCHED

Do you realise we = DO YOU REALISE WE ARE BEING WATCHED?

HE IS BEING FOLLOWED

1. You
2. made a fool of
3. Am I
4. filmed
5. Are we all
6. Is he
7. guarded
8. that man
9. beaten up
10. I'm sure someone
11. murdered
12. fooled
13. Don't you know you
14. laughed at
15. exploited
16. cheated

Comment

Again and again we have seen how important the tense variations of various patterns are. This is equally true of the Passive which, by the way, is used more frequently in English than it is in many other European languages. This is partly because there is really no clear impersonal form such as 'on' or 'si' or 'man'. English people often use 'you' or 'they' or 'one' for this, but there are many cases in which none of these is really suitable. Study the variations of the Passive here.

123 MIGHT HAVE BEEN/DONE

Three weeks ago an old woman was found dead in her attic in Amsterdam. Among her scanty belongings two large paintings were discovered, each with the name "Rembrandt" at the bottom. An art expert is examining the paintings now. He cannot be sure about them yet. Certainly, however, the style is right and it has been established through various tests that the paintings are the right age.
THEY MIGHT HAVE BEEN PAINTED BY REMBRANDT

1. Ask when she was found dead!
2. Ask where!
3. How did the paintings come to light?
4. What is happening to them now?
5. Is there any chance the paintings are genuine?
6. What leads you to this idea?
7. Someone has just asked the expert "Were they really painted by Rembrandt?"; what is the only answer he can give at the moment?

124 Practice Situations

Say what MIGHT (or COULD) HAVE HAPPENED for these situations

1. Lady Crocker casually left her car with the keys still in the door. It was still there when she got back.
2. Two drunken sailors started a fight in the Ming china room of the Museum. The only damage was a black eye for the guard.
3. Someone spilt red wine all over Cynthia's beautiful white dress. Max was there with his bottle of Miracle stain-remover.

4. There was a minor fault in your car. You did nothing about it and it is now beyond repair.
5. There was a chance to end the war last July, but nobody took advantage of it.
6. Griggs, the criminal everybody is looking for, carelessly went out without his beard. Luckily nobody noticed.

125 NEEDN'T HAVE BEEN DONE

For some reason several of the new vans used by a huge firm kept breaking down. A number of experts decided that the only thing that could be done was to replace all the engines. This was done at great cost.

A month later a mechanic happened to be tinkering with one of the replaced engines. He found that the trouble had been caused because one small hole in the air-filter was not large enough.

THE ENGINES NEEDN'T HAVE BEEN REPLACED

1. Ask if anyone knew at the time why the vans kept breaking down!
2. What did the experts decide?
3. How was it that the mechanic happened to find the fault?
4. What exactly did he find?
5. What did everyone realise after this?

126 Practice Situations

What NEEDN'T HAVE HAPPENED in these situations?

1. All the trees in the park were cut down. The motorway took up only part of the land where the park had been.
2. During the battle for the old city, hundreds of houses were destroyed. Actually there hadn't been any enemy soldiers in them at all.
3. Thousands of bombs were dropped on the jungle. The guerilla troops were not there at the time.
4. The goods were sent by air. They were not used for several months.
5. Five new schools were built in the area. A year later the two largest factories closed down and a lot of people moved away.
6. The railway station was closed down for lack of traffic. A month later a huge new factory came to the town.

127 SHOULD HAVE BEEN DONE

Illustrative Situations

i. You are in a café. The waitress has just brought you a ham sandwich. The bread is stale and the ham itself is turning rather brown at the edges.
IT SHOULD HAVE BEEN THROWN AWAY LONG AGO

1. Ask what the bread is like!
2. Ask about the ham itself!
3. What are you going to say to the waitress about the sandwich?

ii. The school was built in 1867. The rooms are small and dark and it looks like a prison. It is still being used, although the local authorities have recently promised it will be pulled down.
IT SHOULD HAVE BEEN PULLED DOWN YEARS AGO

1. Ask if the school is still being used!
2. Ask how long!
3. Ask someone if they would send their children there!
4. What have the authorities promised?
5. What do people say when they hear this?

128 Practice Situations

What SHOULD HAVE HAPPENED and when?

1. You ordered the goods for delivery in May. It is July and they haven't come yet.
2. The Franconian Air Force is still using World War II airplanes.
3. There is a hole in the school-roof. It has been there for some time.
4. There are a ton of oysters in the Customs Shed. They have been there for a week and are beginning to smell.
5. The cows are beginning to moo loudly. Nobody has milked them for 36 hours.
6. That wrecked car has been at the side of the road for 3 months.
7. The public garden is completely overgrown with weeds.
8. The paint on the bus-shelter has been peeling for a year.

129 HAD (experienced) SOMETHING DONE

Illustrative Situation

Just as Tom was walking away from his car, a policeman stopped him. He had noticed that Tom had not locked it. There had been a number of car thefts recently. "Pardon me" the policeman said: "YOU DON'T WANT TO HAVE YOUR CAR STOLEN, DO YOU, SIR?"

1. What was Tom doing when the policeman stopped him?
2. What had the policeman noticed?
3. Why was this a dangerous thing to do?
4. What exactly did the policeman say?

We have already learned this pattern in Unit B Eleven. The meaning, however, was not quite the same.

Study the examples. Notice in particular the position of the word like DONE

130 Key Examples

Tom HAD	HIS FACE	SLAPPED
She HAD	HER HOUSE	BROKEN INTO
The baby HAD	ITS BOTTOM	SMACKED
Patrick HAD	A BOTTLE OF GUIN-NESS	BROKEN OVER HIS HEAD in the fight.

131 Illustrative Situations

i. The champion had a great deal of trouble with the courts. Finally the boxing-commission decided that "he was not a fit person to hold the title" and they took it away from him.
HE HAD HIS TITLE TAKEN AWAY FROM HIM

1. Did the champion lose his title in the ring?
2. Ask how he lost it!
3. So, what can we say about him?

ii. Max wrote a book about six months ago. It was called 'Born Unlucky'. A film-producer liked it very much and made it into a film.
MAX HAD HIS BOOK MADE INTO A FILM

1. Ask what the title of the book was!
2. Who saw it?
3. What did he think of it?
4. What happened?

132 Progressive Substitution

Model HE HAD A BOTTLE OF GUINNESS BROKEN OVER HIS HEAD

Molly = MOLLY HAD A BOTTLE OF GUINNESS BROKEN OVER HER HEAD

her pearls stolen = MOLLY HAD HER PEARLS STOLEN

PATRICK HAD A BOTTLE OF GUINNESS BROKEN OVER HIS HEAD
1. he
2. thrown at him
3. his face slapped
4. nose punched
5. his Rolls Royce dented
6. Lady Crocker
7. towed away by the police
8. picture splashed across all the papers
9. Elizabeth Taylor
10. I
11. my windows smashed
12. the writer
13. books burnt
14. has had
15. a lot of writers
16. published here

SUMMARIES AND EXTRA COMMENTS

The purpose of this book has been to give students a chance to get practical control of the language, this is why the emphasis has been on active practice and inducing ones own 'rules' from the range of examples given.

Formal rules, by themselves, are no substitute for this kind of practical control. This is why there have been very few formal rules of any sort given in the book. A student who finds such rules very useful should consult a book specially designed to give formal rules, such as "A Practical English Grammar" by Thompson and Martinet (O.U.P.)

The brief summaries here are meant only to supplement the occasional comments made in the units themselves. They are not a complete grammar of English. Students may find it useful to read them after the practical work has been done in class. Teachers may find it a pleasant variation occasionally to spend a minute or so going over these summaries at the end of lessons. Not all students will want to use them at all. They are here only as an option for those who find formal rules help them to retain what they have learned through practice.

A ONE

i.   The present Simple ("HE DOES. WE DO") is used for what people often, usually, or sometimes do. It is also used with "never." It is not used for actions that are incomplete and going on at the moment.
ii.   The Present Continuous is used for actions incomplete and going on as you talk about them.
iii.   Words like "never", "usually" etc. (adverbs of frequency) go between the subject ("he" etc.) and the main verb ("watches" etc.). With "is/are/am" and "was/were" however, they go after the variation of "to be" (Example: "He is NEVER on time.")

A TWO

i.   HOW MUCH is used with Mass words, like "money, gold, time, oil."
ii.   HOW MANY is used with Unit words, like "coins, pieces of gold, seconds, glasses of milk, people" etc.
iii.   Neither "much" or "many" is used in positive statements. "A lot" replaces both.
iv.   The word "there" in the phrase "There's a lot of oil in Texas" is not a place word, like "here" or the other "there" in a phrase like "I went there."

A THREE

i.   GOING TO DO is used for future actions already growing out of present ones. It is often used when you see the signs of that future action, such as Peter notices in the first situation (18i). It is the most common, general future form, as well.
ii.   There are two imperative forms, the positive ("Go") and the negative ("Don't go.")

A FOUR

i.   Regular past forms simply add an "ed" to the base form of the verb.
ii.   Irregular past forms change either the middle vowel or a consonant at the end. Some verbs do not change in the past at all, like "put."
iii.   The question form in the past uses the base form or infinitive, as it is also called, together with "Did."
iv.   The negative in the past is formed in the same way.
v.   "What . . . . . like?" asks for a description, like "beautiful" or "very good" or "terrible."
vi.   "How . . . . ?" is used in enquiries about a person's health.

A FIVE

i.   Adjectives (words like "good, bad, terrible") describe what something is like or how it is.

ii.   Adverbs describe how a person does something.

iii.   The adjectives that indicate there is a difference of degree, like "Darker", "brighter", "smaller" occur in the pattern "......er than ...."

iv.   Adjectives that indicate there is no difference occur in the pattern "as .....as"

v.   "Better" and "worse" are irregular in that they do not show they are comparatives by simply adding an "er" on to the base form of the adjective, as happens with "dark, darker."

vi.   A form that is not dealt with here but is introduced later is "more ...... than." This occurs with adjectives of two syllables or more. (Expensive. More expensive.)

A SIX

i.   AGO is always used with a past tense. We use this word when we count the time back from the present to the point in the past when an action happened.

ii.   'turn on', 'turn off', 'take off' and 'put on' are typical phrasal verbs. A preposition is added to the verb to give it a definite change in meaning. If the verb is transitive to begin with (that is, can take a direct object in its base form, without a preposition) the preposition part of the phrasal verb can go either before or after the object. (For example; we can say either "They put their overcoats on" or "They put on their overcoats.")

iii.   A number of regular and irregular verbs have been systematically introduced in units A Four to A Six. Here is a list of them. Notice that there are occasional peculiarities in the spelling of some of the regular verbs.

Regular		Irregular	
answer	rob/robbed	buy/bought	put/put
clap/clapped	stop/stopped	bring/brought	read/read
cook	ski/ski-ed	came/came	ring/rang
dance/danced	travel/travelled	do/did	run/ran
hurry/hurried	turn	drink/drank	say/said
learn	wash	get/got	see/saw
like	watch	go/went	sleep/slept
listen	work	has/had	sing/sang
play		leave/left	speak/spoke
prepare/prepared		meet/met	teach/taught
			tell/told
			take/took

iv.   The HAS/HAVE BEEN form and the HAS/HAVE BEEN DOING form (Present Perfect and Present Perfect Continuous forms) are used to bridge the past and the present. If someone started something in the past, and still does it in the present, we use these forms to describe the action.

v.   SINCE is used to point to the time an action started. FOR is used to show the length of time something has been going on.

A SEVEN

i.   If someone says, "I have a Rolls Royce", and you report what that person said later, the "have" becomes "had." Anything said in the present tense goes into the past tense after "said."

ii.   If you want to say not only what was said but also who it was said to, you must use "tell." 'Say' is used only when we do not mention the person something was said to.

A EIGHT

i.   Use 'would' when you ask someone else to do something.

ii.   Use 'may' when you are talking about what you want to do.

iii.   Observe the phrasal verbs, 'turn on' and 'turn off' in Item 74. The prepositions 'on' and 'off' can go either before or after the object.

iv.   Use 'tell someone to do' for instructions or orders. 'Ask someone to do' is used for polite requests.

v.   'How to do' is used when the question is not what must be done but how (the necessary steps) it must be done.

A NINE

i.   The four verbs 'hate', 'stop', 'enjoy' and 'remember' introduced with the gerund here have been selected as examples of typical problems connected with the gerund. 'Hate' can be used with both the gerund (doing) and the infinitive (to do) without any basic change in meaning. It is probably more common, however, to use the gerund after 'hate' than the infinitive. 'Enjoy' always takes the gerund. 'Stop' and 'remember' however are very different. If the infinitive rather than the gerund is used with either of these last two verbs, there is a great change in meaning. This is illustrated in B Nine.

A TEN

Shall I come with you?
help?

i.   'Shall I . . . . . .?' is used to show you are ready to do something for someone else.

ii.   'Shall we . . . .?' is used to suggest something that you and another person or persons can do if the others want to.

iii.   'Would you like . . . . .?' is the most common form used to invite someone else to do something. It is very polite.

iv.   'I'd like . . . . .' is a polite form used to express what you want to do or have. It is also often used to express wishes, which you cannot be sure will ever come true. (See Item 107ii for a good example of this.)

A ELEVEN

i.   Reflexive pronouns ('myself' etc.) are used when a person becomes the object or receiver of his or her own action.

ii.   Observe that the plural (more than one) form of 'self' is 'selves.'

iii.   Reflexive pronouns are rarely used with 'wash', 'shave', 'prepare', 'feel' and 'concentrate' because if no other person is mentioned with these verbs, it is felt to be clear that the object or the receiver of the action must be the same person who does the thing.

iv.   Items 119i and ii show the basic difference between 'themselves' and 'each other.' 'Themselves' is used only when each person in the group mentioned does something only to himself or herself, and not to anyone else in the group. 'Each other' is used to show that the action was within the group mentioned but that the doer (subject) and receiver (object) of the actions were different people within that group.

B ONE

i.   IS/ARE DOING (Present Continuous) is also used to express future actions when the action or event has already been arranged.

ii.   IS/ARE HAVING (Continuous form of 'have') is used when 'have' means to do something, and the action is going on or incomplete at the moment.

iii.   The other 'have', which often, although not always, means the same thing as possess, has no continuous form. (For an example of when this second 'have' does not really mean possess, see Item 6iii.)

She's having her tooth pulled out.
" " a DRIVING LESSON.

B TWO

i.   SOME is used with mass nouns or plural unit nouns in positive statements when you have some idea of the quantity, but do not mention it specifically.

ii.   ANY is always used with mass nouns or plural unit nouns in negative statements.

iii.   The problem of which to use in questions is deliberately not dealt with here. It is safe always to use ANY in questions. However, SOME is also used, particularly when the speaker has an idea of the quantity in mind. For instance, if you say "Would you like some tea?", you probably have a cup of it in mind, and would be very surprised if the person you offer it to took the whole potful. The same is true of questions like, "Would you like some cake?" or "Have you some glue?" In the first, only a small piece of cake is meant, and not the whole cake. In the second, the person asking the question is probably stressing that he or she only wants a certain quantity, perhaps only a very small amount.

iv.   VERY FEW is used with Unit nouns.

v.   VERY LITTLE is used with Mass nouns.

vi.   If you say "I am going to the school/church/hospital/prison/gaol/university", you indicate, by using 'the', that you are going only as a temporary visitor, and that you are not a pupil, member of the congregation, a patient, etc.

B THREE

i.   One of the main uses of 'I'll' is to show that you are willing to do something or promise to do it.

ii.   In sentences such as you find in items 26—36, the part of the sentence that comes after 'before', 'if', 'when' and 'as soon as' is always in the present simple, even though the action is in the future. Words like 'if' etc. are called co-ordinating conjunctions of time. Some more examples are 'until', 'by the time', and 'as long as.' The principle just described is true of these as well.

B FOUR

i.   Notice that in items 39—42, all the actions that take the WAS/WERE DOING form (Past continuous) had already started before the action in the DID form (Past simple) and were going on when the other action happened.

ii.   WHILE is used before clauses (example: 'I was teaching') and DURING is used before nouns (example: 'the lesson.')

iii.   Notice, however, that DURING is not used with time-nouns, like 'five years' etc. FOR is used before such time-nouns.

B FIVE

i.   Notice that in item 48, "He never drinks very much wine", 'very much' refers to the quantity of wine. Whenever "very much" is put immediately before an object noun, it indicates the quantity of the thing.

ii.   Notice that in item 48, when "very much" comes after the noun, as in "He likes wine very much", it does not refer to the quantity of wine someone likes but how much that person likes it. Always use "very much" after the noun if you want to say how much you like something and not the actual quantity you like.

iii.   'Hardly' means 'almost not at all.'

iv.   In item 58, "Sam is boring", describes the effect he has on other people. Whenever an adjective ending in 'ing' is used with a person or thing, it describes the effect that person has on others.

v.   If, however, we say "Sam is bored" we are not talking about the effect Sam has on other people, but the effect something or someone else has on Sam.

B SIX

i.   Observe that we do not use the past tense simply because we have some other clear indication of the past such as the word "yesterday" etc. in our sentence. The past is used even without these words if in our minds we clearly see that the action has no connection with the present and clearly belongs to the past.

ii.   The word "ever" is used in a question when we want the person we are asking to look at the whole of his or her experience or life.

iii.   Notice that this is also why we use the Present Perfect (have done) form with "ever." The period of time in focus is from the past to the present.

iv.   This is also why the Present Perfect is used with 'yet.' In a question with 'yet', the word means 'up to now.'

v.   Notice in Items 73–75, "He did it for . . . . . ." (Past Tense with 'for') means that the person no longer does the thing mentioned. "Has been doing it for . . . . . ." (Present Perfect with 'for') means that the person still does the thing.

vi.   Notice that in Item 76, we again have a focus on a period from the past to the present. When the judge says "It's the strangest case I've ever handled" he is talking about all his experience, from the past up to the present moment.

B SEVEN

i.   In modern spoken English it is very unusual for a preposition to go before 'who', 'what' or which.' It's normal position is at the end of the question.

ii.   The 'who did that?' type of question is used whenever you do not know who does or did something and want to find out.

iii.   The normal question-construction ("Do you speak English?" etc.) is used whenever you already know who the subject (the person who does the thing) is. Some people still say "whom" instead of "who" when the word does not indicate the doer or subject. However, "whom" seems to be disappearing slowly from spoken English. It has no real function in the language, since word-order and not case-inflection shows whether the word is a subject or object. In the two sentences "Who loves Mary?" and "Who does Mary love?" we can tell from the 'does' in the second question that 'Mary' is the subject.

iv.   Always use "to" with the word "explain" when you want to say not only what was explained, but who it was explained to.

B EIGHT

i.   In the construction WANT SOMEONE TO DO, the person who actually should do the thing is always put just before the infinitive ('to do'). Also, if the person is not mentioned by name, object pronouns are used ('me', 'him', 'us' etc.) and never subject pronouns ('I', etc.)

ii.   Notice that 'You mustn't do that' means that "It will be very bad if you do it." 'Mustn't' is a stronger form of 'shouldn't.'

iii.   If you want to say "You can do it if you want, but it isn't really necessary", use DON'T/ DOESN'T HAVE TO. You can also use 'needn't' in this sense.

B NINE

i.   If we say "He stopped typing" we mean he no longer typed, but did something else. A gerund ('doing') used after 'stop' shows what the person stopped.

ii.   However, an infinitive 'to do', after 'stop' is used to show what the person did after he or she stopped something else. That is why "He stopped to go to bed" means that he stopped something else (typing) and then went to bed.

iii.   The same distinction is true of 'remember.' The gerund shows what was remembered, the thing that came into the person's mind as a memory of a past action. The infinitive shows what the person did after he remembered.

iv.   As items 108–114 show, a verb is put into gerund form after prepositions. (The preposition 'to' in 'to do' is really part of the whole verb itself, and not a separate item, as in "for doing" etc.)

B TEN

i.   The form I WOULDN'T . . . . . . IF I WERE YOU, is often used to give advice, when you wish to put yourself in the person's place you are giving the advice to.

ii.   In all conditional sentences like the ones in Items 116 – 120, the verb in the 'if'-clause (the part of the sentence beginning with 'if') is put into the same form as the past tense. It is not really the past tense, in meaning, however, as is shown by the irregularity 'were' for all persons. However, many English speakers now say 'was' with 'he', 'she' and 'it.'

iii.   COULD is the conditional form of 'can.' MIGHT is used to express the fact that something is uncertain.

iv.   In items 124–127, the form like the past is used for the thing you wish were true now but is not.

v.   WOULD DO is used after 'wish' to express the future action you wish other people would take. It is often used in anger or irritation, such as in a sentence like "I wish you would stop making that noise!" etc.

B ELEVEN

i.   [Passive forms like 'has been done' are used when it is either impossible or unnecessary to say who the person was who did the thing.] In situation 130i, for instance, it is clear that the wind has blown down the tree. In situation 130iii, the salesgirl could not possibly mention all the different salesgirls who have sold the clocks.

ii.   HAVE SOMETHING DONE is used to show that you did not do the thing yourself, but were the cause of another person doing it, at your request.

iii.   Notice in items 140 and 141 that the same distinctions in tense are made with the passive as with any other form.

C ONE

i.   ALWAYS DO/DOES is used for things that are done regularly, at the same times each day, week, month, etc. It is an unemotional statement.

ii.   IS/ARE ALWAYS DOING is used to show not only what is done but often how you yourself feel about the thing. It often expresses irritation or anger.

iii.   Notice that in items 5—12 the same distinctions in tense are made with modals like 'should', 'can', 'must' etc. as are made with full verbs.

iv.   MUST in items 11—12 is used to express the fact that you do not know something as a fact but that it is the only explanation or assumption you can make in the situation.

C TWO

i.   Do not use 'the' with concrete nouns like 'women', 'wine', 'money', 'people', 'men', etc. when you mean the things in general, and not some particular members of the group indicated by the word. *ie. a set, class.*

ii.   The use of 'the' with such words means that you have some particular members of the group indicated in mind.

iii.   Notice this is basically the same distinction we make with abstract nouns such as those in items 15—19. Words like 'war', 'life', 'mathematics', etc. mean the thing in general, the idea of the thing, and no particular concrete example of it. 'The war', however, is a particular war. Do not use 'the' if you mean the idea of the thing and not some very concrete example of it.

iv.   Do you think you are giving a particular example of the thing simply by putting an adjective like 'modern', 'English' etc. in front of it. In the invention drill in Item 18, 'Modern Art' is still an abstract category. "The modern art I have seen in museums" would not be.

v.   The words in Item 20 like 'news', etc. are mass nouns in English. In many other languages they are treated as unit nouns. In English, however, they are never used with 'a'.

C THREE

i.   WILL DO (Future Simple) instead of WILL HAVE DONE (Future Perfect) is often used with 'until' as well. WILL HAVE DONE simply stresses the fact that the action will actually be complete.

ii.   The distinctions between WILL DO and WILL BE DOING shown in items 27—30 are exactly the same as those shown with DID and WAS DOING. The only difference is that those shown in this unit are future rather than past in time.

iii.   MIGHT DO and MIGHT BE DOING are often used in the future for things you cannot be certain about.

C FOUR

i.   If, in the same sentence, one action is in the HAD DONE form (Past Perfect) and the other is

in the Past Simple, the action in the Past Perfect was already over when the other happened.
ii.   WAS GOING TO DO as used in items 40—44 is often called 'the future in the past.' It is used for an action that was in the future from the viewpoint of the past, but no longer is.

C FIVE

He had no idea he was going to have so much trouble.
She didn't know he was going to buy her a ring.

i.   When we say someone else 'looks ill', the verb 'look' does not refer to anything that person does. It is we who look, and use our senses to tell ourselves the state that other person is in. The same is true of 'sound' (we hear something, and form a judgement), 'smell' (we use our own noses when we say a flower "smells nice") and 'feel.' Adjectives are used here because they do not refer to the way the subject performs the action, but to what the subject is like.
ii.   Items 56—60 again illustrate how incomplete actions are always put in some continuous form. Here they are in the past and linked to the modal 'should.'   *'...should have been weaning...'*

C SIX

i.   The basic distinction between HAS BEEN DOING and HAS DONE is explained immediately after item 62.
ii.   HAD BEEN DOING FOR . . . . . . is used to show how long one action had been going on when another one happened. It is sometimes called the 'Pre-Past' because it looks further back into the past than an action in the past simple.

C SEVEN

i.   SUPPOSED TO DO/BE DOING/HAVE DONE is used here in the sense of "This is not what I know from direct experience but because people have told me." Notice again how important it is to make the correct tense distinctions.
ii.   There is a second meaning of SUPPOSED TO DO. "You aren't supposed to get up yet" a nurse might tell a patient. This means "You shouldn't get up yet because the doctor told you not to!"
iii.   The two types of questions illustrated in items 77—80 have been introduced separately before but not contrasted. An explanation of the basic distinction between them is given in the summary for Unit B Seven and is repeated after item 80 in this unit.
iv.   Notice that in sentences like 'It was too big for him to play with' we do not put any object after the preposition at the end of the sentence.

C EIGHT

i.   MAKE SOMEONE DO is explained formally after item 86.
ii.   LET SOMEONE DO is explained formally after item 87.
iii.   GET SOMEONE TO DO is closely related to ASK SOMEONE TO DO in meaning. The difference is that ASK SOMEONE TO DO stresses the request, but does not by itself make it clear whether or not the person you ask actually does the thing. GET SOMEONE TO DO makes it clear that the person you ask does the thing.
iv.   Notice that the two future forms WILL HAVE TO and WILL BE ABLE TO DO in items 92—93 are the only examples of future constructions with modals in English. In other words, only CAN and MUST have special future constructions. The other modals ('should', 'might' etc.) are used in the future without any change in their construction.

C NINE

i.   The examples given in items 95—99 illustrate a common construction in English. Other frequent examples of this construction are 'save someone from drowning' etc., 'talk someone out of doing something', 'be used to people doing something', and 'insist on someone doing something.'
ii.   We use TRY TO DO when we are not sure if we will be able to do the thing.
iii.   We use TRY DOING when the action represented by DOING is a means of reaching some other aim.

(i) HAS DONE   (ii) HAS BEEN DOING.

C.6(i): — When you want to talk about Quantity of Things done in a time rather than How long the Thing has been going on.
He has been smoking constantly for the last 2 hours.
He has smoked 20 cigarettes in that time.

195

C TEN

i.　We use IT'S TIME someone DID when we think something should already have happened but has not. The DID here is not a past tense. It is the same form as "It would be better if you did that" in conditional sentences.

ii.　WOULD HAVE DONE IF HAD DONE is sometimes called the 'Perfect Conditional' or the 'Past Conditional.' It is used for things that are in the past.

iii.　Notice that with this form, 'would have' is never used in the part of the sentence beginning with 'if.'

iv.　WISH + WERE and WISH + WOULD DO have already been introduced as contrasted in unit B Ten. Only WISH + HAD DONE is new. Notice that this last form is used for things you wish had or had not happened in the past.

C ELEVEN

i.　Items 101—106 again illustrate how important tense variations are in English. This has been one of the key themes of this book and part C in particular. Students often learn to handle the main tense variations with simple forms but not with more complex ones, like SHOULD DO and SHOULD BE DOING etc., and the passive. Yet tense variations are just as necessary and as frequent with these more complex forms as they are with simple statements like "He works in a bank."

ii.　Items 107—109 illustrate another use of HAVE SOMETHING DONE. We use this form as a kind of double passive. There are really two passive subjects in each sentence. We see this in Item 108i. We could divide the example "He had his title taken away from him" into two parts.

(a) Something was done to him. (b) His title was taken away from him.

INDEX